Mark Hopkins

Teachings and counsels: Twenty baccalaureate sermons

With a discourse on President Garfield

Mark Hopkins

Teachings and counsels: Twenty baccalaureate sermons
With a discourse on President Garfield

ISBN/EAN: 9783337242664

Printed in Europe, USA, Canada, Australia, Japan

Cover: Foto ©Suzi / pixelio.de

More available books at **www.hansebooks.com**

PREFACE.

THE following baccalaureate sermons were originally published in pamphlets at the time they were delivered. With one exception they were subsequently modified, their order was changed, and they were published in a volume entitled "Strength and Beauty." The exception was the discourse on "Providence and Revelation," delivered in 1865, containing my estimate of President Lincoln and some remarks on the war. The texts are now restored, the discourses are placed in the order in which they were delivered, and, though the more immediate address to the class is still in some instances abbreviated or modified, they are yet substantially as they were Thus all the published baccalaureates are now given in their order, and to these is added, as being in the same line, and as a tribute to the most distinguished graduate of the College, the discourse on President Garfield.

The subjects of the discourses are of permanent interest, and the favor with which the former book has been received leads me to hope for a permanent interest in this. The change is made in accordance with the expressed wish of some of those who heard them, and also because it may be of interest in the future history of the College to know what final teachings and counsels were given from 1850 onward to so many classes.

M. H.

WILLIAMS COLLEGE, *July,* 1884.

iii

TEACHINGS AND COUNSELS

I.

FAITH, PHILOSOPHY, AND REASON.

Who through faith subdued kingdoms, wrought righteousness, obtained promises, stopped the mouths of lions, quenched the violence of fire, escaped
the edge of the sword, out of weakness were made strong, waxed valiant
in fight, turned to flight the armies of the aliens.—Hebrews, xi. 33, 34.

WHAT more heroic action have we on record than
those of the men who through faith subdued kingdoms. The word "hero," does not occur in the Bible.
Nothing can be more opposite to its spirit than that self-
sufficiency and recklessness of human rights and sufferings which are commonly associated with this term. Still,
there are no higher examples of a true heroism than the
Bible presents. These exploits were performed, indeed,
in ancient times, but are such as we should be glad to see
emulated in the midst of the light and advantages of our
day. We have a right to expect, as the stream of time
rolls on and pours its accumulated wealth at the feet of new
generations, that there shall not only be an increase in the
knowledge of nature, but that there shall be, at least, no
failure in the breadth and compass of a comprehensive
wisdom, or in the might of a true manhood that is ready to
do and to suffer in the cause of humanity and of God.

But not only may *we* expect this ; it is also intimated
by the Apostle that it is expected and watched for by those
who have gone before us. He represents, those worthies
and veterans who had finished their own course, as gathered
into a vast assembly, forming " a cloud of witnesses," and
watching with intense interest the bearing of those who

⁎ AUGUST 18, 1850.

follow them. "Seeing then," says he, "that we are com-
passed about with so great a cloud of witnesses, let us run
with patience the race that is set before us."

This race, my friends, I would now invite you to run.
You are especially called upon to emulate the example of
the great and good,—to do deeds that shall not only cause
joy on earth, but shall send a new thrill through the vast
assembly of those who have gone before you.

But if you are to do the deeds of these ancient heroes
you must be girded with the same armor, be controlled by
the same principle, must have the same prize in your eye,
and be sustained by the same power.   Fruitful as the nineteenth century has been in inventions, it yet furnishes none
for making great and good men.   The great tree must
grow now from the same earth, and under the same sun,
and by the same processes and ministrations of dew and
rain and storms, as the great tree of old ; and so, now, as
of old, must the life and might of true greatness be drawn
from the same fountains, and work themselves out by essentially the same processes.   Were these deeds performed
of old only by faith? then only by faith will they be performed now.

What then is Faith?   Avowed by Christianity as its
peculiar principle of action, ridiculed by the philosophers,
is it indeed some new, or peculiar, or blind, or fanatical
principle?   Or is it one of those grand and universal principles which underlie human action, which are necessary
to true heroism, to a right philosophy, to individual and
social perfection, and which must, in the progress of light,
come more and more into distinct recognition and general
acknowledgment?

Whatever faith may be, it must be conceded that
the accounts given of it by its advocates have been neither
uniform nor consistent.   It has been said to be simple

belief founded on evidence, and not differing from any
other belief; to be belief in testimony ; to be belief for
reasons not derived from intrinsic evidence ; to be a belief
on the ground of probable, as distinguished from demon-
strative evidence; to be a belief in things invisible and
supernatural ; to be a trust ; and more recently, and
transcendentally, it has been said to be an *organ* of the
soul by which it becomes cognizant of the invisible and
the supernatural.

To some, this diversity of statement may seem to indicate that there can be nothing in faith very definite or
important. To me it indicates the reverse ; for while men
do certainly differ about things which are indefinite and
obscure, yet it is also found that they come latest, if at all,
to the investigation of those principles which are the most
intimate and essential, and that they are nowhere less
likely to come to a uniform and satisfactory result. As
in mathematics the truths that are most nearly intuitive
are the last and the most difficult to be demonstrated, so
here the principles and processes which are so essential
that they seem inwoven into our being, are the last to be
investigated and the most difficult to be satisfactorily
explained. Men are no better agreed what reason is, or
what personal identity consists in, than they are what faith
is ; and yet as those who think wrongly on these subjects
may, and do, exercise their reason, and continue the same
persons precisely as they would if they thought rightly, so
those who make different statements in regard to faith,
or exercise faith, receive the benefits of faith in precisely
the same way.

That the term faith may not be used loosely and popu-
larly to designate the ideas just mentioned, and also
others, I would not say ; but the inquiry now is, What,
generically, and specifically, is that Faith upon which the

Bible insists as essential to salvation, and by which the
great deeds it records were performed ?   Can this faith be
so defined that our idea of it shall be distinct, that it shall
harmonize with philosophy and with reason, and that it
shall be adequate to the great offices assigned to it in the
Bible ?

I propose, first, to answer these inquiries ; and secondly, to speak of the offices of faith—more particularly,
of its office as a principle of action to be adopted by every
young man.

The generic definition of faith which I would pro-
pose, is, that it is *confidence in a personal being*.   Faith lives
and moves and has its being only in the region of personality.   Whatever we may believe respecting things visible
or invisible, on any other ground than our confidence in a
personal being. does not seem to me to be faith.   It
implies the recognition of a moral nature, and a conviction of the trustworthiness of the being possessed of such
a nature.

This definition of faith implies a division of this universe
into two departments, that of persons, and that of things ;
and, in connection with this division, will give us a clear
distinction between philosophy and faith.   The sphere
of faith is the region of personality, that of philosophy is
the region of things.   Each of these spheres addresses oui
sensibilities and calls for investigation, but in accordance
with its own nature and laws.

By things, are called forth in the region of sensibility,
the emotions of beauty, of sublimity, and of admiration ;
by persons, in addition to these, confidence, affection,
passion.

In her investigations in the department of things, philosophy is concerned, not with all knowledge, but chiefly

with resemblances in those things that exist together, and with uniformities in those that exist in succession. These are the basis of all classification, of all inductive reasoning—and it is through these that we get all our ideas of physical order and law.

Philosophy presupposes a knowledge of things as they exist separately. This being given, she neglects all individual peculiarities, and proceeds to group them according to their resemblances, and to give them collective names. In doing this she acquires for man power, and practical guidance, because a resemblance in external signs denotes a resemblance in essential properties. This gives value to the signs of nature, and shows that in the department of resemblances she is constituted on the basis of truth.

But not only does philosophy notice resemblances in beings and phenomena that exist together, she also notices uniformity of succession; and is thus enabled to foretell the future, and to act wisely with reference to it. She believes in a uniformity of succession according to the order that is established. She investigates the laws in accordance with which this succession moves on. As among things that exist together, she knows nothing of individual peculiarities, so in phenomena that exist in succession, she knows nothing of exceptions, and admits with great reluctance, or not at all, that such exceptions really exist.

Such, except as she may be said to investigate causes, is philosophy.* She stands in the centre of things that coexist, and passes onward and outward to the farthest star, stepping more or less firmly as the resemblances, by which alone she proceeds, are more or less perfect ; she stands at the present point in things that succeed each other, and binds the future to the past by what she conceives to be an inexorable law.

* When this was written philosophy had not, in this country, been distinguished from science, as it has since been. Writing now, the word science would be substituted for philosophy in many instances in this discourse.

But it may be inquired whether philosophy does not extend to the domain of mind. Yes, so far as mind is a thing, and hence under the law of an absolute uniformity, but no farther. The moment a personal being is placed under that law of nature by which that which follows is *necessarily* the product of that which precedes, personality ceases, and you have mere nature—a thing. The very idea of that necessary uniformity upon which philosophy is based, precludes that of personality. It also precludes the idea of faith ; for whatever we may believe without the range of personality, and on whatever grounds, there is always wanting that element which enters into faith by which a person may be said not only to have confidence, but to be *confiding*.

The sphere of faith, as opposed to that of philosophy, is, as I have said, the region of personality. Here we find affections, and a moral nature, and a free-will. In the sphere of things we deal with similarities, and uniformities of succession, and laws, and do not necessarily know anything back of these. We *may* indeed refer them all to a personal agent, but for the grounds of our belief we are not necessitated to go beyond the uniformities and laws themselves. We have in these nothing of the great element of character. But in our dealings with personal beings, whatever ground we may have for belief, either of what they say, or of what they will do, must be found, not in any law, not in any unvarying uniformity conceived of as necessary but in the *character* of the personal being. This is an element entirely different from any found in the sphere of philosophy, and it is upon this that faith fixes. This is the grand peculiarity of faith ; it is confidence in a personal being. Like belief, it admits of degrees. As the highest form of belief is certainty, so the highest form of faith is such a confidence in the character of any being as will lead us to believe whatever he may say *because he says it*, and to commit implicitly into his hands every interest of our being.

And as that without us which calls forth faith, is so different from that which is the basis of philosophy, so, it may be remarked, is that within us which is brought into action also different. Doubtless the nature of man is pre-conformed to the state into which he is to come, and as he naturally conforms himself to the uniformities of nature, so does he, though by a different principle, naturally confide in those to whom his being is intrusted. It is not to be supposed that that feeling of confidence with which the infant looks up into the eye of its mother, with which the new formed angel must look up to his God, is the same as that by which he is adapted to the blind and unvarying movements of nature. It is not to be supposed, as these two great spheres of persons and of things are so distinct, that our nature should not be equally preconformed to each.

If the spheres of faith and of philosophy be thus distinct, it will be obvious that they can come into conflict only at a single point. A personal being may make assertions about facts that lie within the domain of philosophy, and these assertions may seem to conflict, and may conflict, with evidence respecting those same facts derived from philosophy. But in such a case man is not left to the alternative of a blind faith or a presumptuous philosophy. His reason is to decide. By this he is to ascertain, on the one side, that a personal being has spoken, what he has said, what means he had of knowing the truth, and what confidence is to be placed in his character. On the other side, he is to inquire whether he knows all the facts and their relations, and is sure of his inferences. If, after this, there shall seem to be a conflict, or a contradiction, reason must strike the balance, and say whether, under the circumstances, it is more rational to put confidence in a

personal being, or to believe in facts and deductions for
which we have another species of evidence. Reason recognizes both these grounds of belief; and she, and she
only, can decide in cases of apparent conflict between
them.

Having thus considered the relations of faith and philosophy, let us now look at those of faith and reason.

It is strange with what pertinacity the opponents of
Christianity have insisted that there is, and must be, a
conflict between these ; and how readily many advocates
of Christianity have assented to this view. So far has this
been carried, that a recent and much-lauded article in the
Edinburgh Review is entitled, " Reason and Faith ; their
claims and *conflicts.*" But such conflict is by no means to
be admitted. There is just as much opposition between
reason and faith, as there is between reason and philosophy, and no more.

If we regard reason as giving us only intuitive and
necessary truths, then it will act equally in the domain of
philosophy and of faith, and there can be no opposition
between either of them ; unless, indeed, a personal being
should assert an absurdity. But if, as is more common,
we regard reason as comprising what is rational in man,—
those high attributes by which he is distinguished from
the brutes, and which must enter into, and preside over,
every legitimate act and process of the mind,—then, the
sphere of faith and philosophy being different, there can be
no conflict between reason as employed in the sphere of
philosophy, and as employed in the sphere of faith. Reason presides over both spheres, and can therefore be in
conflict with neither. The only possible question is, whether we may, in any case, just as rationally reach conclu-
sions and grounds of action by that process which we call

faith, as we can by that which we call philosophy. But on this point there can be no question. We act as necessarily and as legitimately with reference to personal beings by faith, as we do in reference to things by a belief in the uniformity of nature. It is just as *rational* for a man to have confidence in the character and consequently in the word of a personal being, as it is for him to believe in the facts of observation or experience or in those forms and systems of knowledge deduced from these which are called philosophy. It *may*, perhaps, be found to be *quite* as reasonable to believe a fact because it is asserted by God, as to believe one because it is inferred by ourselves, or even as to believe a fact made known to us by those senses which God has given us.

Is there not then such a thing as faith that is not in accordance with reason ? Certainly, just as there are inferences and philosophies that are not in accordance with reason, and perhaps it would be difficult to say whether there has been more folly and absurdity under the name of faith or of philosophy. My reason tells me that I may confide in the facts given me by my senses, that I may classify these, and build up a system of knowledge which we call philosophy. Under this impression, men have built up systems of philosophy which we can now see were exceedingly irrational and foolish, but this does not show that there is any conflict between reason and philosophy ; but only that reason is not infallible in this department. My reason also, all that is rational within me, tells me that I may, and ought, sometimes to confide in personal beings, and that such confidence is a rational and sufficient ground of knowledge and of action. We may, indeed, here repose confidence where we ought not, and receive irrational dogmas, and submit to useless or ridiculous rites ; but this would only show that reason is not infallible in this department.

So far then from separating faith from reason and bringing them into possible and actual conflict, we would say that the sphere of faith is one of the two great spheres over which reason presides, and that faith itself is one of the great and indispensable methods in which reason is manifested. It is a libel upon religion to say that it requires a blind faith, or any other than a rational faith, or that it requires us to believe any thing which is not more rational to believe than it would be to disbelieve it. There is no tendency in faith to a blind belief. It does not say, and has no tendency to say, " I believe because it is impossible." That is mere Quixotism and folly. Faith may, indeed, take hold of the hand of a father, and be willing to step where it does not see ; but then she is willing thus to step, only because she has a rational ground for believing that her father will lead her right. Christianity discards and repudiates altogether, any faith that can come into conflict with reason.

This view of faith gives it a definite sphere, it shows distinctly its relations both to philosophy and to reason, and removes from it all that mysterious or mystical appearance which has sometimes been thrown around religious faith. As an exercise of the mind it is, generically, no way different from that to which we are constantly accustomed. When a child follows implicitly the directions of its father, when a client puts his case into the hands of an advocate, there is an element in the act that is different from simple belief, it is an element that puts honor upon the father and the advocate. This is faith. Faith, then, generically, is confidence in a personal being. Specifically, religious faith is confidence in God, in every aspect and office in which he reveals himself. As that love of which God is the object, is religious love, so that confidence in Him as a Father, a Moral Governor, a Redeemer, a Sanctifier, in all the modes of his manifestation, by which we believe whatever he says because he says it, and commit ourselves and all our interests cheerfully and entirely into his hands, is religious faith. Surely there is in this, nothing irrational, or hard to be understood.

The distinctive element of faith, then, is not belief, but it is confidence from that perception and appreciation of moral character upon which the belief is based. Involved in this there must always be a belief of the trustworthiness of the object of our faith. Hence, if faith were perfect, it would involve, not merely a belief in testimony, but an obedience like that of Abraham. In his case there was simply a command, and strictly no testimony ; yet the faith was perfect.

It is this complex nature of faith that has caused the confusion respecting it. It does imply a movement of both the rational and the emotive nature. In this, sometimes the one, and sometimes the other may predominate, but it is never due either to the intellect simply, or to the feelings simply. When outward appearances, as in the case of Abraham, are opposed to the dictates of faith, it will be an affectionate confidence. When there is no such opposition, it will be a confiding affection in which the confidence may seem to be entirely absorbed and transfigured into love. The belief involved in faith, is based on those very qualities which necessarily call forth emotion or affection; and hence, in this act, the two are fused and inseparably blended. Hence too the moral element in faith, which is not necessarily in mere belief, and hence its power as a principle of action. Nor is there any thing strange or anomalous in this. Pity is a complex act, consisting of sympathy for distress and a desire to relieve it. These may exist in different proportions, but if either be wanting there is no pity; and yet no one finds any difficulty in understanding what pity is.

Having thus considered the nature of faith, we now proceed to its offices.

Of faith in general, the great office is to underlie all the social intercourse of personal beings. It is to this higher and distinct sphere of personal intercourse, what a belief in the uniformity of nature is in our intercourse with nature. Without confidence society is impossible. It is the great element and condition of social prosperity and happiness. Universally it will be found that all the ends of society are reached, in proportion as there is mutual confidence between husbands and wives, parents and children, rulers and sub-jects, buyers and sellers, friends and neighbors. Remove but the single element of distrust, and who does not see that the great cause of human wretchedness would be taken away. Let but the one element of a general and perfect confidence be poured into the now heaving mass of human society, and its agitations would subside, and it would be at once aggregated and crystalized into its most perfect forms. In connection with this, every form of human at-tachment would strike deep root, every mutual affinity would have free play, and every capacity of man for happi-ness from intercourse with his fellow-men would be filled.

Of the more specific offices of religious faith we will first consider that, so much insisted on in the Scriptures, by which it accepts a gratuitous salvation. From the na-ture of faith as now stated, it is easy to see that its relation to such a salvation is a necessary and not an arbitrary one. To be accepted, a gift must first be appreciated, and desired *as a gift*. This, in the case of salvation from sin, involves repentance. And then there must be full confidence in the sincerity of him who offers the gift. This is faith, and, the gift being desired, there can be a completion of the confidence only in its acceptance. In this view of it, faith is not that in consequence of which we receive the salvation as if the faith existed first and accepted the salvation afterwards, but faith is the very act of confidence by which the salvation is accepted. It is a confidence which can become complete only as it accepts the offer, because it is only as He makes the offer that the Saviour can become the object of our confidence. Faith then, in its relation to salvation, is that confidence by which we accept it as a free gift from the Saviour, and is the only possible way in which this gift of God could be appropriated. How simple ! how rational ! how strange it should fail to be understood !

A second office of religious faith, as stated in the Scriptures, is to unite man to God, and in so doing, to give him power with God. To this, faith, as now explained, is perfectly adapted. As our relations to God are so numerous and intimate, and as confidence in him can be based only on a perception of those perfect attributes which would call out the highest affection, it must be an affectionate confidence. But it is only by an affectionate confidence that such a being as man can be united to God, or, indeed, that any one moral being can be united to another. Let this exist, and everything in the relations of the two beings must be pleasant, the relation itself will be the ground of the highest satisfaction which our nature can know, and will lie at the foundation of a higher and nobler idea of being and of order than any other. What is the idea of myriads of orbs circling in harmony together, compared with that of myriads of intelligent and moral beings united to God and to each other in a mutual and affectionate confidence ? Here we find the true end of this universe —an order of which all other order is but the symbol.

And while faith thus unites us to God, it is natural and rational to suppose that it should have the great power ascribed to it in the Scriptures. It is one of the strongest impulses and principles of a rightly constituted nature never to disappoint any confidence that is justly reposed in it. This seems to be even the instinct of a generous nature without reference to principle. Who is there that would not protect a dove that should come and nestle in his bosom? An appeal by innocence, by helplessness, by distress, in which the individual abandons himself with entire confidence to *us*, is one of the strongest that can be made to our nature, and will often be met by the greatest sacrifices, not only by individuals, but by whole nations. Let Kossuth escape and come to this country, and confide himself to our protection, and let him be pursued by the combined power of Russia and of Austria, yea by the power of the world, and the nation would rise as one man, would form a living wall around him, and he would be taken only as his pursuers should pass over the dead bodies of those who would stand in his defence. Shall *men* do thus, and shall not God defend those who come to put their trust under the shadow of his wings? Shall any *innocent* creature of God that is in distress come to him, and confide in him, and shall not the resources of Omnipotence be held ready for his deliverance? Shall any guilty creature of God, however debased and wretched, yea, though he were dyed and steeped in sin, come to him with a confidence authorized by the death of Christ, and cast himself upon him for pardon and adoption, and not be received even as the prodigal son? Shall any servant of God, in this world of conflict, be hardly beset, and, feeling that his own strength is weakness, look up to God with an eye of filial confidence, and shall he not send him succor? Shall his servants say, in the very face of the flames, " Our God whom we serve is able to deliver us from the burning fiery furnace, and he will deliver us, O king," and shall he not deliver them ?   What are the laws of nature in a case like this ?   They are but as a technicality compared with a mighty principle.   One glance of a confiding eye is mightier than all the laws of nature.   Heaven and earth may pass away, but not a hair of him who puts confidence in God shall "fall to the earth."   Sooner, far sooner, would God sweep this material framework, with all its laws, into utter annihilation, than he would disappoint the authorized confidence of the most inconsiderable of his creatures.   How different is this universe when thus viewed by the light of faith in its relation to a controlling personal being, a Father, and a Friend ; and when viewed in the light of philosophy, as mere nature—as an unvarying, undiscriminating, crushing uniformity !

The third office of religious faith is to be a principle of action.   And if there be any one thing which a young man about to enter upon life ought to consider thoroughly, it is his principles of action.   Upon these his own character, and that of his enterprises, will depend.   As you, my friends, adopt, from this time, right principles of action, so, and so only, will you promote your true usefulness, and permament good.

But certain it is, referring to the distinction already made, that the highest principles of action cannot be found in the sphere of things.   The study of these may train the intellect, and make men mere philosophers ; they may awaken the desire to possess them as property and make men misers ; they may call forth the emotions of beauty and sublimity ; and that is all.   There is here no confidence, no affection, no sympathy.   But bring man, now, into intercourse with free, personal and moral beings, and every high faculty of his nature will come into play.   The intellect, and the heart and the moral nature will act together and strengthen each other. And as the basis of all such intercourse must be faith, so the basis of all intercourse with God must be religious faith.

As a principal of action, religious faith is contrasted with those adopted by the heroes of this world, because it tends to form a complete character. Recognizing an omnipresent and omniscient God, it acts equally at all times, and bears as well upon the minute, as upon the greater actions of life. Minute actions and details must make up the whole life of most men, and the greater part of the life of all men ; and what we need above all things, is a principle of action that shall embrace all acts equally, as the law of gravitation embraces the atom and the planet, and that may dignify the smallest act by the principle from which it proceeds. Such a principle is religious faith ; and nothing but this can carry the life-blood of principle into those minuter portions of human conduct on which our happiness here chiefly depends. This would attune the chords of domestic life and make them discourse sweet music; it would substitute the freshness of sincerity, and the flush of benevolence, for the paint and frigidity of a false and conventional politeness. Carrying out such a principle, an individual may be truly great, however humble his sphere ; and this greatness will bear the test, and grow as it is examined ; while that which takes human opinion as its standard and reward, dwindles and becomes contemptible the more it is known. This latter cultivates the art of concealment; it is great, and generous, and kind, in public; and mean, and selfish, and unamiable, at home. Long enough has the world been filled with pretences, and shows, and fair seemings, and whited sepulchres ; but the remedy for these is to be found, not in any ridicule or denunciation of hypocrisy, nor in any splenetic or contemptuous decrial of " shams," but only in the cultivation of a true religious faith.

This will be the more obvious if we notice a second, and grand peculiarity of religious faith, which is that it can work only in harmony with the moral nature. No man can expect to be aided or sustained by God, when he is doing any thing which he is conscious is not well pleasing to him. Confidence in God must imply a constant endeavor to know his will, and must, hence, quicken the conscience, and, as the Scriptures express it, purify the heart. I have already spoken of the essential connection between faith and love, and it is by its intimate alliance with conscience on the one hand, and love on the other, that religious faith is capable of becoming a principle of action so ennobling and so mighty. It is rational and intelligent as recognizing, sometimes the plans of God, and always the grounds of trust in Him ; it quickens the conscience as necessarily adopting the law of God for its rule of action ; and it gives full play to the affections, by drawing its very life from the holy and infinitely amiable character of God. Thus he who is actuated by this principle must have the strength that comes from the consciousness of acting rationally ; from peace with God ; and peace of conscience. Thus has it every element that can be needed to sustain great and heroic action. Let a man feel that he is in sympathy with God in the object of his pursuit, that God approves the means he adopts, and let him have a filial confidence in him, and what deed of a true heroism is there, whether of action or of suffering, which he may not perform ? Thus moved and sustained, is it any wonder that they of old " subdued kingdoms, wrought righteousness, obtained promises, stopped the mouths of lions, quenched the violence of fire, escape the edge of the

sword, out of weakness were made strong, waxed valiant
in fight, turned to flight the armies of the aliens "? And
what this principle was of old, it is now. The same God
is above us, and his response to any confidence reposed
in Him will not be less full. This only can support the
martyr, the moral hero, the hero of meekness, and righteousness, and love unconquerable. This only can lead
men to originate and sustain those great moral enterprises,
on the success of which the welfare and progress of the
world must ultimately turn. It cannot be that man should
set himself fully against the wickedness of his own heart,
and the wickedness of the world around him, and resist
the allurements of temptation, and defy the powers of
nature wielded by persecution, and endure to the end,
and overcome except as " seeing him who is invisible."
" This is the victory that overcometh the world even our
faith." Only this can enable the true missionary to forsake country and friends, and devote his life, in a heathen
land, to the good of those whom he knows but as
redeemed by the blood of Christ ; only this can sustain him
in attacking forms of sin that seem as ancient and firm as
the hills ; this alone can enable him to labor on till death,
and die in hope, while yet the darkness of midnight lies
upon the mountains. Such a faith has nothing to do with
nature. She comes down from above into the sphere of
nature, she contemplates objects of which nature knows
nothing, and when she acts rationally with reference to
these objects—to a kingdom and laws that are above
nature—nature says she is mad. She is not mad ; the
might of the universe is with her ; God is with her ; eternity shall vindicate her. This, not money, not machinery,
or confidence in them, but this it is that the church needs.
Let her come directly to God in the strength of a perfect
weakness, in the power of a felt helplessness and a child-

like confidence, and then, either she has no strength, and has no right to be, or she has a strength that is infinite. Then, and thus, will she stretch out the rod over the seas of difficulty that lie before her, and the waters shall divide, and she shall pass through, and sing the song of deliverance.

From the view of faith now taken, it is easy to see that every system of negations, and distrust, and scepticism, must tend to lower the tone of human action and enjoyment, and must be uncongenial to our nature. Such systems may be useful in pulling down error, but have no constructive power. Their effect must be like that of withdrawing the vital element from the air ; and not more certainly will languor and feebleness creep over the physical system in one case, than over the spiritual in the other. There can be no robust and healthy life, either social or spiritual, without a strong faith.

Let me then first counsel you, my friends, to place a generous confidence in your fellow-men. Not that you should be weak, or credulous, but, if you must err at all, let it be on the side of confidence. For your own sakes repress the first risings of a suspicious and distrustful temper. It will unstring the nerves of your energy, and corrode your very heart. Far from you be that form of conceit which attributes to itself shrewdness and wisdom by always suspecting evil. Far sooner would I make it a part of my philosophy and plan, to be imposed upon and cheated, up to a certain point. Let not even intercourse with the world, and the caution of age, congeal the spring of your confidence and sympathy. So doing, you may find much that you would wish otherwise, some you may find that will be as a briar, and sharper than a thorn hedge, brethren that will supplant, and neighbors that will walk in slanders ; but you will also find answering confidence, repose for the soul, green spots, and fountains in the des ert.

Let me also warn you especially against all those pan- theistic views, virtually atheistic, which are setting in upon us in these days in connection with certain forms of a tran- scendental philosophy. The great result, if not the object of all such schemes, is to obscure and exclude the idea of personality in God ; and hence, of accountability in man. It is around this banner, more than any other, that the migratory hordes of infidelity are gathering, and uniting against the religion of the Bible. These schemes assume the garb of a high philosophy ; they put on the sheep's clothing of a religious phraseology. In their outward as- pect, they are contemplative, reverent, and especially phi- lanthropic. Their advocates believe in God—but then all things are God, and in the working of all things hitherto, nothing higher than man has been produced. They be- lieve in inspiration—but then all good books are inspired. They believe in Jesus Christ—and so they do in Confu- cius, and Socrates, and Mohammed, and Luther, and in all *earnest* and *heroic* men. They believe in progress—but in a progress which neither springs from nor leads to, moral order. They make the ideas of guilt and retribution a bugbear, redemption an absurdity, repentance unneces- sary, and faith impossible. Making such pretensions, to philosophy and giving such license to passion, these schemes have great attractions, and form the chief specu- lative quicksands which the currents of this age have drifted up, and on which the young are in danger of being wrecked. They merge personality into laws, the operations of a wise agent into necessary uniformities. They make the order and stability of God's works testify, not to his wisdom and immutability, but to his non-existence. They change the truth which the creatures thus tell, into a lie, and say, " No

God." Thus are the heavens disrobed of their glory, and infinite space becomes a blank, and faith finds no object, and the tendrils of affection find no oak, and human life is without a providence, and conscience is a lie, and death is an eternal sleep. To all such schemes, and their abettors, how appropriate and overwhelming are the reproof and the argument framed expressly for them long ago : " Understand, ye brutish among the people ; and ye fools, when will ye be wise ? He that planted the ear, shall he not hear ? He that formed the eye, shall he not see ? He that chastiseth the heathen, shall he not correct ? He that teacheth man knowledge, shall not he know ? "

And now, my Friends, what can I wish better for you personally, or for the world in your relations to it, than that you should take for your actuating and sustaining principle Faith in God. Without this, you will lack the highest element of happiness, and the only adequate ground of support ; life will be without dignity, and death without hope. Only by faith can you run that race which is set before *you*, as before those of old. In this world your courses may be different ; you will choose different professions, and diverge widely in your lines of life. To some of you, the race here may be brief. But whatever this may be, and whether longer or shorter, before you all there is set the same race under the moral government of God ; to you all is held out the same prize. Why should you not run this race? Never was there a time, in the history of the world, when moral heroes were more needed. The world waits for such. The providence of God has commanded science to labor and prepare the way for such. For them she is laying her iron tracks, and stretching her wires, and bridging the oceans. But where are they ? Who shall breathe into our civil and political relations the breath of a higher life ? Who shall couch the eyes of a paganized science, and of a pantheistic philosophy, that they may see God ? Who shall consecrate, to the glory of God, the triumphs of science? Who shall bear the life-boat to the stranded and perishing nations? Who should do these things, if not you—not in your relations to time only, but to eternity, and to the universe of God?

And as seen in the light of faith, what a race ! what an arena ! what a prize !

Faith places us under the inspection and care of the eternal and omnipresent God, and accepts of him as a Father, a Redeemer, a Sanctifier, and Portion. She enthrones Him above all laws, and to that utterance which she hears coming as the voice of many waters from around the throne, saying, The Lord God omnipotent reigneth, she says, Amen. She introduces us to a spiritual family of our own race, and of superior orders of beings, before whose numbers and capacities the imagination falters. She accepts the suggestions of analogy, that the moral and spiritual universe is commensurate with that physical universe which night reveals, the outskirts of which no telescope can reach ; and for the unfolding and sweep of a goverment embracing such an extent, she has an eternity. Such is the scene in the midst of which this race is to be run. What is the prize ? It is likeness to God—sonship —the inheritance of all things to be enjoyed forever. That such a prize might be offered, Christ died ; that it nay be striven for, as the one thing needful, the Holy Spirit pleads. Gird yourselves, then, for this race ; run it with patience, "looking unto Jesus." The world may not notice, or know you ; for it knew Him not. It may persecute you, for it persecuted Him ; but in the Lord Jehovah is everlasting strength. He will be with you ;

He will sustain you ;—the great cloud of witnesses will encompass you ; they will wait to hail you with acclamation as you shall reach the goal, and receive the prize. That goal may you all reach,—that prize may you all receive.

II.

STRENGTH AND BEAUTY.

Strength and beauty are in his sanctuary.—Psalm, xcvi. 6.

THERE are some things, both in nature and in character, that are incompatible with each other. Such are light and darkness, moral good and moral evil, hope and despair. One can exist only as the other is excluded. There are also some things, as drouth and sterility, integrity and firmness, stealing and lying, which are naturally associated, and which we expect to find together. Again; there are qualities which, though not incompatible, have yet a tendency to exclude each other, and which are seldom found combined in any high degree. Such are flexibility and firmness, weight and velocity, energy and good temper, imagination and judgment, judgment and feeling, versatility and concentration, patience and the power of rapid combination and execution.

That the highest excellence, either mental or moral, can be reached only by blending, in their most perfect proportions, qualities which have thus a tendency to exclude each other, may be easily seen. An acute intellect is justly reckoned a perfection, but there is in it a tendency to exclude broad and comprehensive views. The power, on the other hand, of taking the most broad and comprehensive views, not only tends to exclude, but often leads us to despise that acuteness and subtlety of analysis

₄ AUGUST 17, 1851.

without which no investigation is perfect. But these are not incompatible, and a perfect mind would be able to act equally well in either direction. As a perfect eye would possess both a telescopic and a microscopic power—now ranging through the universe, and now adjusting itself to the minutest object—so will mind be perfect only as it can embrace at once the most expanded generalizations and the minutest details. In a perfect mind, great logical power would be united with an affluent imagination ; but these tend to exclude each other, and the combination is so rare that he in whom it occurs is always a distinguished man. In moral character, economy is a virtue ; but there is in it a tendency to the exclusion of generosity, which is equally a virtue. Boldness is not easily combined with caution, nor sternness with a melting pity, nor zeal with toleration. How seldom is a Boanerges at the same time a Barnabas !

Among the qualities which may thus exclude each other, but which are yet often combined both in nature and in character, are strength and beauty.

In nature, how beautiful is the lily, the tulip, the rose, the honeysuckle ! How beautiful is the humming-bird, that poises itself upon its almost viewless wings, and draws from that same honeysuckle its sweet food ! How beautiful is the oriole, that weaves its hanging nest in the tree above ! These are beautiful, but have not strength. On the other hand, how strong is the ox, and the elephant, and the rhinoceros, and the whale ! These have strength, but not beauty. The hugeness of these contributes to their strength, but would seem to exclude beauty ; while the lightness and fragility and exquisite structure of the others constitute their beauty, but would seem to exclude strength. This separation of strength and beauty is perhaps more striking when they are contrasted. Of this we find instances in man and woman, in the vine and the oak, in the violet sheltered in the cleft of the rock, in the rainbow overhanging the cataract.

But these qualities, so often separated and contrasted in nature, are also often combined. They are so in the tree. In the oak strength predominates. Its sturdy and gnarled trunk is the emblem of strength; and yet an oak, with its full coronal of glossy leaves, is not without beauty. In the elm, beauty predominates. With its light form compared with its height, with its symmetrical top and pendent branches, it stands like a veiled bride in her beauty ; and yet the elm impresses us with the idea of great strength. The green valley is beautiful, the mountain is strong. The mountain covered with verdure, is strength clothed with beauty. In a horse, to pass to the animal kingdom, these qualities are sometimes strikingly blended. A fine horse is among the most powerful of animals ; but when he is left as nature made him, with his flowing mane and tail, and moves with the apparent consciousness of the admiration he excites, he is among the most beautiful. But it is in the human form that these qualities are capable of their highest and most perfect combination. This is the central idea in that conception of the Apollo by the Greeks, which must always remain the model of the physical man. In that, nothing that would contribute to beauty is conceded to strength, and everything that contributes to strength is beautiful. Let the body of man combine these qualities as it may, and it is evidently a fit dwelling for that immortal spirit which is made in the image of God. Such a body, filled with life, the features radiant with intelligence and love, would realize the highest conception that man can form of the power of the material, both to veil, and to reveal the spiritual.

But while we thus find this combination in each

separate department of the works of God, it is perhaps most striking in the general impression which those
works make upon man. To the whole structure and
movement of nature, the Greeks gave the name "*kosmos*,"
signifying beauty ; but looking as they did upon the earth
as fixed, what could give a stronger impression of strength
in the form of stability ? But if we look upon the earth
and planetary system as now understood, this impression
is greatly heightened. While we have the same round of
the seasons, the same "pomp of day" and glories of the
night, the same green hills and sparkling waters, and the
same bow in the heavens with them, nothing can be more
beautiful than the conception which our astronomy gives
us of the uniform, circular, harmonious movements of the
shining orbs above us, and nothing can give us a higher
conception of force, or strength exerted, than their amazing
velocity.

With such a combination of these elements in the
works of God, we might expect that they would be combined in any physical structure which he should direct
men to build. Accordingly we find that strength and
beauty were in his sanctuary. Probably these were more
perfectly combined in the temple of Solomon, than in any
other building ever erected. This, however, was not for
its own sake ; but, under a typical dispensation, it was
doubtless intended to symbolize that spiritual strength and
beauty which were to belong to the spiritual, and only true
temple of God.

Let us then look at strength and beauty as they may
exist and be combined in the character of man.

The idea of strength is simple, admitting of no analysis ;
but strength itself may be manifested in either of two ways.
It may either make an impression, as when the "sun
shineth in his strength ;" it may overcome obstacles,

break down barriers, and march forward to the attainment
of a proposed end ; or it may stand firm as the hills, when
it said that " the strength of the hills in his also ; " it may
bear burdens, it may resist impressions that are attempted
to be made upon it.

The whole strength which any man will be able to
exert in either of these modes will depend in part on the
faculties he may possess, and in part on the energy of the
will.

The faculties will vary in their power according to their
original constitution, and their training.   Nothing that I
see would lead me to suppose that the powers of all men
are originally alike.   In this respect, as well as in others,
God gives to one five talents, and to another one.   But
certain original powers being given, their subsequent
strength will depend on their training.   Here the great
and only law is, that the legitimate use of any power given
by God strengthens that power.   This is true of the body
and of the mind ; and here we see the difference between
the works of God and those of man.   The works of man
are impaired by use ; those of God are improved.   For
his original faculties man is not responsible, but only for
their improvement.

But while there is nothing praiseworthy in the possession of great original powers, we yet contemplate them
with admiration and delight, as we do a great tree, a great
mountain, a great river, as we do the ocean.   We watch
with delight the march of the mind of Butler, we wonder
at the apparent intuitions of Newton, and at the spontaneous creations of the genius of Milton.   It is vain to
complain of the admiration of men for talent and genius
as such.   That admiration is legitimate.   It may be over-
whelmed and merged in sorrow, or in horror from their
perversion ; but interest will concentrate where great

power is manifested, whether it be physical or mental, whether for good or for evil. A tornado, prostrating trees and unroofing houses, a volcano pouring forth its destructive lava, a burning city even, regarded simply as a display of energy, are witnessed with pleasure. But this strength of the faculties, this energy with which they are capable of working, however impelled, is entirely different from strength of character. This it is for which we are responsible, and with which we are chiefly concerned.

But man can have strength of character only as he is capable of controlling his faculties ; of choosing a rational end ; and, in its pursuit, of holding fast to his integrity against all the might of external nature.

Without self-control there can be no strength of character. Its first condition is the subjection of the impulses and appetites and passions, of all the faculties, to the control of the personal power—of the man himself. "He that hath no rule over his own spirit is like a city that is broken down and without walls." He has no strength to do, or to resist.

This power of self-control being supposed, strength of character may be manifested by a continued and concentrated energy put forth for the attainment of a given end. This strength, however, can be manifested fully only as obstacles are met, and external influences are resisted, and the power, not only of active effort, but of patient endurance, is tested to the utmost.

Of such strength of character, both in active effort and in patient endurance, Washington is a good example. During the long years of the Revolution his activity was incessant, and that too in the midst of every form of discouragement ; yet he never faltered. Still, strength of character was not as severely tested in him as it might have been. There were many who understood his object,

and sympathized with him. The eyes of a nation were
upon him. It never came to be a question whether
he should relinquish his purpose or his life. But if we
suppose one of exquisite sensibility, the most keenly alive
to suffering and to every form of reproach, whose object
is great and worthy but not understood, who has no sympathy from any human being, who is either opposed or de-
serted by all mankind, and that the question with him is
whether he shall abandon his purpose or go to a death of
torture and of ignominy, we shall then have the highest conceivable test of strength of character. Of this there has
been but one perfect example in our nature ; but of this,
man is capable. He was once in harmony with nature
and with all external agencies. In a perfect state he
would be. But through moral, and consequent physical
derangement, all expressed sympathy, and all external
agencies may be against him, and they may press him to
the last extremity ; but still he may have such a sense
of duty, and such faith in God, as to enable him to stand
firm, and to meet certain death. The spiritual may triumph over the sensual and the material—the immortal
over the mortal. If man is not the master of nature, as
here he is not, he is not yet her slave. Against his own
will, no power on earth or in hell can make him so. As
spiritual and free, he is not properly of nature, but stands
over against her. He is no part of a linked and necessary series of cause and effect, but may find in himself
grounds of activity that will enable him to resist every
impulse and motive that can be brought from without.
When pushed fully up to that line where degradation and
slavery commence, he has only to stand firm, and God
himself, by the hand of death, will open a gate by which
he may pass out unstained and unhumbled into perfect
freedom. Here is his true dignity, here is strength. So

have the martyrs stood. What is the strength of the hills compared with this?

Strength thus shown in resistance to impressions, and in standing firm, is in some respects less striking, and at the time is less admired, than that which shows itself in active effort, producing directly great results ; but it may be doubted whether, in a world like this, it is not more heroic, and ultimately more fruitful of good and more honored. To illustrate this, and express for it the admiration of mankind, the simile of all ages is that of a rock standing immovable in the midst of the tumultuous waters. And certainly when we think of the sea of human passion, and of the fury into which it may be lashed, and of the strong desire for appro- bation, and of the fear of death, and of the natural distrust of men in their own opinions when they stand alone, it is one of the sublimest of all spectacles to see a man stand firm against all possible allurements and threatenings, and, reckless of consequences, hold fast to truth and to duty.

Perhaps it should be mentioned here, that energy in active effort, and the power of patient waiting and endur- ance, may be blended in different proportions, and that they have some tendency to exclude each other.

Such are the nature and sphere of strength of charac- ter. What are those of beauty?

As the idea of strength is simple, so is that of beauty. The emotion can be known only by being felt, and only experience can teach us what it is that causes the emo- tion to arise. Doubtless there is something of inherent beauty in all the forms of moral goodness, but in some more than in others. If it be said, as it may be, that there is beauty in justice, yet other elements preponderate, and it has far less of beauty than benevolence. On such a sub- ject, the imperceptible shading of one thing into another

will not permit us to draw sharp lines ; but it may be said,
in general, that while strength of character depends on
the will, beauty depends on the affections. The affections
are beautiful because they are spontaneous, and the general truth here is that strength is to be found in the voluntary
action of the mind, and beauty in its spontaneous action.

We are all conscious of these two modes in which our
faculties work. A student may pursue a science from fear,
or from the love of praise or of gain. In this case the
faculties will be impelled as by a force from behind, and
the moment that is withdrawn they will cease to act—perhaps will react with strong aversion towards the science
itself. Here the will must labor—it must row against the
current. Much of the activity in this world is of this kind,
and this it is that makes it *labor* and drudgery.

But again, a student may pursue a science from a love
of the science itself. In this case there is an affinity—
an attraction. There is a current of the soul setting in
that direction, which the will may indeed resist, may perhaps wholly arrest ; but it will require an effort to do so.
The will must indeed now give its assent, but it need not
row the boat. The movement of the mind is spontaneous, and without apparent effort. It is as when

“ The river windeth at its own sweet will.”

Such activity and effort are not esteemed a labor. There
will be in it a deep joy. With the movement of the faculties as they perform it, there will be a music like that of
the spheres. It is from the attempt of the will to resist
these currents, that some of the profoundest struggles of
which our nature is capable arise.

Now all such spontaneous movements, if legitimate, are
beautiful. They are beautiful as spontaneous. Such are
all the emotions of taste which respond to the beauties and

sublimities of nature and of art. Such are all the natural affections, and such preëminently are all those high moral affections which find a complacency in their object from its own intrinsic character. Thus it is that benevolence is beautiful, and pity, and tenderness, and a regard for the feelings of others in the minutest particulars; thus sympathy is beautiful, and love, and a clinging trust. Let these be genuine, spontaneous, like the free gushing up of a fountain, and there is a beauty in them such as there is in no verdure or sparkling waters. They are to those sterner qualities which give strength, what the leaves and blossoms are to the tree, making it beautiful in the eyes of men, and sending up a fragrance to heaven.

But spontaneousness is not the only element of beauty. If the beauty be a moral one, as it must, to be strictly a beauty of character, then the affections must be conformed to the law of conscience, and will have an intrinsic beauty as moral. The beauty of holiness is the highest of which the mind is capable, and this implies the conformity of the affections to a perfect law.

What has now been said applies to particular affections ; but beauty of character, as a whole, must include not only spontaneousness and moral rectitude, but also symmetry. There is a tendency in spontaneous movements to extravagance and wildness. This must be repressed. The river, to be beautiful, must indeed wind "at its own sweet will," but it must wind within its banks. A just proportion must be preserved between the affections themselves, and between the affections and the other powers. Symmetry, involving completeness, is a most important element of beauty of character.

With these elements, individual mind possesses a beauty far transcending that of nature. And if this be so in a single individual, how much more in a spiritual system

where every relation is responded to, and every duty met!
What is the harmony of music to the concord of souls in
a true affection? What is the breaking up of light into
its seven colors as it meets with the surfaces of matter,
compared with the modifications of benevolence as it
meets with the varying forms of sensitive and intelligent
life? What is the beauty of natural scenery, with its clus-
tering objects, and contrasted flowers and trees, compared
with the meeting of a family, upon no member of which a
stain rests, and where you see the gray hairs of the patri-
arch, and the infant of the third generation? What is the
beauty of satellities circling around primaries, and primaries around the sun, compared with the order of families
and the State—compared with the order of that moral
government of which God is the centre and sun, and of
which a holy love is at once the uniting force and the
glory and beauty?

Thus the strength and the beauty which impress us
most, are THE STRENGTH OF THE WILL, and THE BEAUTY
OF THE AFFECTIONS.

That the tendency already noticed of strength and
beauty in matter to exclude each other extends also to
mind, is too obvious to need illustration ; and it is equally
obvious that the most desirable character can be reached
only as these are combined in the most perfect manner.
And what is there that this combination would not include ?
As perfect strength and beauty of the body would imply
and include all that is desirable in the body, so would
perfect strength and beauty of the mind and of character
include all that would be desirable in them. What is there
higher or better that we can wish for our friends ? What
higher or better at which a young man can aim ?

The question then arises, how this combination can be

reached. And this brings us directly to the assertion of the Bible, that "strength and beauty are in his sanctuary." Adopting its spiritual import, the doctrine here indicated, and which I wish to enforce, is, that it is only within the fold and under the banner of the religion of Christ, that strength and beauty of character can be perfectly combined. Aside from Christianity there may be strength combined with the beauty of the natural affections, but strength combined with the highest beauty there cannot be.

That true religion would produce this combination appears because God desires it. This desire he has indicated, as we cannot doubt, in the structure of his works already referred to. Does he then value strength and beauty in these? Has he made them the foundation of all that we admire, and of most that we value in material forms? And shall he not value that in mind which is so analogous as to be called by the same name? Yea, is not nature typical? Was it not so constituted for the very purpose of leading us on gradually to ideas of this higher strength and beauty? Is it not but as the Mosaic dispensation to lead us to something higher and better than itself? As certainly as nature was intended to lead us at all to a knowledge of the perfections of God, so certainly were physical strength and beauty intended to reveal to us that in Him which is the substance, and of which these are but the reflection. Hence, only as there is spiritual strength and beauty, can his own image be produced in his creatures.

But on this point, if nature could leave us in doubt, revelation does not. We are commanded to " be *strong* in the Lord ; " and the Psalmist prays that the *beauty* of the Lord our God may be upon us. It is the object of the Saviour to present to himself a glorious church, without

spot or wrinkle, or any such thing. Does God then desire
this ? Then must it be the duty and aspiration of every
religious man to strive for it.   So only is man religious, so
only ennobled, as he strives in coincidence with the purposes and plans of God—as he works "according to the
pattern showed him in the mount."   Does God desire
this?   Then will He who is the foundation of all strength
and beauty ultimately impart them to those, and to those
only, who shall come to Him for them.   Thus coming,
that process of assimilation will take place, by which, as
they behold the glory of the Lord, they shall be changed
into the same image.   Approaching the sun, they will
shine brighter, and the strength of their movement will be
increased.   God will clothe them with strength and beauty,
and thus these shall be the completion and glory of his
spiritual, as they are of his material creation.

Again.   That the religion of Christ must produce this
combination of strength and beauty, is obvious from the
character of Christ.   To be a Christian, a man must not
only receive the doctrines and admire the precepts of
Christ, but must be like him.   He can be a Christian only
as he actually follows Christ and is like Christ.   In this is
found a grand peculiarity of Christianity as distinguished
from other systems.   But there has never appeared on the
earth any character which approximated to that of Christ,
in the union of strength and beauty.   In him we see the
strength of achievement, and the strength of endurance.
He moved with calm majesty, like the sun.   The bloody
sweat, and the crown of thorns, and the cross, were full in
his eye, but he was "obedient unto death."   In his perfect self-sacrifice we see the perfection of strength ; in the
love which prompted it we see the perfection of beauty.
This combination of self-sacrifice and love, thus perfect in
Christ, must be commenced in every Christian ; and when

it shall be, in its spirit, complete in him, then will he also be perfect in strength and beauty.

But once more. That this doctrine is true, appears from the very nature of true religion. This is no mere impulse ; and strength of character is not a blind obstinacy, which, if it does show strength of will, shows also, in equal proportion, weakness of intellect. No : an intelligent *faith* is at the foundation of Christian character. Such a faith will " work," that is, it will produce obedience, and it will " work by love." But it is in obedience to a perfect law, from love, that we find the highest expression of strength and beauty. Law demands the approbation of the moral nature, and the intelligent action of the will in obedience ; but it comes as an external force, and when it conflicts with inclination, obedience will have in it something of constraint ; it will not be perfect freedom ; it will be shorn of its beauty. But let a perfect law no longer stand without as a law of constraint ; let it enter in and become the internal law of the mind, so that every inclination and current of the soul—all its love—shall set in the same direction, and then will there be a confluence of all in man that is rational and moral, with all that is emotive —of all the elements which produce strength with those which produce beauty. This is the consummation which the world waits for, the deliverance and the rest. So only can man be at peace with the law, and at peace with himself. So only can the most intense activity become a harmony and a joy, become rest and peace. So only can the nuptials be celebrated of inclination with conscience, of liberty with law. It is of the essence of Christianity to produce this identification of activity and repose, this union of inclination and conscience, of liberty and law, and thus of strength and beauty. So doing, it must be true ; for it so accords with the nature of man as to embosom his highest good here, and to contain the elements of heaven. If it be not true, falsehood is as good as truth, for no truth could more demonstrably save man. Starting with these combinations, the immortal spirit will need nothing but the expansion of its powers to enable it to move on in its unending way with the strength of a giant and the beauty of an angel.

This is a point on which we may well dwell. You know what a terror to us law is, especially the law of God ; how severe and onerous, even while it commends itself to the conscience, its requisitions seem. You know what that fear of its penalty is that hath torment. Now, could we come to see the stern features of this law so radiant with loveliness that we would not have one of them changed ; could we see within its domain such a perfection of holiness and happiness that no wish would stray beyond that domain ; could we adopt this external law as the law of the mind, so that it should become the life of our life, how plain is it that all the harmonies of the soul would be restored, and that in its every movement there would be strength and beauty. But this enthronement of the law of God, or as I would choose to say, of the God of the law, in the centre of the affections, must come from a perfect Christianity—it can come from that alone ; no other system even proposes to itself such a result ; and hence we may regard the doctrine as established, that strength and beauty are in his sanctuary, and only there.

But if this be so, it may be asked why more of moral beauty has not been manifested in the lives of Christians. It is well known that evangelical religion especially has been regarded by some as distasteful, and the lives of its professors as severe, and harsh, and the reverse of beautiful.

To this two answers may be given. The first is that

the real beauty of Christian character that exists is not
known, nor appreciated. It is not known—for this is no
conservatory plant fostered by human culture and admiration. It springs up under the eye of God on the mountain-
side, and in the retired valley. For Him it blooms, and He
who notices the violet that no human eye ever sees will
notice this. It is not appreciated—for the standards of
this world are wrong. The beauty which the world admires and idolizes, is that beauty of fashion and of art
which may minister to vanity, to sensuality, to superstition
—that beauty of manners which may cover a corrupt heart
—and that beauty of nature which may become a part of
a pervading pantheism. To these the Christian would
give their due place, but he thinks little of them compared
with the beauty of the affections and the life. To him the
character of Christ is supremely beautiful. He is the
" chief among ten thousand," but how is he to the world?
It was foretold of Him, perfect in beauty as his character
was, that he should be a root out of dry ground, and that
when we should see him there would be no *beauty* in
him that we should desire him. This was fulfilled. The
beauty of the character of Christ was not appreciated in
his own day ; it is not now ; and it is to be expected that
the disciple shall be as his Lord. It cannot be expected
that the selfish, the sensual, the ambitious, the proud, the
vain, or the frivolous should admire that which is so opposed to their own temper and character. Especially cannot this be expected when holiness lays aside its abstract
form, and is seen in actual life opposing and casting down
cherished corruptions and interests. Then, instead of
admiration and praise, all history shows that moral goodness and beauty are vilified ; they are cast out as evil ;
are persecuted and crucified. What do bigoted perse-

cutors and infuriated mobs know or care about moral beauty ?

A second answer is, that Christianity is here but incipient, militant, imperfect. It begins in repentance, in tears, in struggles against sin, in self-denial and renunciation of what the heart had clung to. In this state of struggle there is a beauty to the eye of God, but not to that of the world. But beyond this there are many Christians who do not get—nay, they seem to cease to struggle, and stereotype a form and aspect of religion fit for neither a sinner nor a saint, that is neither of the law nor the gospel. There is in it slavery and penance. The face of duty is austere. They abstain from gayety, from fashion and folly, too much through fear, or conventionalism. They have no consistency. They attend church on the Sabbath, but show little of the spirit of religion during the week. They have more of the form of religion, than of the spirit of benevolence. The love of the world in them is not slain by the cross of Christ. There is no free and full and joyful consecration of themselves to God. They know nothing of the "joy of the Lord" as their strength. But religion—if anything with a preponderance of these elements can be called such—can be beautiful only as the conditions of beauty are met. It must be from the heart, and it must be symmetrical. The miserable notion of duty as imposing tasks, which is so prevalent, must pass away. Everything harsh and austere must vanish from her countenance. The Christian must look upon her with the eye of a lover. At her voice his heart must throb, and his chest heave ; her call must be to him as the sound of the trumpet to the war-horse. Then would each individual Christian have not only strength, but beauty ; and that conception in Holy Writ of the embodied church, so beautiful, and so accordant with the spirit of our text,

2

would be realized. In her *beauty*, she would be " fair as the moon and clear as the sun," and in her *strength* she would be " terrible as an army with banners."

In the preceding discussion, a distinction has been indicated between that strength and beauty of the faculties which belong to genius and talent and taste, and that strength and beauty of character which involve moral excellence. This distinction is, perhaps, sufficiently obvious ; but genius and talent have been, and still are, so much deified, and have cast such an illusive attraction around moral deformity, that I wish to draw to it particular attention.

The distinction is that between the agent and the instrument, between a person giving direction and that which is directed. This relative place of these is to be carefully noticed, because of the peculiar difficulty there is, in the present moral state of the world, in combining talent and genius with a high and reverent regard for duty. This is not that there is any natural opposition between them, but because that admiration and influence which are so dear to men possessing talent and genius are expected to follow them without much reference to moral integrity. Now what we say, is, that we are not to over-estimate the mere instrument, however brilliant. We say that our chief regard is due to that sacred personality, that moral presence, which has both the power and the right to direct talent and genius, and before which it is their place to wait and to bow. We say that in any other relation talent is a curse, and that the light of genius can only " lead to bewilder, and dazzle to blind." We would honor genius and talent as gifts of God ; we would make large allowance, if they must have them, or think they must, for their peculiarities, their idiosyncrasies, their weaknesses even ;

but when those who possess them would regard themselves, and be regarded by others, as privileged persons, whose moral delinquencies are to be allowed or winked at, and that, too, on the very ground that should be their highest condemnation, we would utter our solemn protest. We say that the influence of no other men can be so hostile to the best interests of the community—if they be public men, to the liberties of a free people. We say that no rebuke can be too prompt or severe when any man would practically dignify or even palliate meanness, or trickery, or falsehood, or profaneness, or licentiousness, or corruption, by associating them with high intellectual gifts. In the judgment of God, nothing can compensate for the want of moral strength and beauty of character; in comparison with these, everything else is as nothing. This should be so in the judgment of man, and to this position we would fain hope that public opinion is slowly finding its way.

These are the great thing. On these your happiness and influence here will mainly depend; by these your whole interest, under the government of God, will be ultimately decided. My object has been to bring to your definite apprehension a standard of character at which you might safely aim, and to show you how that standard might be reached. I have wished to give you a motto to be inscribed upon your banner, which might give you strength in the hour of conflict. And what can I give you better than *strength and beauty?* What can you do better than to seek the highest combinations of these in the characters you are to form and to manifest?

And in doing this, you are not to suppose, from anything that has been said, that you will be laboring to blend things that are naturally opposed to each other. No; in the deepest view of them they are but the varying forms of the manifestation of one force. They are not one as opposite polar forces are one; but strength, though not necessarily manifesting itself in the form of beauty, though it has a centrifugal force that tends to carry it off from its true curve, does yet underlie it, and is essential to the formation of that curve. Rightly directed, strength seems to attenuate and expand itself into beauty as the trunk of the tree, which is strong, attenuates and expands itself into the branches and the leaves, which are beautiful. It is strength alone that can elaborate itself into beauty ; and only as it does this can we have evidence of the perfection of strength. The exquisite finish of the leaf of the tulip, is from the circulation within it of the divine omnipotence, and is as essential to the perfect evidence for that, as the spheres that roll above. So can you give the highest evidence of strength of character only as that strength can so restrain and control its own workings, as to elaborate itself into beauty. The strength that we want is not a brute, unregulated strength; the beauty that we want is no mere surface beauty, but we want a beauty on the surface of life that is from the central force of principle within, as the beauty on the cheek of health is from the central force at the heart. This is the combination and the character that the world needs, that you need. Going forth with this, the wildernesses and solitary places of the earth will be glad for you. With this you will fill, up to the measure of expectation, and beyond it, every position of domestic and social and public life. You will be more appreciated as you are more known. The natural influence of uncommon powers or acquisitions will not be hindered or marred by those sad blemishes that everybody must speak of in a whisper, but that everybody will know. If you should have greatness of character, it will not shoot up into those isolated and startling peaks that attract notice indeed, but are barren; but it will rise up into those broad table-lands that are covered with verdure, and where the springs arise that gladden the valleys. You will work in harmony with God, and He will give you success.

But you are to remember that the strength and beauty that can do this are not those of nature. The strength is the strength of faith, and the beauty is the beauty of holiness. As I have said, it is only through the religion of Christ that this combination can be reached. Here is our only hope. But through this it may be reached? This combination of strength and beauty you may all reach, every one of you: and eye hath not seen, nor ear heard, nor hath it entered into the heart of man to conceive the blessings that will flow from it in the track of ages. Other strength will decay, other beauty will fade, but this strength will only grow stronger and this beauty more beautiful as eternity shall roll on. "They that wait on the Lord shall renew their *strength;* they shall mount up with wings as eagles, they shall run and not be weary, they shall walk and not faint;" and "the *beauty* of the Lord" their "God shall be upon them." This, my friends, this is the strength, and this the beauty I desire for you. In your characters may they be blended, and in all the pilgrimage of life that is now before you, may you be girded with strength from on high, and may the beauty of the Lord your God be upon you.

III.

RECEIVING AND GIVING.

It is more blessed to give than to receive.—Acts, xx. 35.

A S a dependent being man is, and must be, a receiver.
From God he must receive life and breath, and all
things ; and no one can so elevate or isolate himself, that
he shall not need to receive from his fellow men those
things which only their sympathy and kindness can bestow.

Man being thus necessarily a receiver, we should anticipate, from the goodness of God, that it would be blessed
for him to receive. And so it is. It is blessed for the
creature to receive from the Creator. It is blessed not
only from the enjoyment which the gift itself may confer,
but as awakening admiration, and gratitude, and love. It
is blessed for the child to receive from the parent, for the
friend to receive from his friend. It is always blessed to
receive when the gift is born of affection.

This blessedness our Saviour knew. We are told that
Mary Magdalene, and Joanna the wife of Chuza, Herod's
steward, and Susanna, and many others, ministered to him
of their substance. He received of them what he needed,
and, so far as appears, he consented thus to receive at the
hands of gratitude and affection, and was doubtless blessed
in so receiving his whole support.

But if it is thus blessed to receive, it is more blessed to
give. This is one of those great truths, uttered by our

₊ August 15, 1852.

Saviour, opposed to the whole spirit and practice of the age in which he appeared, which, like his inculcation of the forgiveness of enemies, and universal philanthropy, and seeking first the kingdom of God, showed a divine insight. It is a great practical truth, which, as it is received or rejected, must affect the whole spirit and all the results of life.

This blessedness was that pre-eminently known by our Saviour. " The Son of man came, not to be ministered unto, but to minister, and to *give* his *life* a ransom for many." He gave, not property, but himself. He gave instruction, and gifts of healing, and a divine sympathy. He gave the energies of his being in activity and in suffering for the welfare of man.

But here the inquiry arises, what is it to give. As now used this term carries the mind chiefly, if not wholly, to property ; but this cannot be its main reference, for then neither Christ nor his Apostles would have illustrated their own precepts, or have known, to any great extent, the blessedness of giving, It is worthy of notice, that no direct record is made, that either Christ or his Apostles ever gave any thing in the form of property ; and that would be a sad interpretation which would restrict the pleasures and benefits of giving, to the rich. To give, is not merely to transfer property without an equivalent from him who receives it. This may be done from a regard to public opinion, to quiet conscience, to purchase heaven, to get free from annoyance. Property is not affection, it is not self-sacrificing energy, it is not the heart or the life. No ; *to give, is to impart benefits freely, out of good will.* This Christ and his Apostles did. Said Peter to the impotent man, " Silver and gold have I none, but such as I have give I thee. In the name of Jesus Christ of Nazareth, rise up and walk." Here was a gift which money could not

purchase, and such were all those great gifts which Christ
came to bring. Thus understood, the pleasures and benefits of giving are open to all, even to her who is poorer
than the poor widow who cast in her two mites. All can
impart benefits of some kind, freely and from good will;
and the proposition which we now wish to illustrate
is, that thus to give is more blessed than it is to receive.

That this is so may appear, first, because God is giver
ouly, and not a receiver. Of the modes and conditions
of the divine blessedness we know, indeed, very little. To
our conception, God must have been perfectly blessed in
himself, when, as yet, no creative act had rendered the
blessedness of giving possible. We must conceive of God
as self-sufficing in all respects, as having within himself
the spring of his own activity, and finding in that activity
the source of his blessedness. Without activity in some
form, blessedness is inconceivable, for absolute quiescence
is death. But if we know little of the modes of activity
possible to God, and hence of the modes of his blessedness, we may yet be sure that in all the forms of that
activity there is blessedness, and pre-eminent blessedness
in those which are pre-eminently his. But, as has been
said, he manifests himself only as a giver. He is so in
creation. To the universe of matter, overwhelming us as
it does by its vastness and variety and glory, he gave its
being. From the resources of his own omnipotence he
caused that which was not, to be, and no doubt there was
a sublime blessedness not only in the result, when he beheld and pronounced it good, but also in the energy by
which it was accomplished. And having created this universe with all its properties and adjustments, he gave it to
his sensitive and rational creatures to be the theatre of
their being and a source of enjoyment. To the sensitive
and spiritual universe also, through all its ranks, from the

insect up to the seraph, God has given being, with its infinite diversity of forms, and modes of perception, and capacities, and responsibilities. Throughout the universe there is nothing that any being is, or that he possesses, that is not the gift of God. And not only has God given in creating, but he gives continually. Whatever we may say of second causes, he is the constant upholder and governor of all things, the ever present, conscious giver of every good and perfect gift. This is the highest conception we can form of any being, that he should not only have the spring of activity within himself and be self-sufficing, but that he should suffice for a universe, and find a conscious blessedness in giving without limit and without exhaustion forevermore. Here we find a conception that bears us far above the glories of night, and of all telescopic heavens. Here we find the source of the river of the water of life, clear as crystal, that overflows and sparkles and spreads itself to the outmost limits of the creation. What are the starry heavens to Him who is enthroned as the infinite and only original giver in this limitless universe !

To give thus without exhaustion, would seem to be the natural prerogative of God ; but there is also a form of giving that implies self-denial and self-sacrifice ; it implies that we forego a good for the sake of the good of others. How this may be compatible with what we conceive of the infinite and perfect blessedness of God, it may not be easy to see ; but that he is capable of this form of giving, the Scriptures plainly assert when they say, that He "so loved the world that he gave his only begotten Son." Possibly the highest blessedness of a benevolent being can be known only through self-sacrifice. Blessedness is more than pleasure ; it is the consciousness and exercise of the highest goodness. This is the highest form of giving, and constitutes Christ the great gift of God. It makes him not merely the outflow of his natural attributes, but the manifestation of his heart.

And while God thus gives, he does not receive. "Who hath first given unto Him and it shall be recompensed to him again?" By the right of an original creation, and of a constant preservation, all things are already his. "He is not worshipped with men's hands as though he needed any thing, seeing he giveth to all life and breath and all things." He may be said to accept of our services; that is, he may be pleased with our dutiful affection, but we can bestow upon him no gift; he can receive nothing from us so as to become the owner of that which was not his before. We can never requite him by paying back an equivalent; we can lay him under no obligation.

If then God finds his own blessedness in giving, and not at all in receiving, we should naturally expect, that those who are made in his image would find it more blessed to give than to receive.

But, secondly, it may not be amiss to mention that this is one of those great truths which seem to find their prefiguration and twilight in the material creation. The sun, the grandest and noblest of all material objects, is only a giver. Age after age, from his high place, he imparts, without exhaustion, light and heat, and receives nothing in return. In the coldness of our philosophy we say, indeed, that this involves no blessedness. This is true, just as it is true that there is no color spread over the surface of bodies; and yet is the sun a silent preacher of a truth that is not in him, because we are so made that we must diffuse over matter our own conceptions and vitalize it with our feelings. Let the natural emotions speak, and they say at once, that the sun is "as a bridegroom coming out of his chamber, and *rejoiceth* as a strong man to run a race." We attribute to this sublime body power and dignity, and feel that, if it were concious, it must rejoice in its greatness and in its dispensing power.   This teaching becomes more impressive by contrast.   The sun gives only; the sandy desert only receives, and hence we regard it with aversion, and as fit only to symbolize the drearier desert of a heart thoroughly selfish and absorbing.

But I observe, thirdly, that this truth is enstamped upon our very constitution ; it grows out of the frame-work of our being.

To see this, we have only to examine a little the kinds and sources of the blessedness of which we are capable. As has been said, all blessedness must come from activity and of this there may be three kinds.   One of these we need not consider, because there is in it nothing of giving or receiving.   It is the activity of the mind within itself, in contemplation and thought, when it receives no impression from without, and puts forth no outward activity.   Laying this aside, then, we find that man is a centre of activities, from which influences, originating in his will, flow outward, and affect the world without ; and also that he is a centre of susceptibilities, to which influences flow in from the world without, and by which he is affected.   In the first case he is truly active, putting forth powers, and may be said, in a large sense, to give ; in the second, he is as passive as a perceiving and sentient being can be, and he receives.

It is in conformity with this general idea that the physical frame, even, is constructed.   The nervous system is a railway with a double track.   It is now well known that there are two sets of nerves, those of motion, and those of sensation, running side by side, apparently intimately blended, yet entirely distinct in their origin and office, by one of which influences pass from within outward, and by the other from without inward ; by one of which we receive, and by the other, give. By the one we receive materials of instruction, and impressions pleasing or painful ; by the other, we exert our wills as agents, and give forth our own proper activity.

When we open our eyes to the light, when we behold the trees and the mountains, the waters and the flowers the stars and works of art, we receive ; when there comes to us the perfume of flowers, or the fragrance of the new-made hay, we receive; when we taste the strawberry, the peach, the melon, we receive ; when we hear the song of birds, the rustling of leaves, the rippling of waters, or the music of the flute or of the voice, we receive ; when we open our minds, through the senses, to thoughts and impressions from others, we receive. Here the movement is from without, inward, and if no folly or wickedness intervene, it is always blessed, and only blessed, thus to receive.

To this process God has attached pleasure, as he has to that of receiving food, but both the process and the pleasure are as clearly subordinate in one case as in the other. We receive food that the body may be built up and strengthened, and the pleasure is incidental. So here, the object of the importing railway, or rather railways, is to bring to the mind those materials upon which it may work and be strengthened, which may be elaborated into speech and action and enable man to become a giver, freighting the outward railway with the products of knowledge and of love.

This last is the true sphere of man. He was not made to be merely a passive receiver of pleasure, a bundle of sensibilities, to be madly wasted or artistically and prudently exhausted, beginning with a fountain full and sparkling, and ending, as all mere pleasure must, with the vapid and bitter dregs of decay and exhaustion. He was made

to be an agent, with powers having the spring of their activity within themselves, and having it for their law that
they shall increase in strength by their own legitimate activity.   This it is that allies man to the angels, and makes
him of inappreciable worth, and fits him to become increas·
ingly a giver, and to walk with waxing strength in an upward path, even the path of the just, that shineth more and
more unto the perfect day.   This it is in man that lays
the foundation for that most magnificent of all figures, used
by our Saviour concerning the righteous, that they shall
shine forth as the sun in the kingdom of their Father.

But if this be so, if the sphere of activity and of giving
be higher than that of passivity and receiving, then must
it be more blessed to give than to receive; *for where
should any being find his highest blessedness but in the legitimate exercise of his highest powers ?* This is the law of all
beings ; so, and so only, can their highest blessedness be
reached.

Intimately as the pleasures of receptivity and of activity
are blended, we yet find in the distinction just drawn, a
line of cleavage dividing the race into two classes.   To
the one belong the lovers and seekers of pleasure as distinguished from blessedness or happiness ; for pleasure arises
from some congruity between us and that which is without.
In it the movement is from without, inward, and we are
receivers.   The lovers of pleasure are those who make it
their business to find that without them, which shall act
on their susceptibilities and minister to their passive enjoyment.   To seek this predominatingly is the fatal mis·
take and besetting sin of most.   To do so is compatible
with the highest forms of civilization and of worldly respec-
tabilty.   It rather implies the cultivation and patronage of
the elegancies and refinements of life, and skill in the must
agreeable forms which self-love and selfishness can assume

The elite of the class may worship beauty and art, but the mass will worship sensual pleasure. What they seek for on earth is the highest combination of these, and they would desire no heaven but a Mohammedan paradise. Give them the means of gratification, and they are court- eous, liberal and tolerant ; interfere with these, and they are intolerant, deceitful, malignant, cruel ; and thus vices and cruelties more shocking than those of barbarism may mingle and alternate with the highest forms of luxury and refinement. With such an object of life, immortality and accountablility disappear from its back-ground, and its value is estimated in sensations ; the individual loses his self-respect and his confidence in others ; and though society may seem to be crowned with verdure and flowers to its summit, yet that summit will be the crater of a volcano.

Those, on the other hand, who make their activities the basis of their character, seeking blessedness rather than pleasure, need, indeed, to have those activities rightly directed; but they are on a basis which is capable of sustaining the highest and most solid structure of indi- vidual and social greatness and blessedness.

We have now considered man as having sensibilities on the one hand, and a will on the other,—a receptivity and an activity in correspondence with which his physical frame is formed. But we find a similar correspondence of faculties in the mind itself, with no corresponding phy- sical organization. Man has not only sensibilities and a will, but also desires and affections ; and as he receives by his sensibilities and gives by his will, so does he receive by his desires and give by his affections.

Having shown that to give forth activity and influence is higher and more blessed than to receive impressions, we may now leave behind us, in our search for the highest blessedness, all mere passive enjoyment, and, while we estimate that at its proper value, consider only the different forms of activity. All activity from within, outward, can be regarded as a form of giving only in the wide sense already mentioned ; but all giving is a form of activity that springs from the affections, and we say that this is more blessed than any form of receiving through the desires.

It is of the very nature of the affections that they give, and of the desires that they receive. The affections have persons for their object ; they arise in view of worth or worthiness in them, real or supposed, and we seem in their exercise to give our very being. They are disinterested, they flow out from us, they give, and appropriate nothing. That is not affection which is not disinterested, and it is only because this is not a world of open vision than any outward token, flowing from a secret regard to self can ever be supposed to give evidence of affection. In the sphere of affection every outward token is valued as the evidence of a gift more precious than itself. When we give affection we truly give ; and what is commonly called giving, is really so only as it is an evidence of this.

The desires, on the other hand, have, as their distinguishing characteristics, that they appropriate to themselves the things desired, and that their object is things and not persons. They appropriate wholly ; they receive, and give nothing. Here self is the centre, and nothing is valued except as it can be made to revolve towards the vortex of this whirlpool.

And here again it is blessed to receive, and only blessed, if the desires be kept within their own sphere. Not alone is there the music of enjoyment from the correlation and adjustment of external things with a sensitive organization, of the harp with the breeze, but in the attainment of its object by each of the desires. There is a legitimate enjoyment in receiving wealth, and admiration, and fame and power.

But here, no less than previously, do we find an obvious subordination. Not more obvious is it that food should be received to be given back in strength and activity, or that sensation should minister to knowledge, than it is that the desires were intended to receive that they might minister to the affections. Let a man pursue wealth and power, not for their own sakes, but solely that he may do good to his fellow creatures, and there is no danger that the desires, thus subordinated, will be in excess. But the moment he pursues them, I will not say with some reference to self, for God intended we should provide for ourselves, but the moment he pursues them selfishly, the servant becomes the master and slavery begins.

And here, too, there is made a great and general mistake. The ends proposed by the desires, instead of being held subordinate, become ultimate, and thus the desires become the main spring of activity and the basis of character. We all know how each of the desires creates for itself a world of activity, in which it becomes not only the pervading, but too often the dominant principle ; and when this is so, man seeks to balance himself and society upon a false centre, and can never be at rest.

In the world of business the desire of wealth rules, and in the eager pursuit of this the vision of its votaries becomes narrowed, so that they see and care for nothing else. The fraudulent man, the rum-seller, the slave-trader, the panderer to appetite, the inexorable landlord, have, it may be, no malignity, but in the intenseness of this desire, they bow so eagerly to the god of their idolatry that they see not the scattered wrecks of property and of character strewed around them, and hear not the wail of distress that comes up from fathers and mothers agonized, and from wives and children made desolate. They hear but the cry of this desire, saying, Give, give, and all the better forms of intellectual and moral life are contemned and wither away, and their hearts become as the nether millstone.

In the world of fashion it is the desire of admiration that reigns. The value of dress as a necessary and a comfort, becomes subordinate to that which it receives from the eyes of others, and from the position it is supposed to give. Health and comfort are disregarded. Each desires to become a receiving centre, and the party, the ball, the assembly, where they have been admired, and especially more admired than others, has been a pleasant party or ball or assembly to them. It is in this sphere that vanity, self-complacent, yet meanly dependent and apprehensive, finds its food. Here every thing is on the basis of receiving, and this gives it its heartless and unsatisfying character. Even all copartnerships for mutual admiration, whether between individuals or in regular societies, give, only that they may receive as much again.

In the world of ambition the desire of power is supreme. No ties of kindred, no obligations of faith and sacred honor, no pleadings of humanity, no fear of a righteous retribution, can stay the course of him who has once entered the lists for this glittering prize. Reckless and remorseless as a cannon-shot, he moves towards his object, shattering and prostrating every thing in his way. "The land is as the garden of Eden before him, and behind him a desolate wilderness." A miser of power, if he is less despicable than the miser of wealth, it is only because he is more formidable ; for though he may be admired by the unthinking, he is yet equally false to his nature, and to the true ends of life. He may be a battle-axe in the hand of the Almighty to punish the nations, but a true *man*, knowing his Maker, and voluntarily co-operating with him, he cannot be.

And what is true of the desires thus specified, is true of them all. The slightest knowledge of them will show that they cannot be the basis of either individual or social happiness. The isolated summits which they would reach are glittering and attractive at a distance, but there is there no spring of water for the thirsty soul, and no green thing. Their constitution is such that they grow by what they feed on, never reaching, like the bodily appetites, a limit of satiety. "He that coveteth silver shall not be satisfied with silver." He that conquers one world, will weep that there is not another for him to conquer. Hence a character which has the desires for its basis, must be hard, and dry, and unamiable, and selfish ; and the individual must be restless and unhappy. As, too, the desires are appropriating and necessarily exclusive, if they are the basis of character in the community generally, it must become the theatre of a general conflict, in which every malignant passion and dissocial element will mingle, and society will be dissolved into its original elements.

But with the affections, the reverse of all this is true. In their exercise, we find ultimate ends that are legitimate ; nor is there in them any tendency to excess and disproportion from their own activity. They arise from an apprehension of some worth or worthiness in the person towards whom they go forth ; and the only danger is, that the imagination will clothe their object in false colors. Let the person be seen as he is, and the measure of his worth, or of his worthiness, is the natural measure and limit of the affection ; and in this there can be nothing exaggerated or excessive. If the object be greatly worthy, the affection ought to be great ; and the greater the affection, the greater the blessedness. Among the highest forms of blessedness conceivable by us, is that of a perfect affection resting with full complacency upon a worthy object.

But if the individual will thus be made happy through the affections, much more will society. This scarcely needs to be shown. The affections are not only the true bond of society, the only element and sure guarantee of peace, but as burning coals burn more brightly when brought together, so must there be intenser blessedness where the affections are drawn out by intimate and complex social relations.

From what has been said under this head, it would appear that to give, is to put forth power under the guidance of love. In doing this, there will be a union of the activities with the affections. Hence giving is the culminating point, the blending and fusion of those activities and affec-tions which we have shown to be the two highest sources of human blessedness. If, therefore, we will but notice it we shall find, as was already said, that it is enstamped upon our constitution—that it grows out of the very framework of our being, that it is more blessed to give than to receive.

I cannot leave the discussion under this head without observing, that we may gather from it the limit and law of all our receiving faculties in their relation to those that give,—of all receptivity in its relation to activity. It is that that only should be received, which will enable us to give; that the limit of receptivity should be the point where it ceases to minister to activity.

This gives us the law of temperance in all things—its universal law. Nature is not arbitrary, or capricious, or cynical. We are at liberty to receive into the body anything, and in any quantity, that will, on the whole, best minister to the strength and activity of the body. The mis-take of intemperate men, of every degree, is to receive for the sake of passive impression those things which depress and injure the powers of activity. The student is at liberty to receive into his mind as much promiscuous reading, and to hear as many lectures, as will give him the most active and vigorous mental powers. Let him read as much as he will, provided it be assimilated, and there be nothing of the crudities or tumidity of mental indigestion. Let the desires stretch forth their arms as they may, and gather wealth and admiration and power, provided there be nothing gathered to be hoarded and gloated upon and worshipped; and that the disposition to communicate go hand in hand with the ability, and thus the great law of stewardship come in, and every man, as he has received, be a good steward of the manifold grace of God.

It is, indeed, in this relation and law of receiving and giving, that we find the true ground of the subordination of different enjoyments, and the true theory of human well-being. This last consists, essentially, in the right activity of the powers. The right activity of her powers, is that which makes the King's daughter all glorious within; and if this be so, the King will see that her clothing shall be of wrought gold. For the completeness and fulness of well-being, there is indeed not only the inward harmony and joy, but the investment and regalia of a world without, that shall testify through every sense and susceptibility to the sympathy and approbation of Him by whom that world was organized and is sustained. We reject not, nor undervalue the investment; but we find in this law a necessity, that he who would attain true blessedness at all, should make the basis of his character the activities and the affections, and not, as the many do, the sensibilites and the desires. In the prevalent type of character, reason and conscience and the affections are subordinated to some one of the desires, pleasure being pursued so far as may be compatible with that. But if true blessedness is to be attained, this order must be reversed ; and the love that gives, sustained by reason and conscience must take the place of the desires that would receive ; and all mere pleasure, all desire for passive impression, must give way when love, so sustained, shall call for active exertion.

I have thus illustrated, as I was able, the weighty and comprehensive saying of our Saviour, that "it is more blessed to give than to receive ; " and we find it confirmed by the example of God himself ; by the mute teachings of his works ; and by the best examination we can make of the constitution of man in its relation to the modes and kinds of possible enjoyment. The essential elements, of giving are power and love—activity and affection,—and the consciousness of the race testifies that in the high and approprate exercise of these there is a blessedness greater than any other.

And what is thus taught by precept and confirmed by philosophy and by consciousness, it is most pleasing to find perfectly illustrated by example. With the interpretation now given, it could not be more perfectly illustrated than it was by our Saviour and his apostles. He " loved us and gave himself for us." He saw that the world was in such a state, that by giving himself he could save men ; and with the full knowledge of what was before him, the poverty, the reproaches, the buffetings, the mockings, the scourging, the crucifixion, he gave himself freely. This he did in the conscious exercise of power. He had power to lay down his life, and he had power to take it again. He gave, not as he gives whom giving does not impoverish, but he gave of his heart's blood till that heart ceased to beat. He planted his cross in the midst of the mad and roaring current of selfishness aggravated to malignity and uttered from it the mighty cry of expiring love.) And the waters heard him, and from that moment they began to be refluent about his cross. From that moment, a current deeper and broader, and mightier, began to set heavenward, and it will continue to be deeper and broader, and mightier till its glad waters shall encompass the earth, and toss themselves as the ocean. And not alone did earth hear that cry. It pierced the regions of immensity. Heaven heard it, and hell heard it, and the remotest star shall hear it. testifying to the love of God in his unspeakable gift, and to the supremacy of that blessedness of giving which could be reached only through death—the death of the cross. This joy of giving it was that was set before him, for which he endured the cross despising the shame.

And not only did our Saviour exemplify this precept, but also his Apostles. They were first receivers and then givers. They filled their urns at the fountain of light and power, and then rayed these forth with an energy that made them the great benefactors of the race. Standing simply as men, without wealth, or power, or learning, or genius, they gave their being in its entireness to the diffusion among men of God's method of salvation, and thus took their stand at the head of the mightiest moral movement the world has ever seen. Nor have they failed to have successors in men of a like spirit, faithful, self-denying, ready at any moment to seal their testimony with their blood. All down the ages there have been those who have given, not property only, but themselves, to this cause of God and of man.

My dear Friends. I would that you should be givers. To you the exhortation comes with peculiar appropriateness, " Freely ye have received, freely give." You have received from God high endowments—not merely the

susceptibilities of the animal, by which you are capable of
pleasure, but the powers of the angel, by which you are
capable of an eternal blessedness—not merely.the desires
which would grasp and appropriate their objects, but also
affections by which you may give love and its fruits, voluntarily joining hands in that line of receiving and giving
which begins at the throne of God and terminates only
with animate being. You have received a country, vast,
prosperous, progressive, whose future towers up into an
undefined magnificence. Freely you have received the
heritage of free institutions bought with blood, for which
the nations of the old world sigh in vain. Above all, you
have received " freedom to worship God," and a knowledge
of the way of life and salvation through Jesus Christ our
Lord. O ye plants in the very garden of the Lord, have
ye thus received his rain and his sunshine, and shall ye
not yield fruit? Shall there be among you one empty vine,
bringing forth fruit unto himself; one frivolous, pleasure-
loving, self-seeking, world-worshipping idolater? Are you
not satisfied that the law of giving is the true law of our
being? And do you not see how hopeless it must be to
go against those deep tendencies which God has wrought
into our frame—that to strike against the adamant of his
laws is to be dashed in pieces?" " Freely ye have
received, freely give." Poor you may be, and many of you
are, in the riches of this world. But there is a giving
higher than that decorous giving that meets public expectation, but not the requirements of good stewardship;
there is a giving higher than that of wealth to any extent.
The time has come when a man is " more precious than
fine gold ; even a man, than the golden wedge of Ophir."
Give yourselves, give as Christ gave, as the Apostles gave.
Pierce to the kernel those Christian paradoxes, that we
save by loosing, and live by dying, and receive by giving.

Go where duty calls, where there is ignorance to be enlightened, suffering to be relieved, vice to be reclaimed, character to be improved. These are works which must be done by living men. Wealth alone cannot do them ; the labors of the dead past cannot do them. It is not the touch of the bones of a dead Prophet that can give moral life. In every age it is a sympathizing love that must stretch itself upon the body of this death, and then it will live. So give, and in the day of the Lord Jesus "you shall receive a crown of glory that fadeth not away."

IV.

PERFECT LOVE.

Perfect love casteth out fear.—1 John, iv. 18.

THE happiness which men seek, is not like gold which, when once found, can be kept ; it is the result of some activity ; it must cease when that activity ceases; and the happiness that is highest and best. can spring only from the activity of those faculties tha. are highest and best. Here is the true theory of human happiness. With all normal activity, God has connected enjoyment; and the more exalted the faculties, and the more intense the activity, the higher the enjoyment. If then the highest happiness can come only from those faculties, or forms of activity, that are highest and best, it becomes a paramount question what those faculties are.

The general modes of activity are three. We think, we feel, we will. The will, however, need not be considered here, because it is a means of good only through thought and emotion. Aside from mere sensitive good, it is from thought and emotion that all willing springs, and it is to thought and emotion that it ministers. We have, then, in seeking for the immediate sources of enjoyment not sensitive, to compare only our intellectual and emotive nature ; and our first inquiry is, What is the relative rank of the intellect and the emotions ?

It has been the tendency of the world, and especially of students, to exalt the intellect. Under this, all agree

₊ August 15, 1855.

in including our perceiving and reasoning powers ; and I would also include our powers of intuition, and of comprehension. These, especially those of intuitive reason and comprehension, are high powers. By them we are made in the image of God, we become partakers of his thoughts and purposes, and are enabled intelligently to serve him. They place us in the same rank as the angels, and involve the capacity, and thus the implied promise of an indefinite progression. In their exercise, there is a consciousness of inherent and native dignity that sets us apart from the brutes that perish.

Connected with the activity of the intellect there is naturally an appropriate and a high enjoyment, that still has no name as a specific emotion. Its wheels do not creak and complain, as they revolve ; they sing. Doubtless there might have been a cold and unimpassioned perception, a merely dry insight and comprehension ; but we are not so made. "It is a pleasant thing to behold the sun;" it is pleasant to perceive and trace relations, to discover or follow an argument ; all insight and comprehension are pleasant. Shall we then say that the pleasure thus received is itself an emotion ? In its widest sense, we may ; but not thus can we practically discuss this subject. The pleasure connected with the mere activity of the faculties, is one thing ; the specific emotions, as of admiration, beauty, sublimity, which depend on the activity of the faculties under certain circumstances, are another; and there is plainly no fixed ratio between perception or comprehension on the one hand, and any specific emotion on the other. There are those with great powers of insight who feel little admiration ; who can stand before beautiful and sublime objects with but slight emotion. An astronomer may weigh a planet, or measure its orbit, or cast an eclipse, with as little admiration as a shopkeeper would weigh a pound of sugar, or measure a yard of cloth, or cast up his day-book ; while a person with but little insight, knowing nothing but facts and results, may contemplate the heavens with constant admiration and delight. We even hear of the cold philosopher ; as if ' there were some incompatibility between intellect and emotion · and we constantly observe the greatest variety in the intensity of emotion, when persons are in the presence of the same beautiful or sublime objects. It is true that all elevated and worthy emotion must depend on the intellect ; yet so distinct are they, that we may cultivate the intellect exclusively, and repress the emotions ; or we may riot in emotion, while the intellect is comparatively neglected.

But since both intellect and feeling are essential parts of our being ; since thought is the condition of feeling, and feeling stimulates thought ; it may be asked, how we are to decide their relative rank. This we can do, as in all other systems of related parts that have reference to an end. In these, that which precedes as a condition and a means, is subordinate to that which is accomplished as an end. Hence, that the intellect is subordinate, appears from the very fact that it is the condition and basis of the emotions, and that they are later in the order of nature and of time. In the order of creation, and of all individual development,

"Time's noblest offspring is the last."

Man, in whom all other things are epitomized and culminate, came last ; and that in him which is highest and noblest, the powers of reflection and of reason, with their consequent emotions, also come last to perfection. In the vegetable, the fruit and the flower come last, and all that precedes is conditional for these. Emotion is, indeed, as the flower to the stalk, as the fruit to the flower. It is the verdure, that clothes the skeleton trees ; it is the expression, that lives and glows upon features otherwise rigid and motionless ; it is the sweet-smelling savor of every acceptable offering, that is laid upon the altar of God's service or of the service of man ; it is the incense that should go up as a cloud from this world of marvels and of beauty. To say that there is no happiness without emotion in some form, seems hardly adequate. It might be nearer the truth to say, that it *is* happiness—for what do we know of happiness, except as an emotion ? And yet there is no distinct emotion of happiness that is known by that name, and that can be distinguished from those several emotions by which it is enwrapped, and which it perfumes.

The emotive nature of man, thus preëminent, has a wide range ; and we next inquire what it is in *that* that is highest and best.

In perceiving external nature, every degree and kind of perception has its emotion, from the faintest whisper of beauty, sublimity, admiration, delight, to their highest notes. It is, however, only when we pass to sentient and rational beings, that the emotions take the name of affections, and swell and surge in the passions. Here it is that we find love ; but in assigning its rank, we must make some discriminations.

From the poverty of language, things but remotely related to each other are often indicated by the same word. So it is with love. In its broadest sense, it indicates the tendency of beings capable of enjoyment toward that in which their enjoyment is found, whatever it may be. It includes all animal appetencies and instinctive affections, as well as that attachment which has its primal seat in the will, and involves rational and moral elements. The ox is said to love the grass, the mother bird its young, the

ambitious man loves fame, the miser loves money, and the
seraph loves God.   It is used to express the purest affections of spiritual beings, and to sanctify the grossest and
most criminal passions.   Like " fitness," it is used to express a general relation, and not the nature of the things
related ; and the attraction of gravitation is not more unlike that of two loving hearts, than are some of the different forms of what is called love, from each other.   But that
perfect love that casteth out fear has no connection with
appetite, or passion, or instinct, or anything sensitive ;
but springs wholly from our rational and moral nature, and
is drawn forth wholly by that which is rational and moral.
It is the love of man for the spiritual and unseen Creator.
It is love, not as an instinctive tendency, or a mere affection,
but as a principle.   There is in it a rational apprehension
of both worth and worthiness, an act of choice and commit-
ment, and that peculiar and strong and undefinable emotion which connects itself with this act, and which is modified by the characteristics and character of the being loved.
These may be distinguished from each other, but they cannot be separated and the love remain.   It is their union
that constitutes the one substantial and working principle
that we call love, as it is the union of oxygen and hydrogen
that constitutes water ; and it is this fusion of the intellect
and the affections, that is called " love " in the text.   This
is the highest form of human, and we may say, of rational
activity.   The light of the intellect is cold and cheerless ;
it is the warmth of love that brings out the verdure, and
awakens the voice of the swelling song.   This is the high
and pure principle by which we are drawn toward all that
is capable of happiness in its proper sense, by which we are
not only attracted toward all that is amiable and generous
and pure and holy in character, but by which we abide
steadfast in our attachments.   It is the highest form of

activity drawn out by the highest objects. Taken with the happiness which it enfolds, which pervades and forms a part of it, it is the highest result, the brightness, the crown and consummation of the works of God—nay, it is the great mode of activity and ground of happiness in God himself. "God is love, and he that dwelleth in love, dwelleth in God, and God in him." "He that loveth not, knoweth not God."

But perhaps we may best gain a conception of the true rank and functions of love, from the agencies of nature which are required as its symbols. No one of these is adequate. To symbolize it fully, requires the three great elements or agents, on which all enjoyment, and life, and order depend.

Of these, the first is light, which represents the intellectual element in love. How grand a symbol is this all-encompassing, all-revealing element! It gives to the earth and heavens all their beauty and glory. Without it, the distant universe would be to us as though it were not. This is the only symbol of that conscious certainty and satisfying knowledge, without which all affection is degraded to an instinct. But as there may be and is, knowledge without love, as light without warmth, we will not dwell upon this.

The second great element needed to symbolize love, is heat. Not chiefly as concentrated in fire, or as radiating immediately from it, is heat known as a beneficent agent. It pervades all matter, giving fluidity to water, to the sap of vegetables, to the blood of animals, quickening every seed that germinates, and is an indispensable condition of all life. Without it the universe would be solidified in eternal frost, and motionless in death. But suppose, now, there were in this universe no warmth of affection, no throb of kindness in any heart; that God himself were, as

some would make him, but an iceberg of intellect, chilling
the universe, and that men were made in his image ; and
there would be a frost and a death, which the withdrawal
of its vital heat from the frame of nature could but faintly
shadow forth. Not one pulsation of love in the universe!
How awful the desolation! But where love is, all icy
chains are dissolved, all dormant life is quickened, every
rivulet sings, every flower opens its petals, and to breathe
is to be happy. An intelligent love is the blended light
and warmth that gives to all things in the spiritual world
their life and beauty.

But not less essential in nature than light and warmth,
nor less perfect as a symbol, is another power that pervades the universe, and binds all nature together. This
is the power of attraction. It shows itself in various
forms, now uniting the particles of smaller masses in the
embrace of a cohesion which no force can sever, and now
binding together families of worlds as they pay homage to
their centre, and move on with reciprocal attraction and
seeming affection in the fields of space. Without this,
particle would be loosed from particle, and world from
world. The earth, the planets, the sun, the fixed stars
would be sifted into space, and would disappear. Not a
spot where the foot might tread would remain in the universe. And this does but represent the uniting and harmonizing power of love, in an intelligent and moral system. Within a limited range, and under higher control, a
system of balanced selfishness may move on for a time ;
but as a great uniting principle, that will hold every individual in his place and sphere, and work out any rational
good, nothing but love can be imagined. This only can
unite the family, the church, the state. Only this can
insure harmony among nations, only this can bind the
creature to the throne of the Creator. With a God thus

enthroned and reigning by love, and every rank and order
of being walking his circuit by the attraction of love, not
merely around the throne of God, but around all those
social and governmental centres which God has ordained,
we have moral order, the only order that can be permanent, or that has intrinsic worth.

The union thus of three, and perhaps even of two great
elements in nature, as the symbol of a principle or mode
of activity in the spiritual world, is entirely without example. Of these three great elements and forces, the sun is,
in our system, the centre. From him goes forth the light,
from him the warmth, from him chiefly, though it be reciprocal, the attraction. What a fountain of radiance!
How does that radiance stream forth as in genial marriage with the vitalizing heat! What a centre, we might
almost say, of loving attraction! And when we look at
the splendor and pervasiveness of these elemental forces,
at their gentle, yet ceaseless and resistless agency, and at
their results in the sphere of matter, we may form a conception of the place which that love must hold in a moral
and spiritual system which can be symbolized only by all
of these ; and we may realize more fully the grandeur and
force of those most simple, yet most sublime expressions
of the Bible, " God is a Sun," and, " God is Love."

It is to this great principle of love, thus shown to be
the highest form of human, and indeed of rational activity,
that I would now call your especial attention. It is of
this, that I desire you should become radiating centres ; it
is under the control of this, as flowing out from the great
centre of all, that I desire you should fully come. In order
to this, then, let us consider first, what it is that love must
exclude.

And here I observe, in the first place, that love would
exclude fear. " Perfect love casteth out fear." It is

chiefly in fear, and not without reason, that the son of Sirach makes that "great travail" to consist, which he says "is created for every man, and that heavy yoke which is upon the sons of Adam, from the day that they go out of their mother's womb, till the day that they return to the mother of all things." "Their imagination of things to come," says he, "and the day of death, trouble their thoughts, and cause *fear* of heart ; from him that sitteth on a throne of glory, unto him that is humbled in earth and ashes ; from him that weareth purple and a crown, unto him that is clothed with a linen frock." How then may fear be removed? Its opposite is commonly said to be hope, and it is by this that most would attempt to exorcise this spectre. But the philosophy of the Bible is profounder than this. Hope is so far from being the opposite of fear, that it implies it. So long as there is that want of certainty which hope implies, there must be some lingerings of fear. Nor is it all love that can cast out fear. On the contrary, much of our love tends to increase and multiply our fears. The more objects of affection we have in a world like this, and the more tenderly we love them, the more open we are to suffering, and the more ground we have to fear. It is only the love of God as a Father, involving perfect confidence in his wisdom and goodness, and almightiness, that can stay the risings of distrust and apprehension. This, a perfect filial love not only can, but must so do, that all fear shall flee away, as the mists of the morning before the sun. To him who loves *thus*, God will be a "refuge and strength." He need not, and he will not fear, " though the earth be removed, and though the mountains be carried into the midst of the sea."

And not only would perfect love exclude fear, but also hate. This it does toward the being loved, by the very

force of the terms. But he who has a perfect love of God,
can have no more hatred of any of his creatures, than God
himself has. He may—from the very fact of his loving a
moral quality, he must—have a strong hatred of its opposite ; but in that there will be no corroding passion, no malignity, which alone is properly hate, and in which alone, and
in remorse, is there involved essential misery. As love is
pervaded by an inseparable happiness which, as an original part of it, emanates from it, as the fragrance from the
flower, or the light from the sun; so malignity is pervaded
by an inseparable and an inevitable misery. This element love would exclude ; and thus, under its sway, both
fear and hate, those two great foes of human good, would
disappear.

Once more. The perfect love of God would exclude
that undue regard for self, into which all malignity properly human strikes its roots. Both fear and hate are passions, and imply intense feeling ; but selfishness is a principle, and may be the basis and substratum of life. Practically, this is, indeed, the great antagonist force to love.
Consciously or unconsciously, impliedly or avowedly, we
must make either self or God the centre; and in the conflict of self with the claims and will and interests of God
consists the great moral battle of this world. Originally
self has the ground ; but the entrance of divine love is as
the opening of spring, where the winter has reigned. The
beginning of the spring is often unperceived ; its progress is
slow ; there are long and fierce struggles of contending
forces ; sometimes it may seem to go back. But the sun
does not go back. His advance toward the northern
tropic is steady; the snows disappear, the conflict of the
winds ceases, the earth is quickened, and in due time the
long, quiet, fruitful days of summer are sure to come. Such
is the progress, the triumph, the summer of a divine love

reigning in the soul. Now it will bring forth fruit unto God, and all undue regard to self will be excluded.

Having thus spoken of what a perfect love would ex-clude, we now come to that which is positive, and will first consider it as a motive to action. As such, it is higher and purer than any other. To work from fear, is slavery ; to work under the compulsion of animal want, is a hardship, and if not a positive, yet a relative curse ; to work for personal ends, as for pride, or ambition, or the accumulation of property, either for *its* own sake, or *our* own sake, is compatible with freedom, but has in it no-thing either purifying or ennobling ; it finds and leaves the soul dry and hard. But activity from love, is the perfec-tion of freedom and of joy. Love has the power to make the greatest labors seem light, and the greatest obstacles trifling. When Jacob served seven years for Rachel, " they seemed unto him but a few days, for the love he had to her." How free and cheerful is the labor of a mother for her child ! And even among animals, where instinct simulates and foreshadows moral love, we are attracted toward it, we sympathize with it, we think it beautiful, we regard it as wanton and cruel to disturb its natural flow. Its very semblance is the highest form of animal life ; and when the rapt seraph adores and burns, it is this that gives to the flame its brightness and its power.

But in a world and a universe where obedience is so required by the cardinal relations in which we are placed to parents, to civil society, and to God, the place of love, as a motive to obedience, requires special attention. In a moral system it would seem that the point where obedience is required, must be that and that only, where there can be pressure, friction, derangement. Obedience requires the sacrifice of will, of pride, often of apparent self-interest.

And of these there is no solvent but love. Fear may hold them in abeyance for a time; policy may disguise and temper their workings; but only love can come up and undermine them, and float them away, and dissolve them in its own depths. Obedience from love, is that alone which is honorable to him who is obeyed; and there is no other principle, there can be no other, that will bind a free and rational being to obey, and make that obedience a source of happiness. Hence the Bible, always true to the constitution and wants of our nature, anticipates and recognizes no other obedience. " This is the love of God, that we keep his commandments." " If ye love me, keep my commandments," making the love first, and the keeping of the commandments a natural fruit and outgrowth of that. Thus it is that love, where action is not possible, and where it is, love expressed in action—"love, is the fulfilling of the law."

Nor may I omit to mention the relation of love to the intellect as a moving power. All high emotion is indeed preceded by the action of the intellect, yet that emotion reacts upon the intellect, and from it alone must come the impulse that will lead to steady and intense application. Here, as in the body, the powers act in a circle. Digestion forms the blood, the blood gives power to digestion. It is a prejudice, as disastrous as it is unfounded, that there can be a schism between the heart and the intellect, to the advantage of either. The world is not ready to receive it, but it lies in our structure, and must ultimately appear, that the love of God is the highest ground of enthusiasm, not only in the study of his word, but of his works. They may indeed be studied from curiosity, from ambition, from a desire even to disprove the being or the moral govern-ment of God; and thus we may have sharp, disputatious, dogmatical partisans of theories; but the genial, patient, comprehensive, all-reconciling thinker, will be most often found where the pale and dry light of the intellect is tempered by the warm glow of love. How can he who has no love, interpret a universe that originated in love? The works of God are all expressions of his attributes, and thoughts, and feelings. Through them we may commune with him. So far as there is thought in the works of God, it is his thought. He it is that, through uniformities and resemblances and tendencies, whispers into the ear of a philosophy, *not* falsely so called, its sublime truths; and as we begin to feel, and trace more and more those lines of relation that bind all things into one system, the touch of any one of which may vibrate to the fixed stars, this communion becomes high and thrilling. Science is no longer cold. It lives, and breathes, and glows, and in the ear of love its voice is always a hymn to the Creator.

And not only is love a motive of action, it is also a guide. The modes in which conscious beings are guided to their good, are two. They either comprehend the good, and the means of attaining it, and so are guided by reason; or, without comprehension, are guided to the good by a blind and unreasoning instinct. Of these, reason is the higher, but instinct is the more sure; and proud as we are of our reason, it not seldom happens that that very reason would call upon us to give up the guidance of ourselves, not merely to faith in God, which some object to, but even to the instinct of a brute. The traveller on horseback, returning home and losing his way in the darkness, will most wisely give his horse the reins. He who winds his way over the fearful passes of the Andes, on the back of a mule, where a single misstep would precipitate him a thousand feet, must interpose no suggestions of reason between the sagacity of instinct and his own safety. Now

what man needs, is a guiding principle, that shall combine
the security of an instinct with the ardor of passion, and
the freedom and dignity of a rational wisdom. And such
a principle he has in the love of God. It is rational and
free, because, in the fullest light of his reason, man chooses
God as the object of his confidence and love ; it has in it
the element and impulsion of passion, because we are drawn
toward him by his own inherent loveliness, as the river to
the ocean ; and it is sure, because God must deny himself,
before he could suffer an action, prompted by genuine love
to him, to result in ultimate disaster. It is through this
irresistible conviction of security, that a perfect love must
cast out all fear and its torment. In a world like this,
where we know so little of the connections and dependen-
cies of things, a case can never occur in which the highest
reason would not require us to follow the promptings of
love to God, rather than any calculations of what we may
call prudence, or understanding, or reason. It may lead
to the martyr's stake ; but the end will justify it. It is
from the predominance of love in the character of woman,
that what seem to be her instincts, but which are something higher, are often so much wiser than the reason of
man. Woman loves, and trusts, and so prays ; man reasons, or thinks he does, and scoffs. The perfection of
character and of action will be found, as it was in Christ,
in the highest combination of reason and of love.

But not only is love a motive and guide of action, it is
the basis and essential element of character. The *characteristics* of a man, are those things by which he is known ;
his *character*, is his moral state, and this depends on the
paramount love that is in him. If the paramount love be
of sensual pleasure, the man is a voluptuary ; if of fame,
ambitious ; if of money, a miser ; and if of God, he is a
religious man. According to his paramount love, will be

the image and superscription that shall be set upon every spiritual being ; according to this the quality of his inner life, his affinities, his companionships, and his ultimate destiny. The perfect love of God, is the Christian religion perfected in us : it gives us affinity for him, complacency in him, and gives us naturally, the inheritance not only of all things which he has made, but also of the direct brightness and glories of his character.

And this leads me to speak, in the last place, of love as a source of enjoyment.

Happiness, as has been said, does not consist chiefly in the possession of anything, but in the activity of the faculties upon their appropriate objects. The intellect is not for itself; it apprehends objects adapted to produce emotion, and the emotion comes to us loaded with happiness, as the air with fragrance. We seem at times, indeed, to know it only as happiness.

But of the emotions, the moral love of a Being that is infinite and perfect, is the highest possible. Has man the capacity to apprehend such a Being directly, and can such a Being thus become, by his own presence, the immediate cause of emotion ? That he can, the Bible clearly asserts ; and this is the Christian solution, unique and grand as the telescopic heavens, of the great problem of the highest good of man. No philosophy and no religion had conceived of anything so lofty as this. It is his chief distinction, his highest dignity, that he is capable of such direct communion.

In this life we see all things by reflected light, often in utter unconsciousness of the source of that light. The tendency is to see the creature, and forget the Creator. Men behold all things in their unity and beauty, the " cosmos," without reference to God. The world is in their heart. But infinite love has provided for his creatures something better than this. We shall not only, as here, see God by reflected light, we shall behold his face. The light that is now below the horizon will arise full-orbed, and shine with direct rays. It shall flood the universe, and shall never go down. There shall be no night there. Not that we suppose that the whole joy of heaven will consist in the direct contemplation of God. Christianity excludes no source of happiness of which our higher nature could render us capable. It includes the pleasures of knowledge, of the social state, and the swelling anthem. But all must see, that if we are admitted, not only to an apprehension of the universe, but also to an immediate and direct apprehension of that goodness in which the universe originated ; if we may know the Infinite as a friend knows his friend, the emotion must be far higher. This is the goal, the limit of imagination and of possibility. Than this nothing higher, nothing more ultimate or more satisfying can be conceived.

And now, my friends, what better can I do than to commend to you the cultivation of the affections, and especially of that highest of all affections, the love of God. I do not give you advice, but seek to bring you under the guidance of a great principle, that will bear you on to your true good, as the river to the ocean. Adopt this, and I would simply say to each of you, by way of advice, as Samuel said to Saul, " Do as occasion shall serve thee, for God is with thee.' So far as instructors can give direct aid in education, it is in that of the intellect. In this you have, to a great extent, walked with each other, and with us ; and if the way has been toilsome, it has also been pleasant, and the toil is strengthening. We rejoice to have walked with you ; we hope it has beeen profitable for you, and that it may hereafter be pleasant in the remem-

brance, that you have walked with us. But when the
intellectual part is finished, and the point of transition
from thought to emotion and affection is reached, there is
no longer unity. We have then the expression of the individuality of each, and the same appearances and facts
and knowledge may be transmuted into emotions and
affections, as different from each other as an anthem is
from a sneer. I exhort *you* to sing the anthem, and if there
must be those who scoff and sneer, not to be of their number. There is no source of happiness like a loving heart.
He that has found a worthy object of a true affection has
found a treasure, and he that has found one of infinite
worth has found an infinite good. Therefore it is that I
address you in no language of stoicism, of caution, of
repression, such as age and experience often adopt. It is
peculiar to the love of God, that there is in it no danger
or possibility of excess. It is with loving, as with glorify-
ing him. " When you glorify the Lord," says the son of
Sirach, "exalt him as much as you can ; for even yet will
he far exceed : and when you exalt him, put forth all your
strength and be not weary, for you can never go far
enough." Here there is no need of repression, no conflict
of reason with the affections. The highest office of reason
is to minister to a divine love, and if this, in which there
can be no excess, be enthroned, there can be no danger
of excess in any other affection or passion. It is not reason, that is the natural governor of the passions. The
office of reason is to enthrone an affection rightfully supreme. When this is done, all other affections take their
proper places. Then light, and warmth, and attraction,
coalesce ; then, not from coercion or repression, but from
co-operation and harmonious action, will there be peace,
and an infinite joy. I exhort you, then, to no cold caution, but to the intensest energy, both of thought and of

feeling. Let reason tread her outermost circuits; she shall gather nothing that will not kindle and go up as incense at the touch of divine love. Have zeal, have enthusiasm. There is a sphere for you; there is a true treasure. There are gold and pearls and diamonds and rubies that perish not. There *is* something worth living for. Mount up as on eagles' wings, up—up—to the expanse above you there is no limit.

But while I thus exhort you to this love, as the permanent good of man, I would also urge it as especially needed now in our relations here—in the present tendency to sectionalism in politics, and to sectarianism in religion. If discordant elements are to be fused, it can be only by love. Entire unity of view, in regard to modes and rites and forms, may be hopeless; but may not these be put and kept where they ought to be? May not minor points be so merged in essential truth, that harmony shall not be disturbed? May not God be so loved, that all who love him shall be loved also—that all shall be loved as he loves them? And who should do this, if not you? This is demanded of you by the spirit of your training here; the age demands it of you; God demands it. Who can better bring the diversity that springs from free thought into the unity of an intelligent love? Diversity is before unity, as chaos is before order, as solution is before the crystal. But has not diversity touched its limit? Is it not time that thoughtful and good men should find a common centre in Him who foretold the diversity, but prayed for the unity. To Him we must look. He is the true head, the leader, the champion, the restorer of the race. Not human systems or organizations, but Christ only, can be a living centre of unity. His kingdom is one of obedience and love—of obedience from love. Of these he set the great example. He became obedient unto death; he loved us

unto the end.   My friends, I feel deeply that the complacency of God in us—that our coöperation with him—that
the results of our living that will stand the fire, will be as
our love.   This will purify us.   This will strengthen us for
self-denying labors.   This will make us missionaries wherever we may be.   This will enable us to unite substantially
with all good men.   This will make it light when we go
down into the dark valley.   And when your work is done ;
when, one by one, you shall go down into that valley, may
that light be around you ; may you each have that "perfect
love" that "casteth out fear."

V.

SELF-DENIAL.

For it became Him, for whom are all things, and by whom are all things, in bringing many sons unto glory, to make the captain of their salvation perfect through sufferings.—Hebrews, ii. 10.

If any man will come after me let him deny himself, take up his cross and follow me.—Matthew, xvi. 24.

WHAT is it that makes a hero? Not simply labors performed and sufferings endured. The slave labors and suffers. The labors and sufferings must be voluntarily assumed. Nor is this enough. The fanatic, the superstitious devotee, voluntarily assume labors and sufferings ; but they are not heroes. The labors and sufferings must be voluntarily assumed, from benevolence, a pure affection, or a sense of duty. Labors and sufferings thus assumed and perseveringly sustained, make a hero ; and it is the turning-point in the destiny of men, when they freely decide whether they will, or will not, assume that self-denial and suffering, without which nothing great or good can be accomplished. Not more surely does the tree come to its flowering and its fruitage, than man comes to freedom of choice, intelligent action, moral responsibility, and through these, to that moment of decisive and governing choice which shall control his professional career here, to that which shall give direction to the current of his moral life forever. At this point, the *set* of the current may be undecided. It may be as water on the summit of the Andes. A pebble, the finger of a child, may turn it ; but that moment decides whether it shall mingle with the stormy Atlantic, or rest and glitter on the bosom of the broad Pacific.

₊ AUGUST 3, 1856.

This connection of heroism with labor and suffering preferred for a high end to ease and pleasure, and this turning-point in life, heathen mythology has presented in the choice of Hercules, between Virtue and Pleasure. I wish to present them to you under the clearer light and higher sanctions of the religion of Christ. This would make every man a hero. The work of Christ was accomplished through suffering, which we know he chose to endure, and those who would follow him must deny *themselves*, must *take up* the cross ! Is then the end worthy of these sacrifices ? Are they inherent in the system ? How does this principle of self-denial compare with those which regulate the world ? That we may answer these questions, let us look

I. At the object of Christianity, which is, as presented in the Scriptures, to bring " many sons unto glory."

II. At the process by which this is to be accomplished—a process of *salvation* implying a previous liability and tendency to ruin.

III. At the consequent fact that self-denial and suffering, voluntarily assumed, must enter as essential elements into Christianity.

And IV. Compare the principle of self-denial with those which regulate the enterprise and pleasures of the world.

FIRST, then, the object of Christianity is to bring " many sons unto glory."

This is its more immediate and direct object, though, as has been said of the atmosphere, it "consolidates uses." The atmosphere evaporates water, distributes it, reflects light, bears up birds, wafts ships, supports combustion, conveys sound, is the breath of our life, and the azure of our heavens. So Christianity, while it magnifies the law, and enthrones mercy, and reconciles us to God,

and makes known to principalities and powers in the
heavenly places his manifold wisdom, is also the regu-
lating and renovating spirit in the relations of time. It
alone inspires and guides progress ; for the progress of
man is movement towards God, and movement towards
God will insure a gradual unfolding of all that exalts and
adorns man. It excludes malignity, subdues selfishness,
regulates the passions, subordinates the appetites, quickens
the intellect, exalts the affections. It promotes industry,
honesty, truth, purity, kindness. It humbles the proud, exalts the lowly, upholds law, is essential to liberty, and would
unite men in one great brotherhood. It is the breath
of life to our social and civil well-being here, and spreads
the azure of that heaven into whose unfathomed depths
the eye of faith loves to look. All this it does, while yet
its great object is in the future. The river passes on, but
the trees upon its banks are green and bear fruit.

The glory spoken of in the text, and which is the
direct object of Christianity, consists in an immortality,
in the moral likeness of God, and in the consequent enjoyment of him and of all that he has to give. It implies
conscious rectitude, and the approbation and love of all
the good in the universe of God. This is true glory;
and the love of this, Christianity does not repress. That
love *is* Christianity, and it calls out in its pursuit the whole
strength of the human powers. It opens to the flight of
the eagle a boundless firmament. Here is one difference
between the Christian and the worldly hero. " Now they
do it," says the Apostle, " for a corruptible crown, but we
for an incorruptible." It is a " crown of glory that fadeth
not away." It transcends, as it should to be most effective, as it must to be adequate, our highest conceptions.
Even inspiration can only say, as only inspiration would
say, " We know not what we shall be." " Eye hath not

seen, nor ear heard, neither have entered into the heart
of man, the things which God hath prepared for them that
love him." This is the highest possible object for man,
and hence there is in it his true end; for the true end of
anything which God has made, is the highest of which
it is capable.

Christianity does not, indeed, claim that it shall bring
all unto glory. Here is a mystery that hangs over this
revelation, and a ground of its rejection by many. It
speaks of sin with a sternness, and of its unaverted results with a terror, with which those who have but slight
conceptions of the holiness of God have no sympathy.
Still, it is entirely a system of salvation, and will bring
unto glory every one who will receive it. Men may reject
it, and then charge upon it the very ruin from which it
came to deliver them ; but it is wholly beneficent. Through
it must come all the ultimate good that shall come to the
race ; and if there must be those who perish, yet the sons
that shall be brought unto glory shall be many. They
shall be "a great multitude which no man can number,
of all nations and kindreds and people and tongues."

Such is the object of Christianity ; and, in the SECOND
place, this object is to be reached by a process of *salvation*,
implying a previous liability and tendency to ruin.

This proposition all do not accept ; and, among those
who believe in the being and agency of a personal God, the
question respecting its truth involves a division more radical than any other. It involves a difference in the foundation on which men build, in all the aspects of the present
system, in the supposed tendencies of our nature and of human affairs, and in all plans for reform. This is the parting
point between the Evangelical system of religion and all
others ; for Evangelism, being the proclamation of good

tidings, can properly involve only what is announced from
without as coming into the system, and not anything already
in the system, and that could be evolved from it. Is the
ship moving toward the port, or drifting upon the rocks.
Left to itself, will that aggregate of capacities and tendencies which we call human nature reach its true good as instinct reaches its end? Do we become sons of God, and
shall we be brought unto glory by our first birth, or must
we be born again?

I know well how strange the state is in which this
doctrine supposes our world to be, and into what myste-
ries of the past, and perplexities of the present, and fears
of the future, it must run ; and how strong in us all, is
that naturalism by which we hold, as with the grasp of
death, to what is called the world. I know with what intense hatred and scorn this doctrine and its adjuncts are
regarded, often by learning and philosophy, and especially
by genius, that well knows how to weave its bitter derision
of them into the tissue of its fiction and its poetry. I
know how strong the argument against it is, both from
feeling and from a seeming analogy.

How bright and beautiful is that nature by which we
are surrounded, and with which we feel ourselves in sympathy? We stand abroad when the day is gone, and the
stars are coming out in the clear heavens, and the crescent
moon hangs in the west, and the dark foliage sleeps in
the still air, and the faint light lies upon mountain and
valley and river like a white veil upon the face of beauty,
and Feeling asks, Can it be *this* which revelation has written, " Reserved unto fire ? "

We see the orbs of heaven moving, unerringly, as if of
themselves ; we see the tree pushed upward by an internal force, and the animal following its instincts, and thus
reaching their ends. They have no need to be born

again ; and Analogy asks, Is not our nature also good?
If we give ourselves up to the guidance of its instincts and
impulses and passions, shall it not be well with us? To
enjoy, is it not to obey? May we not give nature her
bent, and eat and drink and enjoy ourselves and die, and
feel that death is but a sleep before a pleasant waking?
Oh, what joy it were to mingle ourselves with the elements
and forces around us, in their on-going, without responsibility, or care, or fear. Can it be that we must deny ourselves? Have we that in us which needs to be repressed,
crucified, and must we make strenuous effort or be lost?
Oh, how gladly would we believe that the broad road of
nature does *not* lead to destruction—that her current
would float us down to no rapids, and to no cataract.

But not so speaks the revealed word. That says that
the broad road does lead to destruction. Not so says
conscience. When the still night of reflection comes, she
does hear the roar of the cataract towards which sin is
floating. Not so say history and fact. When we contrast
the idols of heathen nations, and their objects of worship,
with the true God ; and their frivolous and debasing superstitions with his holy and spiritual worship ; and their
aims and hopes with the Christian heaven ; and their
wretched forms of intellectual and social life, their wars
and licentiousness and revenge and deceit, with the
intelligence and purity and love which Christianity would
produce ; when we see how Christianity itself is thwarted,
baffled, perverted, rejected ; we must feel that here is
moral perversion and moral ruin. Not so speaks the
voice of nature, in her sterner and more terrific aspects ;
not so in the uncertainty and hazard upon which she puts
us in regard to our interests here ; not so in her unswerving laws and unpitying inflictions when the fatal point in
transgression is reached. Not so speaks death, in its

13*

present aspect and form, with its sin-envemoned sting. Not so speak the law of God, and those dreadful words, guilt, and remorse, which are in human speech because what they indicate was first in human consciousness. Not so, especially, speak Gethsemane and Calvary. There can be no healing without sickness, no redemption without captivity, no pardon without guilt, no finding of those that are not lost, no salvation without exposure to ruin. If nature and Christianity did so speak, the first altar built by the gate of Paradise, and every bleeding victim under the Jewish economy were a lie, and Christianity would deny the necessity of its own existence. There would not be, as there is now, a salvation, and a Captain of our salvation made perfect through sufferings.

With such ground for the proposition that the process of Christianity is one of *salvation*, let us look,

III. At the *consequent* fact that self-denial and suffering, voluntarily assumed, must enter as essential elements into Christianity.

The self-denial and sufferings essential to Christianity as redemptive and restorative are those of Christ, and of his people. Both were necessary, but on different grounds. When the Apostle says of Christ that he was made perfect through sufferings, he must mean, not that he was made perfect as a man—for as a man he was always perfect—but that by these he became officially perfect, that is, qualified for his work. Why it became God thus to qualify him, we are not here told ; but this expression implies that in his qualification the sufferings were an indispensable element. That they did meet an exigency in the divine government, and are of peculiar efficacy, appears from the fact that he did *so* suffer ; from the whole sacrificial economy, patriarchal and Jewish ; from most direct assertions

of the Bible ; from the peculiar basis of Christian obligation ; and from the songs of the redeemed.

But all the sufferings of Christ were not redemptive.
He met with opposition and reproach, and felt under them
as man may feel. He "was in all points tempted like as
we are," and there are self-denials and sufferings which his
people must share with him. The soldier must follow his
Captain.

That self-denial enters into the preceptive part of Christianity, no one can doubt. It is remarkable how unflinch-
ingly she proclaims her gate of entrance to be strait, and
her path to be trodden, narrow. She calls upon men to
count the cost before they begin to build. Unqualifiedly
and universally does Christ announce the condition of dis-
cipleship : "If *any man* will come after me, let him deny
himself, and take up his cross and follow me." "It is enough
that the disciple be as his master." "If they have persecuted
me, they will also persecute you."

But is not this a harsh and an unexpected feature in a
religion which originated in love? Is there not in it something of arbitrary appointment? Might not Christ have
endured all? We say, No. We say that self-denial not
only may, but must enter into Christian life—that so far
as Christianity is redemptive and restorative, every act
originating under it is, and must be, an act of self-denial.
Christianity is not the absolute religion. That is freedom,
health, strength, joy. That is the religion of heaven, where
every power sings in the joy of a spontaneous activity. But
as redemptive and restorative, Christianity exists only as
antagonistic to sin ; and hence there must be conflict and
consequent self-denial till sin shall be eradicated.

Self-denial is not, as some seem to suppose, a conflict
between different forms of selfishness. It is not self-denial
when the miser concentrates his selfishness into one

absorbing passion, and through that denies and subjugates his appetites; but self-denial is the triumph in man of that which is higher over that which is lower. It is, first, the exclusion of selfishness, and then the renunciation of any form of enjoyment, or of natural good, from duty or from love. Christian self-denial is the denial of self for Christ's sake. It is love going forth to reclaim the sinful, and re‑lieve the wretched.

Now Christianity finds man in the intense activity of a spiritual death, and her work is to make him spiritually alive and healthful ; but all moral death and moral disease so involved a love of sin and its pleasures, a wrong bias of the will, that conflict must attend every step of the process in eradicating sin and restoring the image of God. The disease is in the will—in the very self. Hence that self must be denied ; and it is the beauty of Christianity that the great transition-acts by which man passes over to it are not abitrary, but imply just this denial. Repentance, especially in that element of it by which we forsake sin, is always the denial of self ; and this must continue as long as sin shall remain. The very act of faith by which we receive Christ is an act of the utter renunciation of self, and all its works, as a ground of salvation. It is really a denial of self, and a grounding of its arms in the last citadel into which it can be driven, and is, in its principle, inclusive of every subsequent act of self-denial by which sin is forsaken or overcome.

But if it must require self-denial to resist and overcome sin in ourselves, so must it when the sin is in others. To a sinner, the very life of his life seems involved in the selfish bent of his will, and hence the war between sin and holiness is one of extermination. The true expression of the opposition of sin to reproof, of its blind determination and unfaltering malignity, is to be found in the crucifixion of Christ. It slew the Son of God. ⸜When man saw perfect goodness, he crucified it.⸝ That act showed the character of man ; the life and sufferings of Christ showed the kind of effort needed to reclaim him. His mission was wholly for the good of others, including their radical reformation, and was *therefore* one stupendous act and manifestation of self-denial. Of the same general character were the labors of the Apostles and their successors, and such must be all true missionary labor. In doing this, men renounce the love of property, of ease and enjoyment, and give, and labor, and suffer, for the good of others.

This essential inherence of self-denial in the Christian system is a doctrine that has faded, perhaps is fading, from the consciousness of the church, and greatly needs to be freshened and revived. Having its root in the moral ruin of man and his possible restoration, it must enter into the elimination of sin and its consequences from any system. It is the distinctive characteristic of Christian activity as opposed to a life of mere nature, or of absolute wickedness. It excludes, on the one hand, all penances and self-righteousness; and, on the other, the love of ease and self-indulgence. Thus viewed, there is about it nothing arbitrary, or harsh, or austere. It is no mere negation of good for the sake of the negation, but rather the regimen necessary for the restoration of health. Not with the eye of a cynic or of a stoic is any enjoyment scorned or rejected, but only as duty and love fix their eye upon something higher and better. God is not a hard master. The infinite love of the gospel is dashed with no spirit averse to enjoyment, or that would mar the unspeakable gift.

But if self-denial must thus enter into the Christian life, let us, as was proposed in the FOURTH place, compare it with the principles which govern the world, especially with that which governs it in its enterprise and business.

The principle which regulates the enterprise and business of the world, is that of *demand and supply;* and the spirit of the time requires, when this would come in conflict with self-denial, that they should be brought fully into contrast, that you may choose intelligently between them.

That this principle of demand and supply has a legitimate sphere, I do not question. Among beings capable of supplying each other's wants and demanding nothing injurious, it would be wholly legitimate. It does now, and must always, regulate trade, as gravity does the level of the ocean; and to apply it skilfully, is the great means of success in honorable traffic and in all forms of business. The young man inquires what it is that the world demands and is willing to pay for—whether to supply its wants, or to gratify its tastes—and as he can furnish this, and the world is willing to pay for it more than it costs, his gains will increase. In doing this, he can meet with no opposition from the very fact that there is a demand; and though he may thus accumulate a fortune, he is often regarded, if not as a benefactor, yet with complacency and approbation. Especially is this so if he have met a want unsupplied before, thus opening new sources of enjoyment, and new channels of industry. How long did the ice of our rivers and lakes form and dissolve, and contribute nothing to industry or comfort? And he who first had the enterprise to take it to the tropics, deserved a fortune. Thus we trust it will be, more and more; that as the great ocean currents circulate the waters of all zones and equalize temperature, heat creating the demand and cold supplying it, so, in the legitimate application of this principle, the productions of all zones shall more and more contri bute to bring unity into the seeming diversity of nature, to supply the wants and augment the comforts of man.

But wholly legitimate as this principle would be in a race unperverted, it has its root in the doctrine that the world needs no moral change—that we are to take it as it is, and make the most of it. This it is that supplies, and insists on its right to supply whatever demand may exist, regardless of the wickedness or the woe it may cause. This it is that will sell the assassin his knife, and the drunkard his drink, and the slave-dealer his slave. It says, there is a demand; I only supply it; if I do not, another will. Thus the business of great companies and firms, nay the very institutions of society become impregnated and cemented by iniquity, till interest conspires with appetite and passion to blind the conscience and silence rebuke. Confining yourselves prudently within the range of this principle, you may pass on easily, and gain wealth, and be respected. Men will praise him that doeth well for himself. You will not be of those who turn the world upside-down. You will not trouble the world, and the world will not trouble you.

But, my friends, when the Captain of our salvation came into this world, he came not to supply a demand. There was none. He came to meet a deep, though unacknowledged want. He came to those who did not receive him, who rejected him and his teachings, and crucified him. Universally it is the characteristic of wickedness and of the ignorance it engenders, that they desire to be let alone. Unhallowed traffic says, let me alone, and slavery says, let me alone, and drunkenness, and licentiousness, and Sabbath-breaking say, let us alone, and superstition and heathenism say, let us alone. If we wait till there come up from these a call for reclaiming influences, we shall wait forever. And not only do they not demand these, but they will resist them, and persecute those who bring them, and the unconsciousness of need and the strength of resistance will be in proportion to the depth of the igno-rance and of the wickedness. In the face of a state of things like this, what is your sagacious, prudent, prosper-ous, demand-and-supply man good for? His principle is that the supply should be as the demand, and when the demand is great his labors are great, and so is his har-vest. But just the opposite of this is the principle of self-denial. Not in proportion to the demand but to the want of it ; to the depth of the insensibility, or the fierceness of the opposition, will its sensibilities be quickened, and its energies stirred. It will run at the articulated cry for help ; but when there is no cry, it will abide long, even as the missionaries in the South Sea islands sixteen years, and chafe the temples of seeming death. Said one who proposed to be a missionary, " Send me to the darkest and hardest and most degraded place in your field." There spoke the spirit of the Captain of our salvation ; there the spirit of every true missionary and minister and pastor. Where is the pastor even, who so preaches the truth as to search the conscience, and enforce every duty and exalt God, and lead to a life of humility and self-denial because there is a demand for such preaching? Where is there one who is not constantly tempted to sub-stitute the principle of demand and supply that calls for smooth, or learned, or entertaining, or exciting preaching, instead of that which would fix his eye steadily on the true end of preaching? The object of this principle is, not to take the world as it is and make the most of it, but to transform the world ; and it can never rest till that world shall reflect the image of heaven. The leaven, if it *be* leaven, must *work* and cause *fermentation* till the whole be leavened.

After the contrast now drawn, it will hardly be necessary to compare this principle of active and voluntary self-denial with those which govern the seekers of pleasure and of personal distinction. For the principle of demand and supply, there is a legitimate sphere; but a love of pleasure or of personal distinction as a paramount end, has no such sphere. They have self for their centre. Their object is to *use* all things, not to improve them. Incidentally and casually useful, they are necessarily disturbing forces in any great system of order. They link not themselves with God, or with any rightly constituted community, and so, when the springs of nature fail, they wither. There is about them nothing redolent of immortality. No man, whatever his wealth, or position, has a right thus to live in himself. No man has a right to excuse himself from active self-denial for Christ's sake. " If *any man* will come after me, let him deny himself, and take up his cross, and follow me."

From what has been said, it appears that if there is in Christianity an element of self-denial and suffering, it is because there is also in it the heroic, and the redemptive element.

The heroic element is a firm purpose to do and to endure all that love may prompt and duty require; and implies obstacles great and long continued. It is born of conflict, is manifested through labors and sufferings, and hence, but for sin and its consequent evils, could have had no place. It is not rash, or quixotic, or vain; it is not superstitious or ascetic. Needless conflict or suffering it avoids; but when its hour is come, it dares to the utmost, it endures unto death. Its full perfume is known only when it is crushed. What wonder, then, that there has been hero-worship? What has the pantheist that is nobler? Yea, what is the very highest manifestation of being, the sublimest object of contemplation ? Not oceans, not mountains, or precipices, or cataracts, or storms. Not the blue vault above us, with planets and satellites and countless suns ; not the awful depths of infinite space. It is not power in its creative or upholding agency ; it is not skill in its minutest or in its broadest exhibitions ; it is not even God himself ruling by love over an intelligent, free, harmonious, happy universe. No ; it is *self-sacrificing Love*. Clothe this and the issues connected with it, as does Christianity, with the attributes of infinity and eternity, and you have a manifestation of God such as nothing else can give. It is Love unto death ; Love conquering through death ; Love conquering death itself, and bringing up from the struggle, and bearing aloft the.gift of eternal life for a race that was lost. Here is the power of a divine Redeemer—in this the voice of the Captain of our salvation to a redeemed race, calling upon them to follow him. For something of this—for self-sacrificing love according to his measure, there is a capacity in every man, and to this, in the great conflict between moral good and evil of which this world is the theatre, every man is called. It requires no favoring exigency, no special endowment, no applauding throng, no results even which may not seem to sleep with the body of the humblest Christian till the resurrection. Its theatre is time, its issues are in eternity. This is the true battle of life. That is, not with the elements, to gain food and shelter ; it is, not with the selfishness around us, to gain wealth and position ; it is the conflict of every man with that within and around him which would drag him and others down, and would debar him and them from their rightful inheritance and position as children of God. And what element of heroism can there be which does not here find theatre and scope ? There is an enemy to be con-

quered, great struggles are required, great results are pend-
ing.   Here are needed both endurance and achievement ;
and if hitheıto, in Christian heroism, endurance has seemed
to preponderate over achievement, it ıs to be remembered.
that they spring from the same root, that endurance is
often the nobler and more difficult, and that in this cause
endurance *is* achievement.   " He that endureth unto the
end, shall be saved."   Wonderful is it that Christianity,
which so humbles man, should also stimulate and exalt
him—that it should be the only thing that brings within
the reach of all, the struggles and rewards of a true
heroism.

    We see also, from the preceding discussion, the pecu-
liar source and character of *Christian* joy.

    Man is naturally capable of joy in its lighter forms.
There is a joy in wit, and pleasantry, and mirth ; and with
these Christianity is not incompatible, except as the sight
of the great mountains, or the piloting of a boat down the
rapids, or earnest engagement in any business is incompatible with them.   They are a part of our humanity ;
they have their place, and let them have it, varying with
temperaments and with times.   There are also the more
serious and deeper joys of success, of gratified desire and
affection in any form.   But Christian joy is joy under the
Christian system, which exists only in opposition to sin
and in conflict with it.   It is not, therefore, the joy of the
absolute religion, when the kingdom shall be delivered up
to God, even the Father, but of a cause yet militant, moving on in discouragement and perplexity, and often meeting with apparent defeat.   It is the joy of repentance, of
humility, of hope, of conflict ; for in the conflict itself there
is often a stern joy not to be exchanged for those that are
lighter.   There is in it the joy of earnestness, which is
man's natural element.   Negation, skepticism, distrust,

have no joy. There is joy as the truth grows brighter, as temptation is overcome, as appetite and passion and evil habits succumb, as there is news of success and of the power of God's Spirit over the vast and varied field. An Apostle could say, " I have no greater joy than to hear that my children walk in truth." The Christian is in sympathy with Christ ; and as the captive Jews remem- bered Jerusalem, so he remembers his cause, and weeps and rejoices with the alternations of its success. He is as the patriot soldier watching the turns of parties and the fate of battles. This may give him a sober and an appre- hensive eye, but there is in it a deep and solemn joy. This is high in itself, but is chiefly to be regarded as pro- phetic of that which shall be, when these straits and shoals and currents of time shall be past, and we shall look upon the calm ocean. That will be the time for joy. And oh, what joy, when, in view of the full range of this mighty conflict, of the parties engaged, and of the issues involved, we shall see the last enemy destroyed, and many sons shall be brought unto glory. That will be the time for joy ; now is the time for labor, self-denial, if need be, for suffering.

Once more, we may see what must be the characteristic of effective labor in the Christian ministry.

Something is said at the present day, perhaps not too much as it is intended, of making the ministry an inviting field of labor to young men, and thus in these days, when the world draws so strongly, of inducing more to enter it. But nothing is gained by fighting the world with its own weapons. The ministry has its own joys and rewards, higher than any other ; but let me say to you, my friends, who propose to enter it, that in its true spirit it can never be made an inviting field to flesh and blood ; and unless you expect to take upon you this burden of self-denial, and

to look for your reward chiefly to the Captain of your salvation when the conflict shall be over, let me entreat you
not to enter it.

But not only in the ministry is self-denial required ;
there is one rule and standard for all.   And now, my dear
friends, let me ask each of you, standing where you now
do, Will you deny yourselves in this world for Christ's
sake ?   I call you to no superstition, to no austerity, to no
fostering of pride and self-righteousness, but to the acceptance of this essential element of the Christian system
as Christ left it.   As you answer this question, you will
settle the cast and general direction of your influence for
life.   So far as you are Christian men, and have insight
into your own state and moral wants, you must adopt this
as an element of your own secret, spiritual life.   Only thus
can you be transformed into the image of Christ.   Only
thus, too, can you do anything to hasten the triumphs of
a redemptive and restorative system on the earth.   In proportion to this, must be your interest and ownership in the
future kingdom of Christ.   This is the spirit in which Paul
prayed and labored, the spirit in which Mills and his companions prayed under the "hay-stack" fifty years ago, and
devoted themselves personally to the work of missions ;
and only in this spirit can you be associated with them.

The voice of your great Captain is calling you to other
posts in the ranks of his army.   Go to your posts.   You
are needed there.   Long has that army marched in feebleness and in gloom.   Through the long night of the past
I hear its muffled tread, and the low notes of its complain-
ing music.   I hear the groanings of its prisoners, and see
the light of its martyr fires.   But now the morning is
spread upon the mountains.   Catching the strains of prophecy, the music strikes up inspiring notes, and the tramp
of the host as it emerges from the gloom, begins to shake

the earth. Eveiywhere the standard of the Captain of our salvation is thrown to the breeze, and the ranks are defiling as on the plain of the final battle. Go to your posts ; take unto you the whole armor of God ; watch the signals and follow the footsteps of your Leader. That Leader is not now in the form of the man of sorrows ; not now does the sweat of agony rain from him. Him the armies of heaven follow, and he "hath on his vesture and on his thigh a name written, King of kings, and Lord of lords." The conflict may be long, but its issue is not doubtful. You may fall upon the field before the final peal of victory, but be ye faithful unto death, and ye shall receive a crown of life.

VI.

HIGHER AND LOWER GOOD.

But seek ye first the kingdom of God, and his righteousness; and all these things shall be added unto you.—Matthew, vi. 33.

THE blessings which man can enjoy may be divided into two classes. Of these, one class comes to him without his seeking them. If he is to live at all, he *must* see the light and feel the warmth of the sun; he must breathe the air, and smell the fragrance of flowers, and hear the voices of men and of birds. These things he may, indeed, seek; but for the most part they come to him without any seeking or agency of his.

But there is another class of blessings in respect to which the voice of nature and of revelation is, "Seek, and ye shall find." They are to be had *only* by seeking—often only by the most assiduous and energetic application of those powers which God has given for their attainment. To most men this is true of wealth and its advantages; and it is universally true of all high knowledge and of all those personal acquisitions and qualities of mind by which a man becomes truly great.

But these blessings that must thus be sought, may also be divided into two classes, according to the *direction* in which they are sought. We may either seek to produce outward changes and to acquire possessions, or we may seek to produce inward changes—to become wiser and better. We may seek to derive our happiness chiefly from

⁎ AUGUST 4, 1857.

what we *possess*, or from what we *are*. The greater part
of men evidently direct their activity chiefly to the production of outward changes and the acquisition of possessions. This, as it is the sin, is also the great error of the
race. A few only seek first to make the tree good, and
leave the result with God.

That "the kingdom of God and his righteousness " are
among those blessings that must be sought, is very plain.
In this respect they differ even from knowledge. Some
knowledge is gathered unconsciously and involuntarily,
but the kingdom of God and righteousness *can* come only
through the activity and consent of the affections and the
will. It is also equally plain, that the direction of the
activity to be put forth in attaining these must be within.
"The kingdom of God," says our Saviour, "is within you."
It does not consist, in any degree, in the possession of
anything. It has nothing to do with wealth, or station,
or learning, or place, or time. It consists wholly in our
state ; in what we really *are* in our relations to God as he
is revealed in his law, and in his gospel.

And such a state—a right state in our relations to
God—is not only to be sought, but is the highest end
which man can seek. That this is so regarded by God,
is evident from the very fact and plan of redemption.
All the motives and efforts and energies of his moral government have been, and are, adapted to produce in man a
change of *state*. For this Christ came ; for this the Spirit
is given ; for this the gospel is preached ; for this angels
minister ; this causes joy in heaven ; in this God is more
glorified than in all the works of his hands. What God
desires of us, is a right state of the affections and the will
—that we should take the place of his children, and *be* his
children. Such a state, moreover, is the perfection of man
himself in that which is most intimate and essential to

him.   It constitutes him a centre of light and of power.
It is the brilliancy of the diamond, and all else is but the
setting.

Having thus seen what the kingdom of God is, in what
direction we are to seek it, and that it is the highest end
at which we can aim, we now proceed to inquire whether
it is not a general truth, that he who in any department
aims at and attains the highest good, will also, and in so
doing, attain, not merely an adequate amount, but the
highest amount of subordinate good ?   This we suppose
to be a general principle, and we propose to show that it
is confirmed, first, by the Scriptures ; secondly, by all that
we observe in life ; and thirdly, by the very constitution
and processes of nature itself.

And first, if we test this principle by the Scriptures, we
shall find it fully confirmed in the Old Testament.   Of
this no more striking instance could be given than that of
Solomon.   When he was permitted to ask what he would,
and asked an understanding heart, " the speech pleased
the Lord, that Solomon had asked this thing.   And God
said unto him, Because thou hast asked this thing, and
hast not asked for thyself long life ; neither hast asked
riches for thyself, nor hast asked the life of thine enimies;
but hast asked for thyself understanding to discern judgment ; behold, I have done according to thy words ; lo, I
have given thee a wise and an understanding heart ; so
that there was none like thee before thee, neither after
thee shall any arise like unto thee.   And I have also
given thee that which thou hast *not* asked, both riches, and
honor."   He sought that which was higher, and God added the lower.

But of this principle the whole history of the Israelites
is an exemplification.   During the periods of the Judges,
whenever they sought the Lord and served him, they pros-

pered. The earth yielded her increase, and their enemies were subdued ; but when, ceasing to seek the higher blessings, they turned to idolatry, the lower were also removed. So in the history of the Kings, whenever one of them " did that which was right in the sight of the Lord," the Lord was with him and made his way prosperous ; and when one of them " did evil in the sight of the Lord," disaster was sure to follow. This is the one great lesson taught by their whole history, and intended for the warning of individuals and of nations.

In the New Testament, spiritual blessings are more regarded ; but even there, this principle does not fail of being announced in its general form. We are told that "godliness is profitable unto all things, having the promise of the life that *now is*," as well as " of that which is to come."

Being thus confirmed by Scripture, let us test this principle by a reference to the common objects of desire and pursuit in life.

Health is a subordinate good. To some extent, certainly, it is a good in itself, but it is chiefly so as enabling us to perform fully the duties and labors of life. How then is health best promoted ? Not by making it a direct object, and exercising for the sake of exercise, but by seeking, through all the exercise of body and mind which they involve, to accomplish those higher ends for the attainment of which health was given. It was not by attention to health, but by labor, that our fathers secured the constitutions they had. It is when people have little to do, or do little, that they become nervous, and make out a daily bulletin of their feelings ; and if they are not sick think they are, and in the end become so. It is recognized by every physician as a general principle, that the best condition and means of health is such activity in the pursuit of other ends as shall cause health to be unthought of.

Again, sensitive pleasure is a subordinate good, and how may this be best obtained? The body may be used either for the higher purpose of promoting the moral ends of life, or as a machine with the direct object of manufacturing the various forms of pleasurable sensation; and what we say is, that it will yield more of this form of good in its higher, than in its lower use. Pleasure results, not from the body alone, nor from that which acts upon it alone, but from the relation of the two. It is as the music from the Æolian harp. Let the harp be well strung, and it matters little what wind may blow. So of the body. It is only when this is well strung by temperance, and has that general vigor and perfection of all the senses by which it is best fitted to serve the mind, that it is most perfectly in harmony with all those natural objects which are adapted to give it pleasure. The sensitive organization of man was made to respond to the whole of nature. It is all his counterpart, and natural inheritance. But when he begins to make upon his system drafts of artificial excitement for the express purpose of pleasure, his relations to those sources of temperate and lasting pleasure which God has provided are changed. Quiet and simple pleasures become insipid; passive impressions become weaker; stronger and still stronger excitement is required; and the dividends of pleasure are increased only by drawing on the capital stock. The natural birthright of the senses is then rejected—sold for a mess of pottage. Thenceforward the man knows nothing of sun-risings and sun-settings, and the glories of night, and the march of the seasons, and the singing of birds. Sensation is more and more divorced from that union with intellect and sentiment by which it may be transfigured. Instead of being

mingled in the feast of life as a condiment, it is concentrated into an unwholesome drug that stimulates and
bewilders its victim for a time, and then palls upon the
sense. Even Epicurus could say, that the greatest amount
of pleasure could be reached only by temperance.

Thus it is that the use of the sensitive organization for
a purpose lower than that for which it was intended, is not
only wickedness but folly. This point should be fully
settled by every young man, for it is just here that many
make shipwreck.

We next inquire how this principle applies to the acquisition of wealth.   Would a lawyer, or a physician, or an
artist gain wealth, how will he do it most successfully?
Certainly by attaining something higher—great excellence
in his profession or skill in his art—and then wealth will
flow in as a matter of course.   But if any should say that
the skill is subordinate to the wealth, let me speak of a character for prudence, for energy, for high integrity and honor,
for righteousness generally.   To such a character wealth is
certainly subordinate, and yet the cultivation of that will
be found one of the surest ways of acquiring wealth. This
includes all that is meant by the proverb, that " honesty
is the best policy," and something more.   Not only is
honesty the best policy, but there is a tendency in all
righteousness, or, as the Scriptures term it, wisdom, to
produce wealth and the outward means of enjoyment.
" Length of days is in her right hand, and in her left hand
riches and honor."   Righteousness must exclude all habits
of vice and of vain and injurious expense ; it would insure
industry and a sense of responsibility, and would secure
that confidence which is so important an element of success with business men.

In the present disordered state of things, there may be,
and are exceptions to this in individual cases ; but, on a

large scale, where alone the principle can be fairly tested, there can be no exception. Let a nation, let this nation become righteous, and it is as certain as any law in physics, that it would be the most effectual means of increasing its wealth and worldly prosperity. The heavy weights of crime and pauperism, that now drag society down, would fall off; its productive power would be greatly increased; property would be more valuable as more secure ; and the imagination can hardly conceive the extent to which such a nation might enjoy all that can make this life happy.

Again, how may a man best take care of and extend his reputation ? Not by aiming at it directly, by anxiously nursing it, eager to show every unfavorable rumor to be false, and to fan every spark of good opinion into a flame ; but by going on in an independent course of duty, leaving unfounded reports to die out of themselves, and the sparks to kindle into a flame, or not, as they may.

And if this be true of mere reputation, it is much more so of any great and lasting fame. The highest form of greatness, and, of course, the highest legitimate fame, can never belong to a man who has fame for his chief object. He is no true artist, who pursues his art for the sake of fame. The patriot, whose highest object is fame, is no patriot.

Health, pleasure, wealth, reputation, fame, these are all subordinate objects, and to them all the principle now laid down applies. As a general rule, they are best attained when some higher end is the immediate object of pursuit.

Here, then, we have a great law for human action. It is also a law which God has prescribed for himself, which runs through nature, and is incorporated into all the processes and methods of his natural and moral government ? Does he always, in securing higher ends, incidentally secure the lower ?

In securing specific ends, and giving unity to his works, God has two methods. One of these we may call the method of additions, the other that of development. In the first, he passes onward and upward, from step to step ; at each step adding something new, but also bringing forward, either in itself or its results, all that had preceded.

To illustrate this, we must go back to the beginning of time, when we may suppose matter to have existed chaotically in space, having properties but not laws. And it may be well for our present purpose, to represent the world to be constructed as a pyramid with a broad base, and ascending by successive steps or platforms, each above less extensive than that below.

What then, in such a state, must have been the first and lowest step by which matter could have been rendered available? Evidently it was to bring it together into masses ; and so the first law in the order of nature, if not of time, must have been that of gravitation. This lies at the foundation. It is simple, universal, and seems to pervade all space ; but, acting alone, it would simply hold the particles in proximity.

The object next higher would be, to form from these loose particles solid bodies. This is done by what is called the attraction of cohesion ; and bodies united by this will form the second platform. But here it will be observed, that the higher includes the lower. Not all particles that gravitate cohere, but all that cohere gravitate.

The object next higher would be, to cause particles not merely to cohere, but to combine and to form compounds. Bodies thus united would form the third platform. But here, again, this higher is not attained without the two lower. All bodies united by chemical affinity also cohere and gravitate.

The next higher and more specific object would be,

the production of regular forms, as in crystals ; but every body that has a regular form also gravitates and coheres, and has its particles united by chemical affinity.

These are the first four platforms in the upward pro-gress of the creation, and they include inorganic matter.

The platform next higher is composed of regular forms endowed with organic life. This includes all plants—the whole vegetable creation. But in every plant we find not only organic life, and regular form, but also chemical affinity, and cohesion, and gravitation.

The next step upward is to sensitive life—that which is capable of enjoyment and of suffering, with the instincts necessary for its preservation. This greatly narrows our platform ; but here again the attainment of the higher both includes and presupposes that of the lower. In every being possessed of sensitive life, we find also organic life, and regular form, and chemical affinity, and cohesion and gravitation.

There is but one step more. It is that which carries us from the sensitive life with its instincts, up to the higher rational and moral life of man. Here we find every end attained that we had below, and something added. Man is subject to every law to which the minutest portion of mat-ter is subject, and has, generically, every characteristic of every order of being from the animalcule up to himself. In him we find operating gravitation, and cohesion, and chemical affinity; in him we find regular form, and sensitive life, and instinct, and, added to these, the higher gifts of reason and of conscience, by which he is made in the image of God.

Thus do we pass from that which is subject to law, to that which also comprehends law. Thus is man placed on the summit of the pyramid of these lower works, and fitted to link himself with that which is above. Thus is he the natural ruler, the epitome and crown of this lower world. Thus is he fitted, as partaking of the nature of all, to be the representative and priest of everything below him, and to gather up and give a voice to that inarticulate praise which goes up from every part of it to the Creator. Thus it is that the seven steps of the creation up which I have endeavored to lead you, may be compared to seven notes in music sounded successively, and then in harmony. In the first step, there was a single note ; in the second, the same note was taken up and another that accorded with it was added; in the third, another still was added to these, till man came, and everything was prepared for the full chorus that rang through the arches of heaven when the morning stars sang together and all the sons of God shouted for joy.

We see then how perfectly, in this method of additions, God adheres to the principle which we are now considering. He never does secure, according to the constitution which he has adopted it would seem impossible he ever should secure, a higher end or good, without securing at the same time, incidentally, every subordinate end and good.

But, besides the method of additions, I have spoken of that of development. This applies only to organized beings, each of which is a system having parts and functions, some of which are subordinate and others ultimate. To such a system nothing is added from without, except as there is development from within. It supposes something to be enveloped ; and that to which all the other parts are subservient, will be that which is originally enclosed in all the rest, and which is the last to come to perfection. So it is with the brain in man, so with the flower and the fruit in the plant.

But that the principle in question must hold under

this method is evident because, here, that which is highest becomes perfect only through the ministration of the parts that are lower ; and the more perfect the parts are that minister, the more efficient must their ministration be. This is the general rule. Limitations there may be, but not exceptions. Would God secure to any man the highest, the best balanced, and the longest continued action of the intellectual and moral powers, he does it only by giving him a sound physical constitution. When Moses, the servant of the Lord, was a hundred and twenty years old, " his eye was not dim, nor his natural force abated." So has God constituted every organic being, that " if one member suffer, all the members suffer with it, and if one member rejoice, all the members rejoice with it ; " and if he would secure the perfection of the higher parts that are ministered unto, he must do it by securing the perfection of the lower parts that minister.

So far, then, as we can observe the works and methods of God, there is no exception to the principle now stated. Within the sphere of this world, it is evidently a great, guiding idea, in all that he does. It was so in its construction, giving it unity; it is so in its government, and how much farther it may extend, we cannot say. It may be, taking the universe together, and going back to the very birth of time—not of our time, but of all time—that the first world, or sun, or system that came into being, gave the keynote to the whole. It may be that that note has been repeated with additions from that time onward, till at length it may require the ken of the highest archangel to read the extended scale, and the voices, as of many waters, that surround the throne, to utter the swelling anthem.

But, it may be asked, is not the great doctrine of voluntary self-denial, a doctrine taught equally by nature and by Christianity, an exception to this principle? Is it not of the very essence of self-denial, that instead of attaining a subordinate good by pursuing one that is higher, we attain the higher only by renouncing the subordinate?

This is a difficulty; but it will be observed that it arises wholly from the disorder and unnatural state·introduced by sin. This disorder and perversion are sometimes so great, as in martyrdom, that it is necessary to sacrifice every subordinate good, even life itself, for the attainment of that which is higher. Paul found it necessary to suffer, and did suffer, the loss of all things for Christ's sake.

Still, a fair statement of what is required by the law of Christian self-denial, will show that such cases are but exceptions. This law is not arbitrary. It is no law of fanaticism, or enthusiasm, or self-torture. It simply requires, first, that we deny ourselves everything that is sinful in itself; and, second, that we deny ourselves subordinate good not sinful in itself only so far as it would exclude a higher good. The first of these is no exception to the principle of the text, because pleasures, sinful in themselves, are not a subordinate but an incompatible good—incompatible with any true good. Under the second requisition there may be exceptions, but they commend themselves to our reason and give us our true law at a point where there has been serious error. The Christian may attain any subordinate end, as wealth, may enjoy any subordinate pleasure, as that of the senses, to the highest point of non-interference with that which is higher and better. You are at liberty, my friends, to pursue wealth, and pleasure, and fame, as far as you please, provided that pursuit be not incompatible with the attainment of a higher good. You are at perfect liberty to follow amusements to any extent, if there be nothing higher or better, which, as men, and as Christians, you can do.

While, then, we admit that exceptions may arise in this way, still, the general rule will hold that subordinate good is best attained by the pursuit of that which is higher.

Having thus illustrated and confirmed the general doctrine implied in the text, from the Scriptures, from what we observe in life, and from the constitution of nature, I wish to put into your hands an infallible chart. Here it is : " Seek ye first the kingdom of God, and his righteous- ness." Since the world began, there was never a sentence penned or uttered which I should prefer to give you as your guide. In it is the essence of all wisdom for man, for the individual and for society, the wisdom of all reform and of all growth.

In following this chart you will, first, see the necessity of seeking something. " Seek ye," says our Saviour, " seek." Have an aim, definite, specific. Without this there can be no comprehensive plans, no unity, no true decision, no earnestness, no moral power. The whole history of the race, the arrangements of nature, the con- stitution of man, all proclaim that man can reach his true good only by the voluntary activity of his highest powers in seeking a chosen end. Some things you may have with- out seeking ; some you may seek, and not find ; but there are things, and those which you most need, that you will never find without seeking.

Seek *ye*—ye, who are placed on the summit of the pyramid of these lower works ; ye, who may, if you will, link yourselves with that which is still higher ; ye, who have but one life in which to make the great choice ; ye, who have been redeemed by the precious blood of the Son of God, seek *ye*.

But *what* will ye seek? This is the great question,

here and now. What *will* ye seek? What will ye seek *first?* Not for its own sake, but for its bearing upon this question, have I asked your attention to the preceding discussion. I wished that my appeal to you to seek first the kingdom of God, might come, not only from his word, but that it might be seconded by a voice from all his works. I wished you to see that the principle involved is so inwrought into all those works, that it cannot fail to avenge itself upon those who shall disregard it. I wished you to see that the works of God are but as a great whispering-gallery, along which, if you will but put your ear to it, the words of Christ are constantly echoing. Seek, then, not that which is below you—you were not made for *that*—but that "which is above, where Christ sitteth, at the right hand of God." Seek *first* the kingdom of God, and his righteousness. Seek it first in the order of time. Let no business preclude it. Seek it first in the strength of that purpose by which you devote yourselves to its pursuit. The kingdom of God! His glorious and eternal kingdom! His righteousness! The moral likeness of God! Seek these, and all other things, truly good, shall be added unto you. That this shall be so, there comes a voice, not from the word of God only, but from the very beginning of time, and it is uttered with increased force at every step in the process of the creation. No, my friends, it is not *I* that speak to you; it is the whole process and method and structure of the creation of God. For Him all his works testify. When the Saviour says, "Seek ye first the kingdom of God, and his righteousness; and all these things shall be added unto you," there is not one of them that does not utter its Amen.

And why should not he who attains the kingdom of God and his righteousness, have all other things added? It must be so. If there may be exceptions and limitations

in the present temporary scene of sin and disorder, I beseech you think not so of God as to suppose there can be
any ultimate exception.   " Though it tarry, wait for it; it
will surely come ; it will not tarry."   Think not of God as
unwilling that his creatures should enjoy all from his
works that they can enjoy, without sin.   Vast as this universe is, he has made it, the whole of it, for his creatures.
He owns, not the earth only and the planets, but the sun,
and the milky-way, and the far-off nebulæ.   And what
use has he for all these but to make his creatures happy ?
And whom should he make happy but those who, in his
appointed way, seek first his kingdom and righteousness ?
So doing, you shall become his children ; and if children,
then *heirs ;* and then it is the voice of reason as well as of
Scripture, that utters that promise—the most magnificent
that language can embody—ye " shall inherit all things."
Ye shall be children and citizens in the kingdom of God
and shall have the free range and use of all his works.
The clouds and darkness which now seem to rest over his
moral government, you shall see roll away ; and from the
first faint whisper at the birth of time, to the full and tri-
umphant chorus of a finished creation and redemption, you
shall catch and repeat the song that shall come up to God
from all his works of creation and providence and grace.
With wonder and joy you shall witness every new step in
the process of creative power, and of the manifestation of
the divine character.   You shall be present at that next
and higher manifestation to which all things are now tending and hastening, and of which he speaks when he says,
" Behold, I make all things new."   You shall sit down at
the marriage supper of the Lamb.

VII.

THE ONE EXCEPTION.

Even the youths shall faint and be weary, and the young men shall utterly fail; but they that wait upon the Lord shall renew their strength; they shall mount up with wings as eagles; they shall run and not be weary; and they shall walk and not faint.—Isaiah, xl. 30, 31.

IS there anything that begins to be, and grows, that does not reach an appointed limit, and then go back ? Is not the daily movement of the sun in the heavens the fit emblem of every living thing that he looks upon in his circuit? He comes out of his chamber in the morning; he climbs the eastern sky; he reaches his meridian height, and then declines to his setting. So it is with every blade of grass, with every shrub, with every tree ; so with every insect and animal, from the animalcule to the elephant ; so it is with the physical system of man, and so with his mental faculties. And not only do change and decay affect every organized being, but also the empires of men and their monuments, and even the face of nature itself. " And surely the mountain falling cometh to nought, and the rock is removed out of his place ; the waters wear the stones; thou washest away the things that grow out of the dust of the earth ; and thou destroyest the hope of man." Throughout this universe nothing is at rest. There is permanence only from change. The stability of the heavens is from their motion ; the permanence of our bodies is by constant waste and supply. Whether the movements in the heavens will be perpetual we know

₊ AUGUST 1, 1858.

not, but in the march of life every step is towards death.
The movement there tends to a cessation, and that cessation is death.

It is this certainty of decay that gives a tinge of sadness to the scenes that are most full of life. In the deepest green of the mountain-side, the prophetic eye sees the
"sere and yellow leaf;" in the gayest assembly of the
young, it sees the gray hair and tottering age.

But to this law we find an exception in the Bible
representation of the moral growth and progress of the
righteous. We are told that "the path of the just is as
the shining light, that shineth more and more unto the perfect day"—that "the righteous shall hold on his way, and
he that hath clean hands shall be stronger and stronger"—
—that "they shall go from strength to strength"—that
"they shall mount up with wings as eagles; they shall
run, and not be weary; and they shall walk, and not faint."

So, likewise, the kingdom of Christ is not to be subject
to the decays of other kingdoms. "Of the increase of his
government and peace there shall be no end." "And the
kingdom shall not be left to other people, but it shall break
in pieces and consume all other kingdoms, and it shall
stand forever." "His throne shall be established forever
as the moon, and as a faithful witness in heaven." "His
dominion is an everlasting dominion, which shall not pass
away; and his kingdom that which shall not be destroyed."

Here, in those who wait on God, we have an alleged
exception to the law of decay.

What then is it to wait on God? It is not to wait *for*
him in an indolent passivity. It supposes that "all our
springs are in him," and that there is an open channel of
communication between him and us; so that the resources
of his omnipotence may flow in to us, and supplement our
weaknesses and infirmities. Its elements are expectation

15*

and trust. It implies ends sought in sympathy with God, and a sense of dependence on him actively expressed. It is as when a captive, who cannot redeem himself, waits on and earnestly implores the help of one who can redeem him. We do not suffice to ourselves. On every side we are surrounded by agents and elements that we cannot control. Beset where we stand, opposed when we would go forward, we find ourselves powerless in the presence of obstacles and foes. Then we wait upon God; our strength is renewed, and we go forward. Plainly, those "who wait on the Lord" are the same as "the just," "the righteous;" and the doctrine is, that the moral and spiritual nature of man is an exception to everything else on this earth; and that moral goodness not only need not wane, but that it may have an uninterrupted progress.

To establish the doctrine just stated will be our first object; and to do this, we must find the ground on which the exception is made. This is found in the very nature of moral goodness. Moral goodness has its seat in the affections and the will, and these do not so decay with the strength of the body and the power of the intellect, that that goodness is impaired.

It is a brave and a beautiful thing, if indeed it be not rather sublime, when a man, in the fulness of health and of strength, is required to abjure his faith in Christ, and in the face of the tyrant he says boldly, and even defiantly, No. But when the inquisition puts its victim on the rack, and the power of endurance is tested to the utmost, and there remains only strength of mind to apprehend the question, and only strength of body to whisper the feeblest No, there is in *that No*, a power that is mighty in proportion to the very feebleness of its utterance. Yea, if we suppose any power of apprehension, and of expression even by the feeblest sign, to remain, the indication of firm principle and enduring affection and moral goodness can become strongest and most affecting only at the point where the powers of the body and of the mind flicker on the very verge of death, and at the moment when they go out in its darkness. The love of the Saviour for this world reached the crowning point of its expression only at the moment when he " bowed his head and gave up the ghost."

In these cases the exhaustion and feebleness are indeed from torture, but the principle is the same in natural decay. Had the affections of that aged and dying Christian grown weaker as his powers decayed, who, when he was asked if he knew his friend who spoke to him, said, " No,"—if he knew his children, " No,"—if he knew his wife, " No,"—if he knew the Lord Jesus Christ, " Yes," and a smile from heaven lighted up his countenance ; " Yes, he is all my hope." In such cases, the embers of a wasting animal life gather over the " vital spark of heavenly flame," and obscure it. It seems to be lost ; but when it can be thus reached, as sometimes it may, it is seen to be all aglow, and the light which it shoots up is but the brighter from the darkness out of which it comes.

It is conceded that the strength of virtue and of trust are most tried in adversity, and when the natural desires are thwarted. " Though he slay me, yet will I trust in him," is the strongest possible expression of confidence. Let, then, the decay of the powers from age commence and go on, and let there be perfect acquiescence in this till their apparent cessation ; and how does the power of goodness, as thus seen, differ from that which is seen in submission to a voluntary death, and in holding on, through exhaustion from torture, till the very end ?

The truth seems to be, that an accountable being,

remaining such, can be placed in no circumstances in which moral goodness, the principle of duty, of submission, of faith, may not be brought into exercise ; and if exercised, then, by a natural law, must they be strengthened ; and the more difficult and trying the circumstances are, the more strength may be gained. It is through and in the very weakness of the natural powers, that the moral powers may show their strength. Only at the moment of the seeming triumph of the tyrant, of disease, of decay, can humanity pay its highest homage to goodness and to God.

In the struggle of men against evil and for the right, there is doubtless given the special and supernatural aid of God ; but, in addition to this, it would seem, from what has been said, that the exception made by the Scriptures to the great natural law of decay, is itself sustained by a natural law.

Having thus shown that there may be constant progress in moral goodness, we next inquire whether such progress is not a condition of the highest possible strength and perfection of the intellectual faculties. If we regard man simply as intellectual, will he not, both as an individual and as a race, mount higher, in proportion as he cultivates his moral powers, and waits upon God ?

This is a question that deeply concerns every scholar ; and that it should be answered rightly, is of much consequence, both because it lies at the basis of all right education, and of all true self-culture ; and because there is, to some extent, an impression that skepticism and wickedness are naturally associated with intellectual power.

In what has been said it has been taken for granted that the powers of the intellect really decay. This may be doubted. Of mind in its essence we know nothing, and of the laws of its connection with the body, very little.

What seems decay may be from the body, and be only as a temporary drowsiness. Certain it is that the intellectual are indispensable to the moral powers ; that in the nature and sphere of each, there is equally a provision for an indefinite progress ; and that the aged must be supposed to carry into another state, not the imbecility of a second childhood, but the results of their mental, as well as of their moral action. Still, these powers do *seem* to decay ; between them and the moral powers, as has been shown, there is a broad distinction ; and what we say, in either case, is, that the condition of their highest attainment is the cultivation of the moral powers.

That this is true we believe, first, because of the obstacles to intellectual growth and progress that would be removed by the ascendency of the moral powers.

These obstacles are prejudice and vice, both of which are inseparable from the sway of passion and appetite, and both of which would disappear in the full ascendency of the moral powers. If prejudice may not be said to weaken the mental powers, it misdirects, perverts, and limits their action. The power of the eye is one thing ; a clear atmosphere is another. Prejudice is, to the mental eye, an indistinct, a colored, a distorting medium. But while prejudice misdirects, vice enfeebles, or wholly prevents the action of the intellect. From the drunkard, the glutton, the licentious man, the gambler, we do not look for continuous thought, or for any rich fruit of intellectual culture. They have the instincts and sagacity of the animal, heightened by their connection with rational powers ; but they are engrossed by their vices, and their intellects have no range beyond the activity necessary for self-gratification. Through these vices much of the finest intellect of the race has been lost. And so it must be. If the swallow would fly, its wing must not be draggled in the mud ;

if the eagle would continue to mount up, the animal that is sucking his blood must drop from under his wing.

But that the intellect will be most successfully cultivated through the moral powers, appears, secondly, because it is lower than those powers, and subordinate to them ; and because, in securing a higher good, we best secure that which is subordinate and lower.

That the intellect is lower than the moral powers appears, because it is conditional for their activity. And here we find a criterion which may be universally applied in determining, both in matter and in mind, what agencies and powers are higher, and what are lower. Always that which is conditional for another thing, and so serves it, is lower than that thing. The foundation of a house is conditional for a house, and is lower, in more senses than one. It is indispensable, but of no value without something beyond itself. So of all the powers and agencies of inanimate matter. They are conditional for vegetable life, and are lower. So, again, vegetable is conditional for animal life, and it is lower ; so with the heart and the brain ; so with the body and the mind; and so with the intellect and the moral powers. The intellect is conditional for choice and activity, in which are the end of man, but it does not choose. It does not even know ends, as such. It can judge of their attainability, and of the fitness of means ; but the apprehension and choice of an end, and especially, that highest act of the mind, the choice of a supreme end, belongs to a higher power.

The inferiority of the intellect is also manifest, because it is an instrumental and not a governing power.

We cannot too carefully discriminate those powers in us, by which we choose ends, from those that are merely instruments in their attainment. In the one is wisdom, in the other talent ; in the one is character, in the other capacity ; in the one, the man himself acts in his whole being, and very personality ; in the other, the faculties play on the surface. The end is already chosen, and the whole work is simply executive. But, as has been said, the in- tellect does not choose. It is an axe, a saw, a hammer, a a piece of machinery to be worked by a power back of itself. It is a Swiss mercenary, that may be enlisted in any cause, good or bad, and, as such, is inferior to the employing and directing power.

It appearing thus that the intellect is lower than the moral powers, it remains to show that the well-being of that which is lower can be best attained only as we secure that of the higher.

This was shown in the discourse of last year to be true of health, and pleasure, and wealth, and reputation, and fame ; and also that the principle implied is incorporated into all the works of God. It is a great law of nature, with as few exceptions as there are to most of her laws ; and we may fairly presume, till the contrary shall be shown, that the intellect is no exception.

But, that the intellect will be best cultivated through the moral powers will appear, if we compare those powers with any other force by which it can be worked.

As has been said, the intellect must be worked by something back of it. It is as the muscle, that is nothing without the nerve ; and its efficiency will depend partly on original structure and on training, and partly on the power that lies behind. That power must be some in- stinct, tendency, appetite, passion, taste, feeling, some capacity of emotion or enjoyment ; and if we make a com- parison among these, we shall find that the moral powers have the advantage, both in strength and continuance, and also in the unity and harmony that result from their working.

Man's nature is not a hive of faculties without a queen bee. It is not a mob. It is rather a commonwealth where each has its place, and where there can be strength and continuance and harmony of action only as the moral nature is made central, and as all move and cluster about that.

If any force can compare favorably with the moral nature, it must be ambition. But ambition refers, for its standard, to the opinions and attainments of others; when it has gained its end, or become hopeless of gaining it, its efforts cease. Let that end be but gained, and it does not require the improvement of time ; it knows nothing of working in harmony with God, and so nothing of healthy, symmetrical, beautiful growth and development, as good in themselves. It has no power of self-regulation, and so is often consuming and self-destructive. It puts the mind in conflict with itself, and makes it anxious for the result. It is selfish, repellent, and tends to isolation. That follows here which follows always when the lower faculty is disengaged from the higher, and ceases to act in its light. That which was intended to walk erect by holding on to something above it, becomes a serpent going upon its belly and eating dust.

But the moral nature is stronger than ambition. It underlies all true heroism, all martyrdom, and, by uniting us to God, was intended to be the paramount and immortal force of our nature. Let this, then, lie back of intellectual effort, and we have a permanent, constant, self-regulating principle, that will always bring the faculties up to the full glow of a healthful activity, and forbid them to go beyond. Now, the standard will be fixed, not with reference to others, but by capacity and opportunity. The mind will act in its unity, with no conflict of its higher and lower faculties, and with no fear of the result. Hence

there will be, not only strength, but balance and completeness and order and beauty. Not only will there be harmony among the faculties themselves, with no tendency to
a repellency of others, or to isolation ; but it will be felt
that the activity is with all, and for all. It will be felt to
be a struggling towards that absolute perfection of one
which is necessary to the perfection of all.

But whatever may be said of individuals, of communities there can be no doubt. The spiritual and moral elevation of a people would certainly secure their general
enlightenment. It would not make every individual intellectual, but it would create a summer atmosphere for the
quickening and growth of intellect, that would rest alike
upon the hilltop and in the valley, and would solicit every
latent capacity. The higher faculties would so strike down,
and stimulate and appropriate the lower, that there would
be, if not technical intellectualism, yet a broad, balanced,
directive intelligence which would, as by instinct, bear
society on to its right ends ; and in the light and under
the stimulus of which, individual growth, whether humble
or gigantic, would be most favored. Then would the
necessity of toil be no longer a blessing to man by keeping him from mischief. Leisure would be a blessing. A
community let loose into that, would rise like a bird.
Under the power of moral motives, leisure—the power to
do what we please—would be equivalent to a college education, and the works of God would be to every man a
university. Without these motives, even a college education becomes, within the limits of possible graduation, a
systematic evasion of study, the works of God are a blank,
and this furnished world becomes a pigsty or a pande-
monium. It is in the use to be made of its leisure, that
the problem of the race lies. Who shall drain this bog ?
—hitherto a bog bearing weeds and sending up miasm—

who shall drain it, and make it healthful and fruitful?
Tell me what is to be done with the leisure that a machinery, gigantic and tiny, myriad-handed and half-reasoning,
is beginning to give, and will yet give more fully to the
race, and I will tell you what the destiny of the race will
be.   To the opportunities and facilities it will furnish for
intellectual and social elevation there is scarcely a limit ;
there is none to the sensuality and degradation which may
grow from its abuse.   But intellect in the service of the
passions tends downwards.   Only from the sense of obligation and the free play of those spiritual affinities by
which we are united to God, will there be the broad light
of an intellectual day.

We conclude, then, that the higher intellectual power,
whether of the individual or of the community, can be
reached only by waiting on God, and by the culture,
through that, of the spiritual and moral powers.

If, now, it be inquired how the impression of intellectual power has come to be associated with skepticism and
wickedness, an answer may be found, first in the fields of
literature and speculation commonly entered by the skeptical and licentious.   These are those of imagination, wit,
ridicule, and trancendental metaphysics.   Often, pervaded
by a sneer, and quietly assuming the falseness of religion
and the weakness or hypocrisy of those who profess it,
we have, in novels, in poetry, in essays, a combination of
all these.   Their object, the last excepted, is not truth, but
impression ; and this last is as yet so overrun with strange
terms, so the common ground of truth, falsehood, and non-
sense, each aping the profound, that it is difficult to say
whether it is better as a hunting-ground for truth, or a
stalking-ground for vanity, or a hiding-place for falsehood.
That there is power in this literature, is not denied ; but

the power of imagination, wit, assumption, and even of bathos, it is not distinguished from that of fair and searching investigation.

A second answer we find in the effect upon the mind of all irregular action, especially when combined with daring, or fool-hardiness. The utmost power of a horse, exerted in the true line of draft, will excite no attention. Half the power put forth in rearing and plunging, will draw a crowd about him. A cheap method of notoriety, the world over, is this rearing and plunging. Sam Patch, leaping over Genesee Falls, could gather a greater crowd than Daniel Webster. The great powers of nature, those by which she wheels up her sun, and navigates her planets, and lifts vegetation, and circulates her waters, by which she holds herself in her unity and manifests her diversity, are regular, quiet, within the traces of law, and excite no attention. Here and there the quiet eye of a philosopher expands in permanent wonder, but from the very fact, the greatest wonder of all, that these forces are so clothed in order and tempered with gentleness, they are to the multitude nothing. Not so with volcanoes and earthquakes, with hurricanes and thunder-storms, with water-spouts and cataracts. These are irregular manifestations of the great forces that lie back of them. Compared with those forces, they are only as the eddy to the river ; only as the opening of the side-valve and the hiss of the steam compared with the force of the engine that is bearing on the long train ; and yet these are the wonders of the world. So with the mind. When it respects order and law, when it seeks the ends and moves in the channels appointed by God, its mightiest and most beneficent movements excite comparatively little attention. But combine now irregularity with audacity ; open a side valve ; assail the foundations of belief ; make it impossible for God to work a miracle, or to prove it if he should ; turn history into a myth ; show your consciousness of power by setting yourself against the race ; flatter the nineteenth century ; dethrone God ; if you make the universe God, yourself being a part of it, so much the better,—do thus, and there will not be wanting those who will despise the plodders, and hail you as " the coming man."

I have thus endeavored to show, first, that moral goodness is the only exception, on this earth, to the law of decay ; and, secondly, that it is the condition of the highest intellectual power, both for the individual and the race.

In the light of these propositions we may see, first, what must be the essential elements in the promised kingdom of our Lord Jesus Christ.

They must be righteousness and knowledge. So says the prophet. " The people shall be all righteous : they shall inherit the land forever." " And the work of righteousness shall be peace, and the effect of righteousness, quietness and assurance forever." " And wisdom and knowledge shall be the stability of thy times, and strength of salvation." This gives the line and order of effort for all who would labor for Christ. Not for an unintelligent piety—well-meaning, but blundering—are they to labor ; not for a superstition without knowledge, calling itself righteousness, but weak, sentimental and showy—bolstered up by fine arts and wire-pulled by a hierarchy; not for knowledge without righteousness, sensualized, self-conceited and presumptuous ; but for a combination of righteousness and knowledge working together like the warmth and the light, everywhere pervading society in its free, oceanic, and multitudinous action, and building it up into the order and beauty of heaven.

In the second place you will see what you are to do in carrying out your own education.

That education you have, I trust, entered upon not wholly from worldly ends, but with some reference to the state of your permanent being, and to an immortal progress. For it, many of you have made sacrifices, and have applied yourselves laboriously and faithfully. Grow, my friends; seek to grow. But as a condition of a growth that shall be permanent, healthful, symmetrical, do not ignore that interaction of the higher and lower powers which is like that of the leaves and the trunk of the tree. As in that, elaboration, assimilation and ultimate growth are from above, so it is only through the higher moral nature that the sap of knowledge is converted into wisdom. If your chief sphere of study were to be the abstract sciences, cold and passionless, where, as in mathematics, the relations depend on no will, your moral state would be of less moment; but your chief sphere is to be nature and man, where everything is constituted by design, and where the key to the whole structure and to each particular department is to be found in ends and uses. Here love, trust, sympathy, will be stimulants of thought and elements of moral power. Nature is from God no less than mind. It was made for mind. It reflects the thoughts and feelings of God. It is understood only as the thoughts of God in it are reached, and it must be that, as we are in a right moral state, and in sympathy with God, we shall have a finer sense and a quicker sympathy on the side of nature. She will open herself to us more fully, and become, in a far higher sense, a companion and an educating power. But let now a man study nature with a scoffing spirit, and he must fail of insight. His stand-point will be wrong. Movements that are onward and beautiful when seen from the centre, will seem to him retrograde and perplexing. The sweetest voices of nature, her hymns, he cannot hear ; her highest beauties he cannot see, her profouudest teachings are to him mere babble. Jeers, sarcasm, fault-finding, exciting no enthusiasm, with no re· action on thought, with no element of satisfaction except as they minister to notoriety, will take the place of admiration, love, adoration, by which thought is naturally quickened and rewarded. Would you study the works of God, and yourselves as a part of those works, be in harmony with yourselves, and in sympathy with God.

But thirdly. Not only are you to educate yourselves, opening your minds to all light, and putting forth all effort, but directly and indirectly you will have much to do in educating the community, and you will see, in the light of this subject, your duty in that regard.

You will neither form, nor encourage, any extravagant expectations from what is commonly called education. Not so will society grow up into its true life. If there be that above the intellect to which it ought to be subservient, but is not, then there will be a law of degradation even in its own activity. Education will become, either simply an accomplishment, or a drudge. It will do nothing towards removing the follies and weaknesses of society ; so that you will find, as we now do, communities claiming to be the most highly educated, pervaded, even more than others, with a credulity and a superstition that would have disgraced the days of witchcraft, but without the earnestness which saved those from being contemptible. This we may satirize and deplore, but, under the system, it cannot be helped. The only true method is that of our Saviour. Nothing now on the earth, or that ever has been, can compare with Christianity in its educating power. Wherever it has been in its purity, the standard of general education has always been highest. It is so now. You

cannot have a pure Christianity without general education,
while yet education, as such, is not the object of Christianity at all. Its educating power results solely from its
reaching and controlling that which is highest, and from
the necessary stimulus and rectification through that, according to the principle laid down, of all that is lower.
So has it wrought from the beginning ; so will it work, and
only in and through this can you work effectually. Hence
you will make, simply as educators, a capital mistake, if
you do not seek to enthrone Christianity in all our seats
of learning, and to extend and deepen its influence in
every possible way. Hence no institution, not pervaded
by Christianity, can do much in really educating and ele-
vating the community.

Finally, we see from this subject where lies the permanent strength and the true good of man.

It is much to know, that there is any one thing on this
earth that does not decay ; that while the body is constant only by change, and its identity is only similarity,
there is in the mind a central point that is unchangeable,
and an identity that is absolute. It is more to know that
in this we find our true selves, that by this we are allied
to God. This takes us out of the sphere of that law of
uniformities, in the light of which we have hitherto chiefly
regarded the subject, and brings us into that of free personalities. Made in the image of God, allied to him as
personal and free, we have faculties, call them moral, call
them spiritual, by which we apprehend him, and through
which we become receptive of influences from him.
These influences imply no inspiration of particular truths
as to prophets and seers. but are open to the race.
They come as the tide to the stranded vessel that
gradually surrounds it, and lifts it up, and bears it
into the depths and boundlessness of its appropriate

element. By these influences, respecting the laws of our freedom, and the bounds of our individuality, the Spirit of God enlightens, sustains, purifies, exalts us, and makes us partakers of his own blessedness. This is the Scripture doctrine of the indwelling of the Holy Spirit, that last link in the work of human salvation, by which, all incompati-bilities of justice and mercy having been removed, the law becomes written in the heart, and we are brought to rest in the activity of a full and unceasing complacency in a holy and infinite God. Thus God himself becomes the portion of the soul. Thus do we enter into the "fulness of him that filleth all in all." Beyond this, nothing of good can be conceived of. This is our rest—our ultimate goal. This it is that we yearn after; in the congruity of this to the mind, and in the deep, conscious want of it, it is that we find the solution of those enthusiasms, and extrava-gancies, and distortions of the religious nature, which have made religion a by-word. These suppose a capacity and need of communion with God just as insanity supposes reason, and they will cease only when that communion returns.

Do you, my friends, accept this doctrine? Will you accept it practically? Will you open the way for the com-ing into your own souls of divine light and divine help. Will you put away sin? This is the one condition of a pure light and a true elevation. You must begin with the heart, for only the pure in heart can see God, and only as we see him, and in his light, can we see all other things in their true proportions. Will you then open yourselves fully to the divine teachings, and to the intimacy of a divine communion? Not only morally, but intellectually, will the answer to this question be the turning-point in your destiny. The question involved in this doctrine of a divine communion and help, is the cardinal one for the race. At every point this doctrine meets not only our weaknesses and wants, but also our *sinfulness*, and so transcends all transcendentalism, and all possible philoso- phies and devices of man. It is not merely a philosophy, but a redemption and a remedy, a companionship and a portion. Without this doctrine, man is but a waif upon the waters, a severed branch that must perish. With it he is united to God, and so there is nothing too great for him to hope. With it he may mount up as with the wings of an eagle, may run and not be weary, and walk and not faint.

VIII.

THE MANIFOLDNESS OF MAN.

What manner of child shall this be?—Luke, i. 66.

THE circumstances preceding and attending the birth of John the Baptist, were extraordinary. As his father, Zacharias, then "well stricken in years," "executed the priest's office before God in the order of his course," "there appeared unto him an angel of the Lord standing on the right hand of the altar of incense," and foretold the birth of the child. When Zacharias did not believe him, "the angel answering said unto him, I am Gabriel, that stand in the presence of God, and am sent to speak unto thee, and to show thee these glad tidings. And behold, thou shalt be dumb, and not able to speak, until the day that these things shall be performed." Accordingly Zacharias was dumb until the time came for naming the child. Then, after he had written the name given by the angel, "his mouth was opened immediately, and his tongue loosed, and he spake and praised God." These things "were noised abroad throughout all the hill-country of Judea;" and it is not strange that "all they that heard them laid them up in their hearts," or that they said, "What manner of child shall this be?" Of a child whose birth was thus heralded and signalized, something extraordinary could not fail to be expected.

₊ JULY 31, 1859.

But while this inquiry was thus naturally made respecting John, may it not also be appropriately made respecting every child that is born? There may be nothing extraordinary, either in connection with the birth
of the child, or with the child itself, and yet that child
shall be different from every other child that ever was
born, or ever shall be; and its capacities of development, and the possibilities of its future, shall run in lines
of such divergency from those of every other, that we
may well ask respecting it, "What manner of child
shall this be?"

There is nothing in the works of God more striking
than the differences there are of things that are similar,
and the similarities of things that are different. In the
perception of these two we have the element of science
on the one hand, and of practical skill on the other.
So far as beings or things are similar, they may be
named alike, and treated alike, and so a knowledge
of one becomes the knowledge of all. This is science.
Through this the individuals which God has made, vast
as they are in number and variety, are marshalled, and
ranged in regiments, and battalions, and companies.
In this, and so far as it goes, exceptions and individual-
ities disappear; what seemed promiscuous and irregular
falls into order, and the universe assumes the appearance of troops marching and countermarching in a grand
review. But so far as things are different, each individual must be studied by itself, and treated by itself; and
as differences constantly appear, they furnish the occasion of constant study. Thus it is that through similarities the dictionary of human knowledge is greatly
abridged, while through diversities, the faculties are kept
constantly awake. At the point where we cease to discriminate differences, all interest ceases from uniformity

and monotony.   At the point where we cease to discern similarities, interest again ceases from diversity and confusion.

But while these elements pervade the works of God, while our scientific interest in those works and practical power over them are from these, yet are they nowhere more striking, and nowhere as interesting to us, as in man.   Every man has, and as a man must have, the great features and characteristics which make him a man, and yet how infinite the diversity!   No two are there that look alike, no two that think alike, no two that act alike; and doubtless this diversity will become greater and greater, so long as they shall exist.   Here, and here only in this diversity ever increasing yet not divorced from unity, do we find the basis of a harmony that shall also ever increase.

This diversity it was which was implied in the question of the text.   That referred not merely to the childhood, but to the whole career of John.   What manner of man should he become ?   What part should he perform in the great drama of human affairs ?   Should he be a monarch, a conqueror, a sage, a lawgiver ?   Should he play over again the old games of ambition, and pleasure, and gain? or should he be something new and fresh in the world's history.

The question supposes a great difference between the child then, and what he would become.   And how great was that difference !   Now he is an infant of eight days, with no visible distinction from other infants; just as helpless and dependent.   A Pharisee might have taken him under the enlarged border of his garments, and have borne him through the streets of Jerusalem, and no one have known it.   But pass on now thirty years, and what is he ?   He is " the voice of one crying

in the wilderness, Prepare ye the way of the Lord, make
his paths straight." He cries, and all Judea, and Jerusalem, and the region round about Jordan are stirred,
and go out to him. He is the fulfillment of prophecies
made centuries before, the forerunner of the Messiah, a
bright and shining light, one of whom it could truly be
said, that of those born of women, there had been none
greater than he.

But great as this change was, there was nothing in
it so unusual as to attract attention. The man attracted
attention, but not the change. This was so gradual,
that wonder was superseded by familarity. It was but a
single exemplification of a general law. Hence I observe, in the first place.

That there is a great difference in all organic beings,
between what they are at first, and what we see them
become.

We might ask of any seed just germinating, What
manner of plant shall this be? See; here is a point of
green just visible. Look again. It has become a violet,
with its eye on the sun, suffused with beauty, and throb-
bing with the pulses of the universal life. Here is a filmy
substance; it lies upon the palm of your hand, and a
breath will blow it away. From this, too, emerges a point
of green no larger than the other, and with no perceptible
difference between them. But this shall become the elm
with its pendent branches, towering and spreading, the
pride of the meadow. We may ask the egg, "What manner of creature shall this be?" Now there is in it a beating speck—a mere point that pulsates. The philosopher
is peering at it through his microscope, searching for the
principle of life, as the child chases the foot of the rainbow.
That principle he finds not, he shall not find it, but it em-
bodies and perfects itself, and from points undistinguish

able, it becomes now a wren, chattering and vivacious ; now a golden oriole, warbling and weaving its pendent nest ; now a solemn owl ; a peacock, with its "goodly wings ;" an ostrich, with its "wings and feathers," fleet and powerful ; an eagle, screaming and breasting the storm-cloud far in the sky. It is indeed now said, that every plant, from the lichen to the oak, and every animal, from the insect to man, has its beginning in a single cell. It is in these cells, undistinguishable by us, that Omniscience can see the future, and from them that Omnipotence can call "the things that are not, as though they were."

This capacity of transformation and growth, by which beings seem to us to pass from the very verge of nonentity to great perfection and magnitude and power, is among the most striking characteristics of the present state. It is also one which we think of, and Revelation confirms the impression, as belonging to this state alone. There are not wanting those who believe that this world is the nursery for peopling this planetary system at least, if not the worlds scattered through all space.

The individuals thus starting from what seems a common point, are different in rank, and fall into different classes ; and we next inquire what the rank of each will be.

The rank of each will be determined, first, by its rank in its own class ; and, secondly, by the rank of the class.

The rank of an individual in its own class will be determined by its capacity of development, and by its actual development in one direction. The California pine may reach a circumference of thirty feet, and a height of three hundred and fifty, and so be the first of its class ; but it is by a repetition always of the same processes, an extension and increase in one line. Between the greatest and the least of them there is no difference, except that of de

velopment in a particular direction. Among men, a man
will be really first, who possesses most perfectly what is
distinctively human ; and in general, whatever individual
of a class shall manifest most fully its distinctive characteristic, will be the first in that class.

But while rank *in* a class is determined by development in one direction, the rank *of* a class is determined
by the capacity of individuals in it for development in different directions ; thus giving wide scope to the imagination in answering the question, "What manner of being
shall this be?" The power in a tree of varying from a
given line is as nothing. So it can grow, so only. In
animals, this power is greater ; in man, greater still—and
the more things it is possible for him to become, the more
complex must be his nature, and the higher his rank. As
the scheme of the creation is, that that which is above takes
up into itself all that is below, the more complex the nature
is, the higher it must be, the more directions it may take,
and the greater is the uncertainty that must hang about its
final destiny.

And here I observe, in the third place, that, in sensitive
and moral beings, a capacity of development in one direction involves its opposite, and that in an equal degree. In
this we find startling indications respecting the possibilities of our future. In creatures merely sensitive, perhaps
a different constitution was possible, but we know of no instance of it. A capacity for pleasure always involves that
of pain, and, so far as we can judge, in a degree precisely
correspondent. But whatever may be possible in the region
of simple enjoyment, in a moral being the capacity of development in one direction must imply that in the other.
He who is capable of moral elevation, must also be of
moral degradation. He, and he only, who is capable of
great moral excellence, is capable of great sin. This is the

basis of the maxim universally true, that the best things corrupted,.become the worst. The better, the higher, the purer, the nobler any being is capable of becoming, the more utter and awful may be its downfall and ruin. It requires an angel to make a devil.

From what has been said, it appears that the rank of man will be determined by the range of his possible development in different directions. And how wide is that range! How different in this is man from any other being on the earth! Let us look at the breadth of this range, first, in respect to *belief.* An animal cannot be said to believe at all, but for an infant how wide is the range of possible belief! Wonderful is it, that with the same faculties, thrown into the same world, with the same phenomena, and orders of succession, and similarities and differences, such a range should be possible. Especially is this true of religious belief, where the range is the widest conceivable.

Here are two infants just opening their eyes upon the light, and beginning to gather those materials which are to be the basis of their belief. What manner of men shall they be? They seem alike; but when manhood comes, one of them shall stand upon this earth so full of the good-ness of God, under these heavens which declare his glory, he shall see all there is in them of order, and beauty, and beneficence, and yet be an atheist. Causeless, aimless, fatherless, hopeless, with nothing to respond to his deepest wants, for him the universe shall be whirled in the eddies of chance, or swept on by the current of a blind and remorseless fate. The other shall believe that there is one God, infinite, eternal and unchangeable, omnipotent and omnipresent, holy, just and merciful, the Creator and Governor of all things, to whom he may look up and say, My Father. For him, compared with this God, the universe is as nothing.   In Him it has its being.   It is irradiated with his glory, as the evening cloud with the glory of the setting sun.   Except as expressing his attributes and indi- cating his purposes, it had no grandeur and no significance.

One of these again shall look forward to death, and see in it the end of man.   For him, the sullen sound sent back from his coffin when the sod falls upon it, is the last which the conscious universe is to know of each individual man, unless, indeed, the geologist of some future era may find in the impression of his bones, a record of this.   For him, man has, in death, no pre-eminence over the beast. By the other, death shall be welcomed as a friend.   It shall be for him the beginning of a higher life, of clearer insight, of purer joys, of a greater nearness to God, and of an unending progression.   He shall

> ' The darkening universe defy,
> To quench his immortality."

He shall believe with a certainty that shall enable him to say with one of old, that he *knows* " that if this earthly house of his tabernacle were dissolved he has a building of God, a house not made with hands, eternal in the heavens," and so his great hope shall lie beyond the tomb.   One of these, again shall believe in no accountability after death ; the other shall believe, that " every idle word that men shall speak, they shall give account thereof in the day of judg- ment."

So these two may come to believe, and yet be men. These three great doctrines—of God, of a future life, and of accountability—without which there can be neither religion nor morality, one shall receive, and the other shall reject.   Side by side they may stand, separated by scarcely a point in space ; but in that whole interior life

which is most intimate and essential to them, they are as
wide asunder as the poles.

But here it is to be noticed, that while the possibility
of this divergence in belief indicates elevation in rank, yet
the fact of such divergence indicates for some a low position in that rank.   A perfect instinct is uniform.   So is
perfect reason, and these would coincide.   These are the
extremes, and between these, imperfection and diversity
lie.   Truth is one, and a failure to see it is always the
result either of feebleness or of sin.   Hence, diversity of
belief is not among those needed for harmony, but the
reverse.   A measure of it is compatible with harmony,
that is, such as this world admits of, but the harmony of
the universe will be perfect only when all rational creatures, so far as they see at all, shall see eye to eye.

But if the divergence of men in religious belief, and in
all belief, is great, it is not less, and is even more striking,
in their objects of worship.

One "planteth an ash, and the rain doth nourish it.
Then shall it be for a man to burn.   He burneth part thereof in the fire, and the residue thereof he maketh a god,
even his graven image ; he falleth down and worshippeth
it ; he prayeth unto it and saith, Deliver me, for thou art
my god."   He may worship, as men have done, flies, and
serpents, and crocodiles, and oxen, and the sun, and moon,
and stars, and heroes, and devils ; and worshipping these, he
becomes, so far as is possible, assimilated to them.   How
different these from Him, who is " the Lord, the true God,
the living God, and an everlasting King ; who hath made
the earth by his power, who hath established the world by
his wisdom, and hath stretched out the heavens by his
discretion."   And can the intelligent worshipper of this
God, the holy prophet, or apostle, rapt in vision, or swal-
lowed up in adoration, be of the same race with the idola-

ter casting himself beneath the car of Juggernaut, or with the cannibal savage eating his victim, and dancing before a carved, besmeared, and hideous log? Can it be that those who do thus, might have changed places?

Here, again, diversity is not the basis of harmony. If harmony requires diversity, it has its root in unity, the unity of truth and of God; and so, of belief and of worship.

We may further ask what any child shall be in position, in attainments, and in the extent of his influence. Shall he be a miner, thousands of feet beneath the earth's surface, untaught, unknown, unthanked, uncared for, with a mind as narrow and as dark as the sphere of his labors? Shall he be a slave, whose range is the plantation, and to whom cupidity and fear forbid the knowledge of letters? Shall he be a misanthrope, self-exiled from society, who dies alone, and whose body is found by accident? Shall he be, as probably he will, neither rich nor poor, neither learned nor ignorant, neither widely known nor wholly obscure—one of the countless throng on life's thoroughfare of whom the casual observer would take no note? Or, shall he tread the high places of art, of learning, and of power? Shall the canvas or the marble wait for his touch to become immortal? Shall he be a poet, "soaring in the high region of his fancy, with his garland and singing robes about him?" Shall he govern nations, command armies, sway senates, wrest from nature her secrets, lead the van of progress, and make his thought and will felt over the globe?

But chiefly may we ask concerning any infant, What manner of child shall this be in character, and in the *kind* of influence he shall exert. Upon character every thing depends, and from this, influence flows. And shall these be in the line, and on the level of sensuality and of sense or of a selfish and all-absorbing ambition? or of a pure philanthropy? or of a whole-hearted consecration to the will of God? Shall the child be an apostle of righteousness? a martyr missionary? a preacher like Whitfield, whose eloquence and zeal shall set a continent on fire? Shall he be a fashionable exquisite, admiring himself, and supposing himself admired by others? Shall he be a political intriguer? an adroit depredator upon society? Shall he be a drunkard, and die in a ditch? Shall he be a thief? a murderer? a pirate? Can it be that he who sails under the black flag of death, and whose motto is, that "dead men tell no tales," once drew his life from the breast of a human mother, returned her caress, and answered to her smile? Who is this upon whom every eye in the vast multitude is fixed? Over his face the fatal cap is drawn, and he stands upon the drop just ready to fall. It is but a few years, and his tiny hand held the finger of his mother, and in him were garnered up her fond hopes and high expectations.

At this point the import of the question is deepest, because the dread issues involved in our immortality are here at stake. Here are harnessed the forces that are to move on the plains of eternity. Everything indicates that in the mind, as well as in the body, there is a possibility of RUIN ; that there are there also processes that are cancerous and leprous ; and that they may gradually pervade, and at length utterly pervert and corrupt the whole being. Awful and significant it is, to see such a disease spreading itself over the body, tainting the fluids more widely, and implicating more tissues, till deformity becomes only the more obtrusive, and hideous, and persistent, as the forces of nature were originally greater and more beneficent. And so it may be in mind. Whatever the fact may be, no one can doubt the fearful capacity for this. It belongs to

our conception of spiritual forces that they are indefinite
or without limit in their capacities, in whatever direction
they may move.   It is the natural pledge of their immortality, that whatever point they may reach in knowledge or
affection, in virtue or in vice, it will always be possible for
them to advance still further.   This point, whatever it be,
must be reached under the law of habit, and under that
still more general law that "to him that hath shall be
given," and thus the time must come when there can be
no return.   For the same reason that the path of the just
shall be as the shining light, that shines more and more,
the gloom of to-day shall become the darkness of to morrow, and the deep midnight of the day following.   Selfishness, passion, hate, shall gain a permanent ascendancy,
and the reign of retribution begin.   The immutability of
law is the rock to which the sinner shall be bound; the
ceaseless action of the spiritual powers is the immortal
liver that shall grow as it is consumed, and the diseased
action is the vulture that shall prey upon it.   The worm
shall gnaw till it shall become undying, the fire shall burn
till it "cannot be quenched."   This, not crumbling arches,
not mouldering cities, but this, this is ruin.

What a contrast between this and the possibilities we see
before us and in us, when we look at the *man* Christ Jesus.
In him, in him alone, can we form a right estimate of our
nature ; and that he has enabled us to do this, is no small
ground of our indebtedness to him.   So far as he was man
only, there was in him no excellence or perfection which
we may not attain ; and the perfections in him were not
only an example to us, but were a pledge to his followers
that they shall attain the same.   The disciple shall be as
his Master.   They shall be like him, for they shall see him
as he is.   Christ was the Son of God as Adam was not ;
and in him humanity was glorified as it could have been in

no other way. There was stamped upon it the seal of an infinite value. It was so taken into union with God as to show that God can dwell with it, and that the highest divine perfections may be manifested through it. Christ was the "brightness of his glory," as manifested on the earth, "the express image of his person," and whoever would see the capacities there are in man for elevation and excellence must look to him. "Looking unto Jesus," is the motto of the Christian. He is the only type of normal development for the race. I point you to no heroes or sages, but to Him ; to no abstract conception, but to embodied excellence, living, walking, speaking, sympathizing, suffering among men. The divine image, marred in Adam, was restored in Christ, and is so held in him that it can be lost never more. The gem is now set forever. It will belong to the riches of eternity. *This image we may attain.* Between the attainment of this and any thing else, the differ ence is infinite. This is the true good. And O how great, how infinite is this good! In view of it, how forcible the question of our Saviour, "What shall it profit a man if he shall gain the whole world and lose his soul? Or what shall a man give in exchange for his soul?" Fully attained, this good is heaven. Whatever outward circumstances may be, potentially, substantially, ultimately, this is heaven. He that is like God shall dwell with God. The son shall be in his father's house. He shall abide forever. For this we bless thee, O our Father. Cease, my friends, your disputes about religion. He that is like God shall dwell with God, and he that is not like God, shall not dwell with him.

We thus see that man must be in the highest rank of created beings, and how it is that his manifoldness is a proof of his greatness. Touching the extremes of being, he is capable of development on the level of any nature of

which he is partaker, and at any point along a line that
reaches from the instinct of the animal up to God himself.
He may become an animal, or simply human, or devilish,
or divine. Made in the image of God, capable of indefinite progress, of falling to a depth profound in proportion to
the height to which he can rise, no wider scope could be
given to the imagination than is now given, when the question is asked concerning any child, "What manner of child
shall this be?" You my friends are no longer children,
but men, and in view of the wide range of possibilities now
presented before you, I ask you, What manner of men will
you be? I come to you individually, and with affectionate
earnestness and deep solicitude, ask each one of you, What
manner of man will *you* be?

The question, observe, is not, What will you *get*? but,
What will you *be*? The first is the paramount question
with selfishness; the second, with reason and religion.
In asking the first, you are not necessarily selfish; in
making it paramount, you are. In seeking, on the other
hand, to be great, good, noble like God, you are indeed
consulting your own good most wisely, but are not selfish,
for how can a man be selfish, when his very object is to *be*
benevolent. How be selfish in seeking to be like God, for
God is love. This question, then, I ask with emphasis,
for under the government of God your all must depend
upon it. And not only do I ask it. Your parents and
near friends, to whom you owe every thing, ask it. Your
country asks it. The church of God asks it. The nations that are in ignorance, and under oppression, ask it.
And I doubt not there is, at this solemn moment in your
own hearts, a "still small voice," in which God is, that
asks it. What manner of men will you be?

This question, as put to you, I desire to limit as I have
not done in the general discussion. That was in view of

two kinds of diversity that must be discriminated.   There
is one having its root in repugnance and opposition,
involving elements that can never be brought into harmony, and that can have no unity even, except as there is
fixed between them a great and impassable gulf.   For this
gulf there is provision in the essential difference of moral
good and evil; and while these may be embraced in the
unity of one government of eternal righteousness, yet this
can be only on the condition that that gulf shall be *fixed*.

But there is also a diversity which springs from unity,
and is the basis of harmony; and within this limit diversity is a good.   Only through this can we have the riches
and beauty, as well as the harmony of the universe.   In
this we have the one light refracted into its seven colors,
making the earth green, and the sky blue, and the clouds
gorgeous.   In this is the one sound now parting itself into
its seven notes for music, now articulating itself in speech,
now becoming the chirp of the cricket, and now the roar
of the thunder.   In this is the one water seen in mist, in
dew, in steam, in ice, in snow, in the green heaving ocean,
and in the rainbow that spans it.   In this is the one body
with its organs, the one tree with its branches, the one
universe with its suns, and planets, and satellites, and
comets.   Within this limit, the wider the diversity, the
richer are the fields opening to us in science, in beauty,
and in character.

And now, when I put this question to you, I would
have all your diversity within this limit.   I wish to speak
with you of no other.   This will involve no restriction,
no monotony, or tameness, or repression of any manly
energy, no abatement of the zest and foam and sparkle
of life.   It will only lift you above obstructions, and enable
you to move calmly and freely, as the balloon that floats in
the long upper currents, instead of being whirled in the

lower tempests, and wrecked among the branches. O, could I but know that all your diversity would range within this limit, that you would all be Christians, true followers of the Lord Jesus, almost would I say to you, Be what you please. Certainly I should prefer, since one star differs from another star in glory, that you should not be among those less bright. But only be a star. Shine and, choose your own shade of light. Be Paul, or Peter, or John, or James, or even Thomas; any of them but Judas. Be a Luther, or Melancthon; be Jonathan Edwards, or Harlan Page; be—but I will go no further; I will rather recall what I have said, and say to you, *Be yourselves.* Bring out your own individuality. It is your own. As such, respect and cherish it, only avoiding all affected singularity. If it be different from that of others, do not be troubled. It ought to be. Bring it out in its simplicity, anywhere within the broad light and expanse of the one perfect example. Christ was peculiar, but not singular, except as Mount Blanc and the Ocean are singular. So be you, and you shall polish a gem for its setting in the diadem of Him who weareth many crowns, that shall have in it shades and lines that no other can have.

And while I thus call upon you to bring out your own individuality, let me say to you also, Respect that of others; and not only so, appreciate it, and rejoice in its manifestation. Nothing is more needed among men than the power and readiness to do this, and to accept in religion, in politics, and in social life, those diversities of belief and of forms which spring from this, but which yet have their root in essential unity, and no more cease to be of it than men of different colors cease to be of the race. To do this, is liberality, in distinction from laxness and indifference to the truth. This God intended should be. It is not for nothing, that the notes of birds;

and the colors of flowers, and the outlines of mountains
differ yet are all pleasing.   It is not for nothing, that we
are told that the foundations of the New Jersualem are of
twelve manner of precious stones ; and the Jasper is not
better than the sapphire, nor the sapphire than the emerald, nor the emerald than the amethyst, and all are better
than any one would be, and all are one in their common
nature as gems, and in their common office of adorning
and supporting the heavenly city.   How to draw the line
rightly in particular cases, no rules can be given ; but you
see the general principle, and I beseech you to do this
wisely and liberally, remembering that it is the tendency
of egotism and selfishness to fall into clannishness, and
into a party and sectarian spirit, and to magnify non-
essentials.

In the light of what has been said, let me turn your
thoughts to the provision God has made for the growth and
enjoyment of his creatures as intelligent, and aside from
the affections.   For these the great conditions, in the construction of his works, are, first, unity.   By this is not
meant an indivisible unit of which there may be any number without either unity or harmony, and which must remain unfruitful ; but a unity like those spoken of above,
capable of being parted into diversity, and of returning to
itself again.   The second condition is diversity—not merely numerical, but that which is implied in parts having
relation to a common whole.   The third condition is harmony, that is, such a relation of parts to each other and to
the whole, as to realize and complete our conception of that
whole.   For intellectual growth and enjoyment, a perception of these is all that is needed ; and how inexhaustible
these are, and how wonderfully blended in this universe, I
need not say.   In this view of it, the universe is an organ
that constantly discourses music to angels and to God.

6

The relations of its parts at a given moment, in their adjustment to each other and to ends, are its harmony, and
the succession of its events are its melody. Its harmony
we can begin to study. Of the melody we can know comparatively nothing, for our time is too brief; but we may
be sure that both will forever increase.

In view of what has been said, you will also be able,
not only to estimate the place and value of diversity in the
universe, but also of what has been called many-sidedness,
in the individual. Plainly this is a proof of greatness.
At times the admiration for this has been overdone, and
there has been about it, in certain quarters, something of
cant. On the other hand, there are those who say that a
man can excel in but one thing, and should attend to but
one. Doubtless the greatest effect requires concentration,
and there should be no attempt at varied excellence that
would diminish this ; but there are few occupations in
which all that a man can do may not be done with less
than his whole energies ; the use of the powers in different
directions gives diversion and strength, and there seems
no good reason why a man may not gain excellence in all
the directions in which he is capable of development.
Why may not a man cultivate both muscle and mind, both
mathematics and music, both poetry and philosophy? I
trust you will shrink into no one channel, but will continue
to advance in a liberal culture.

Once more, if the rank of man be so high and his
capacities so great, then is this world a fit theatre for that
great redemption which the Scriptures reveal. Between
him and that redemption there is no want of congruity or
proportion. Some there are who speak of this world as a
mere speck in the universe, and of man as too inconsiderable to be the object of such regard as is implied in the
coming and death, for him, of the Son of God. But so far

as is possible for any creature, man takes hold on infinity.
He is a *child* of God, and in the dealings of God with him
there may be involved all those principles of wisdom and
righteousness and mercy which can be involved in the divine government any where, and so the whole universe,
mighty as it is, may be brought, through man, to the "light
of the knowledge of the glory of God." Little can they
who think thus, have meditated upon those sublime and
consoling words of the Apostle, " Beloved, now are we the
sons of God, and it doth not yet appear what we shall be ;
but we know that, when he shall appear, we shall be like
him ; for we shall see him as he is."

Finally, my friends, if there is, in the *capacities* of man
a fit occasion and ground for the redemption revealed in
the Scriptures, so is there in his *diversities* a fit occasion
and ground for that future and final Judgment which they
also reveal. How could these diversities be greater?
How is everything respecting God and his government,
even to his very being, denied, questioned, challenged,
ridiculed, mocked ? Taken by itself, how tangled, perplexed, and insoluble by reason, is the present state?
What shades of character ! What modifications of responsibility ! What wrongs unredressed ! What questions cut
short by death ! And in connection with these, what scope
for the application, in every delicate adjustment, of every
principle of moral government ! Probably in no other way
than by such a Judgment, could these diversities be re-
duced to the comprehension of finite minds, and the ways
of God to man be vindicated. Here, as elsewhere, the
reality of what God does, and proposes to do, transcends
all that man could have imagined to be possible, and hence
many deny this also. They say, " Where is the promise
of his coming? " " But the day of the Lord will come as
a thief in the night." " The Son of man shall sit on the

throne of his glory, and before him shall be gathered all nations." This we believe, will be the next great epoch in this world's history. And in view of it, I ask the question no longer in regard to this world, What manner of men will you be? This world and its scenes, now so bright before you, will be nothing then. I ask this question in view of that day when there will be but one alternative. What manner of men will you then be?

IX.

NOTHING TO BE LOST.

Gather up the fragments that remain, that nothing be lost.—John, vi. 12.

A MONG the more striking miracles wrought by our Saviour, was that of feeding five thousand men from five barley loaves and two small fishes. But, striking as it was, it was simply a reproduction, in a different form, of the great miracle of nature that is constantly going on around us. The miracle was not at all in the things made, but wholly in the manner of making them. Bread had been made before, and as good bread ; and there had been fish before ; but never before had they been formed at once, by the energy of will, from their original and simple elements. In both cases the elements existed. There was no new creation ; but in the miracle they were brought together in a manner entirely different.

When the sower sows the seed in which is the nucleus, the possibility, and the promise of all the bread that is to be eaten the succeeding year, where are the materials out of which that bread is to be made ? They exist, but are dispersed hither and thither, and are held in different affinities. No human eye can see, and no skill can detect them They are like an army in ambush, ready to come at the appointed signal, but answering only to that.

And now the earth receives the seed. It is buried, but not forgotten. Small as it is, the ocean knows of it and

₊ JULY 29, 1860.

offers it moisture ; and the atmosphere knows of it, and is
ready with its invisible fingers to lift the mist, and fashion
the cloud-car, and transport the moisture to it.   The sun,
too, distant as it is, remembers it, and sends it heat and
light.   These provoke its hidden life, and the roots shoot
downwards, and the stem. upwards.   But in those roots,
and in that stem, there is no particle that will make bread.
There must first be a blossom, and then a receptacle formed, and then the stalk of grain must set itself at work, and
the earth, and the air, and the sun, electricity and magnet-
ism, agents, visible and invisible, must give their aid ; and
then the particles of oxygen and hydrogen, and nitrogen
and carbon, will come from their hiding places and mar-
shal themselves into starch and gluten, and the full seed
will be formed.   The yellow harvest shall lift itself towards
heaven, and wave and toss itself in the wind, a gift from
all the elements and agencies of nature to man.   So do
they all serve him.   Then comes the harvesting, and thresh-
ing, and winnowing, and grinding, and leavening ; and then
the fire does its work, and it is bread.   Through the processes of a year, through changes so slow and minute as to
escape observation at the time, by the combined agencies
of the earth, and air, and ocean, of the sun and the fire, the
materials that were scattered and hidden, have heard the
call that was made for them, and have come forth ; they
have entered into their new combinations, and have become
the " bread that strengtheneth man's heart."

But in all this there is no miracle.   There is nothing
strange.   Oh, no.   We have seen it all, and have eaten
such bread all our lives.   It is nature that does all this ;
or nature and art ; though in reality, art, human art and
skill, can do nothing but to give the opportunity, and provide the conditions for nature to work.   Nature it is, and
there is nothing strange about it.

But now, instead of this complicated and mighty agency extending over months of time, and reaching millions of miles into space, implicating, indeed, the whole planetary system, instead of sympathies and interactions between materials where there is no direct evidence of personality, and so, of anything above what we call nature, there comes One who claims to be the Lord of nature, and as quietly as the sun shines, without even indicating that he is working a miracle, he calls for the elements to come from their hiding places, and enter into their new combinations, and they obey. The materials were all around him, and he controlled their affinities at once, as nature controls the same affinities in her long processes. The simple record is, that " Jesus took the loaves ; and when he had given thanks, he distributed to the disciples, and the disciples to them that were set down ; and likewise of the fishes as much as they would." There was no seeming effort, no ostentation, no production of anything but barley bread, just such bread as was made by the people, and of fish such as were caught in their waters. But this was a miracle, a strange thing, so strange that many cannot believe it. But obviously, if we had been accustomed to this, and then had seen the other for the first time, it would have been accounted by far the greater miracle.

And here we may remark what a testimony the miracles of our Saviour, generally, were to the perfection of the works of God in nature, and so to his own oneness with God. As the bread which he made by a miracle was no better than that made by the ordinary processes, so when he raised men to life, it was to the same life that they had before, and that other men have. When he restored a palsied limb, or a blind eye, it only became as it was before, or like other limbs and eyes. A miracle could make them no better. In this consists the simplicity and grandeur of our Saviour's miracles, and in this the force of their internal evidence for his divine mission. He honored nature, while he showed that he was her Lord.

Thus calling the materials together without effort, the Saviour provided for the wants of five thousand men. Nor was the provision scanty; it was ample and bountiful. They took as much as they would, and the fragments left were more than the original loaves and fishes.

And what the Saviour did at that time, he was able to do at any time. To his power in this respect there was no restriction. Always he could provide for himself and for his disciples in the same free and magnificent manner. And now, when he had just made such a provision, and had it in his power to do so at any time, shall he care for the remnants, the fragments that remain? Not so should we have done. But, and this is not the least remarkable part of the transaction, the Saviour did thus care. "When they were filled, he said unto his disciples, Gather up the fragments that remain, that nothing be lost." The same thing also he did on another occasion, when he had fed a multitude in a similar manner.

What then have we here? Something of penuriousness and smallness? of an undue desire of saving? That can hardly be in him who never owned property, and who had just dispensed his bounties so freely. Have we then a command appropriate only to that time and place? or have we, as in so many other instances of the sayings of our Saviour, clothed in a particular and individual form, a universal maxim, a great principle of the government of God, and one that should regulate the conduct of men? Are these words as the index of a partial and local force? or are they as the magnetic needle that indicates the polar forces of this planet, and, so far as we may conjecture, of all planets and systems? Are they the word of the individual speaking for that time and place, or of the Lawgiver, speaking for all times and for all places? " Gather up the fragments that remain that nothing be lost." Why should *anything* be *lost ?*

Anything once possessed is said to be lost, when it is so concealed or removed from us that we do not know where it is. The piece of silver in search of which the woman swept the house, was lost. The sheep which had wan dered away, and which the owner brought back rejoicing had been lost.

Anything is also said to be lost, when it fails to accomplish the end for which it was made or given. A journey is lost, when the end for which it was undertaken is not accomplished. A day is lost, when in it, no good is done ; an education is lost when no use is made of it ; a man is lost when he becomes hopelessly a drunkard, or is given over to any vice. We know where to find him, but he is lost.

That a thing should be lost in the first sense is acci- dental, and incident to us from the limitation of our facul- ties. Not so with God. To the Omniscient, nothing can be hidden, or obscure, or remote ; and if in his agency he shall fail to cause any past event to be brought to its bear- ings, or any existing thing to accomplish its end, it will not be because he does not know what it is, or where to find it. In our agency a thing may be, and often is lost in the second sense, because it is in the first. We fail to put a thing to its use because we do not know where to find it.

It is plainly in the second sense, that the term " lost " was used by our Saviour in the text. It was not that there was danger of concealment, but of waste. It is in this sense that God would have nothing lost.

The principle involved in the text manifests itself in

4

two forms, both in human affairs and in the divine administration. In the one it respects economy of force when
any thing is to be done ; and in the other the waste of
material or of means when anything is possessed. Let us
look at the Divine administration with reference to both
of these.

And first, of the economy of force.

If we consider those forces that operate in free space,
by which the planets and planetary systems are moved
with such velocity, and guided with such precision, we
have no means of measuring any thing except by the
results. But these will suffice for us. When the earth
comes round to a given star at the appointed and predicted
moment, we must know that not one iota of the force that
brought it there could have been spared. It is just brought
there, and no more. When gravitation draws the earth to
the sun, it is by a force that just retains it in its orbit, and
no more ; and the opposite force that would drive it into
lawlessness and seclusion, is but just sufficient to prevent
it from falling into the sun. As the avalanche is suspended
by a balance of forces so delicate that the traveller who
walks beneath fears even to whisper lest it should be
launched upon him, so hang the heavens. The slightest
difference of adjustment, the least diminution of force, in
any direction, would ultimately bring the system rushing
together to the centre, or scatter it hopelessly.

And what is true of the forces that act at such vast
distances, is equally true of those that are acting around
us, and at distances that are inappreciable. The affinities
by which solid bodies and gases are held together are so
balanced that a less amount in any direction would unchain
their elements, and the atmosphere would be decomposed,
and the earth would effervesce and boil like lime when it
is slacking.

We may notice, also, not only a balance of forces, implying a minimum in both directions, but also the different
and apparently opposite offices which the same agents and
forces subserve. Under precisely the same outward conditions, acted upon by the same outward agents—the same
atmosphere, and storms, and sunshine—a tree that is growing shall be carried up to its perfection, and one that is
decaying shall be resolved into its original elements. It
is in this way that the constant circuit, and interdependent
succession of life and death is kept up.

But perhaps the economy of force is best illustrated in
the structure of animals, where there is not, in the same
way, a balance of forces, but simply mechanism. Take
the skeleton of any animal, and let the problem be to cause
it to perform the same variety of motions that the animal
can perform, and with the same rapidity, and the forces
can be applied only as they are in the animal. In every
animal, regarding its structure, and its position and surroundings relative to that, in the bird that flies, the fish
that swims, the worm that crawls, the insect that creeps,
in the four-footed animal, and in man, the economy of force
is absolutely perfect. In no instance has any mechanician
been able to show how this economy could be greater.
On the contrary, mechanicians have borrowed many hints
from the structure of animals for the economy of force, and
might borrow more ; for her motors are all perfect, both
in their principle and in the mode of its application.
Guided by the principle that nature does nothing in vain,
Harvey discovered the circulation of the blood ; and
guided by the principle that she does everything in the
simplest and best way, the mechanician, if he will but allow for the difference of circumstances, may safely adopt
any of her models and methods.

But on this point there is no need of detail. The

principle contended for is involved in one of those broad inductions of Newton, which has been universally accepted as a law of philosophizing. The law is, " That no more, and no other causes are to be allowed, than are sufficient to explain the appearances."

Having thus considered the economy of force, we next look at that of material and of means. Between these, the relation is intimate, since all material used, and all means put in operation, require force.

As an illustration of economy in both, as thus related, but especially of material, we may take the stems of grasses and of grain. Contrive, if you can, a support for an ear of wheat that shall be adequate, and yet have in it less of material than that now provided. It is hollow and jointed, because, with a given amount of material, it is thus strong- er. The same principle applies to the bones of animals, and to the quills of feathers. How perfectly discriminat- ing, how illustrative of the principle involved, is the differ- ence here between a stem of wheat and the trunk of a tree ! As intended but for a season, the one, though ade- quate, is hollow and fragile ; but the other, as solid, has not too much material for the support of its top, and to withstand the storms ; and then it is needed, and was intended, as a supply for the permanent wants of man. The provision that surrounds the germ of a seed is just enough to support the young plant till it can strike its roots into the earth, and no more. The same is true of that about the vital point in an egg. The quantity of the atmosphere is just sufficient for the density needed to bear up clouds and birds, to give force to winds, that they may waft ships, and for the pressure needed upon animal bodies. The amount of heat and of light are in exact accordance with the demands of vitality and of vision. Vast as it is, the ocean is not too large for the evaporation needed to supply vegetation, and wells and springs; and certain it is that the earth, as a whole, is not a particle too large in its relation to other bodies to hold its place firmly, and exert its due influence amidst the perturbations and actions and reac tions of the system.

Another form of this economy may be noticed in the use of the same structure or substance to subserve differ- ent purposes, and those independent of each other. The lungs have an adequate end in the oxygenation of the blood, a function wholly within us, and so vital that a very brief suspension of it is death. They might seem to have sole reference to that. But see the same lungs in their connection with the voice, circulating fresh thought and sentiment through society, a function wholly without us, and not less vital to it than the renovation of the blood is to the body. The one substance, oxygen, is a main con- stituent of water, of the atmosphere, of all acids, of all vegetable products, and of most mineral substances and rocks as found in nature. It gives its heat to fire, its acidity to vinegar, and to potash its caustic power. It is the vital element of the atmosphere, and its destructive element. Water ! How common it is, yet how manifold in its uses ! It becomes ice, and so a reservoir of cold for the summer ; it becomes steam and so a power in locomotion and in manufacturing ; it becomes vapor, and so fits the air to be breathed, and descends in dew ; it becomes clouds, and so transports the rain ; it becomes snow, and so gives the earth its winter robe. It is the element and home of all fish, and of the monsters of the deep ; it is the chief con- stituent of all fluids of plants and of animals ; it quenches thirst ; it is the great cleanser and purifier ; it is an ele- ment of beauty. With no running water, with no tossing ocean, with no cataracts, no dew, no changing clouds, now dark and seamed with lightning, now fleecy and mottled with the blue beyond, and now gorgeous in the sunset, with no showers, and no rainbow, where would the beauty of the earth be? And all this from the one substance, water! What economy of material! It would seem as if no property or capacity of usefulness in this substance could be lost.

The same principle also appears in the results of all decomposition. This seems a destruction; but in the sense of annihilation there is no destruction. In this sense nothing has ever been lost. The materials merely change their forms, and enter into new combinations. The servants retire, and reappear in a different garb. The partners are changed; and so, like a star in the heavens, each changing particle of matter walks its appointed round. Of this economy in connection with apparent destruction, we find large evidence in geology. There have, it seems, been creations and epochs long since that have come to an end; but when they did so, the command was given to the earth, "Gather up the fragments that remain, that nothing be lost," and the earth heard and obeyed. And now we have these fragments in the form of soil and drift; in granite and marble; in mines and coal-beds; in foot-prints and fossils, for the profit and instruction of those who now live; and probably much more, of those who shall live hereafter.

But while these instances are sufficient to establish the principle, there are objections and difficulties. There is apparent waste. Large portions of the earth are mere sandy plains, deserts, or inaccessible mountains; and upon these the sunshine and rain and dews descend. There is also an apparent and great waste of the germs of life.

In reply, it may be said that deserts and mountains are of use physically. "Were it not," says Maury, "for the Great Desert of Sahara, and other arid plains of Africa the western shores of that continent, within the trade-wind region, would be almost, if not altogether, as rainless and sterile as the desert itself. We are to regard the sandy deserts, and arid plains, and the inland basins of the earth, as compensations in the great system of atmospherical circulation." The inaccessible and snow-capped mountains condense the moisture and form water-sheds. They are as a hand lifted up to compress the distended atmosphere, and to return to the ocean in long, and fertilizing, and navigable rivers, the tribute it had given.

But aside from this, if we admit, as we must, moral considerations and reasons, these difficulties vanish! Those deserts are not too large, or sterile, to be a mirror in which the man who receives the blessings of God and makes no return, may see his own features reflected. Those mountains of rock are not too hard and unimpressible to represent that adamant that can resist a Saviour's love. Those germs of life destroyed are not too many, or too precious, to show what is possible in regard to those powers and capabilities which every man has, and which he may dwarf and ruin. Without a correspondence between external nature and the character of man, the end of probation here could not be reached; and without these and similar features and facts in nature, that correspondence could not exist.

To many, the above would be a sufficient solution of the difficulties. It is so to me. But there is another.

It is plain that there is, in this world, a great work carried on through, or in accordance with, what we call general laws. It is thus that the rain and the sunshine descend, and that the current of life, broad and deep, is kept in its even flow. To this the earth as a whole and the elements minister. In this great work it could not be expected that the sun should withhold his beams from every barren spot,

or that the rain should skip and shun every stone and sand·
bank. This would be petty, not in accordance with the
nature of general laws, or with the dignity of the divine
government. The great work is done. The current of
life flows on, and no more. The nations are fed ; and if
there are outlying facts, the bearing of which upon the result we do not see, we may well class them with fragments
that remain, which will be used at another time, or are used
in other connections.

On the whole, then, we conclude that the economy of
God, both with respect to force and to material, is perfect.
In so wide a reach, where we confessedly know so little, it
is not reasonable that a conclusion so borne out by the
great mass and current of facts should be held in abeyance
out of respect to mere exceptional eddies. Sustained,
therefore, by the science of the nineteenth century, we ven-
ture with the fullest confidence, in regard to every particle
of this universe, the assertion implied in the sublime inter-
rogatories of the prophet: " Who hath measured the waters
in the hollow of his hand, and meted out heaven with the
span, and comprehended the dust of the earth in a measure,
and weighed the mountains in scales, and the hills in a
balance ? "

The principle of economy thus regarded in the divine
administration, ought to be equally regarded by man in the
conduct of life. It ought to be thus regarded, but is not.
Not only is there indolence, and so dormancy of capacity,
but there is great misdirection of force and waste of material. Who is there that gathers what he might ? that be
comes what he might ? that acheives what he might ? In
doing each and all of these, and in that only, would be the
highest success ; and to this, economy is no less necessary
than energy. The monarch who conquers a country pro·

vides for retaining it; without this his victories would be fruitless, and they become available only as he can incorporate it into his own dominions, and, if need be, make it the means of still further conquests. So it is with us. The two elements or factors of success in life, mental capacity being given, are the energy, the will, needed for getting, and for achivement ; and the economy needed for so keeping what is thus gained, that nothing shall be lost. Of these elements the first is more exciting, more naturally attractive of sympathy, and has received, by far, greater attention. Young men are constantly exhorted to energy and enterprise, to perseverance and force of will, while the power of a wise economy and husbandry of resources is disregarded.

This general principle needs to be applied, first, in regard to health and physical energy. In the management of these there has been, and still is, unspeakable loss. Let the pressure of necessity be removed, and men have not sufficient resolution and self-control to comply with the conditions of physical vigor. Civilization, the accumulation of wealth, refinement, leisure, bring facilities for various forms of indulgence incompatible with this vigor in its highest form ; and so uniform is this, that no nation, highly civilized, has escaped physical deterioration. They have not learned the secret of gaining in refinement, without losing in a robust manhood. The population of cities, it is said, requires to be renovated by men fresh from the country every third generation, and that it is such men, or their descendants of the second generation, who hold the wealth and places of influence there. Of course there are exceptions, but this is the general rule. The third generation are inferior, both physically and mentally. They are second or third rate men. Instead of being judges of soils and of oxen, they are judges of actors, and singers, and

4*

neck-ties ; instead of being leaders in a town meeting, they
are leaders of fashion. They become *dilettanti.* They
drink, they gamble, they give themselves up to pleasure,
they are of no particular use in the world, and not seldom
either they or their children are beggars in the streets
where their fathers were merchant princes. Meantime,
everywhere, in the city and in the country, in the count-
ing house, and in the college, men are drawn into " the
old way," or rather, ways " which wicked men have trodden." They becomes victims of licentiousness, or of some
form of artificial stimulation : and with various alternations of hope and fear on the part of their friends, and of
successful struggle and defeat, they become a curse to
society, and go down to dishonored graves. The promises
of early life are not met. The parental hand is pierced by
the reed that it leans upon. Instead of fruit, awakened
hope finds ashes in her grasp.

Of this loss something is due to ignorance, but there is
scarcely any one whose knowledge is not in advance of his
practice ; and where that is the case, the root of the evil,
and generally of the ignorance itself, lies deeper. It lies in
the insane purpose to secure present enjoyment, regardless
of consequences. From this no mere regard to self-culture,
to the laws of health, to enjoyment on the whole, will hold
the masses back when solicitation stands at every corner,
and addresses every sense. Restraint will be spurned, and
caution mocked at, and a pure and efficient manhood will
disappear. This, a pervasive Christianity can prevent,
and nothing else can. Nothing but the cross of Christ can
so startle the spiritual nature from its torpor as to make
it an effectual counterpoise to the debasing and sensual
tendencies of the race. Favored by temperament and education, individuals may measurably escape, but if the race
is to triumph in the conflict between the flesh and the spirit,

between the lower propensities and the higher nature, they must, as Constantine is said to have done, see the cross, and on it the motto, "*In hoc signo vinces*." By this sign you shall conquer.

But, secondly, this principle is peculiarly applicable in its relation to time.

There is a low philosophy which says that time is money. It is more ; it is the interval between two eternities ; it is life ; it is opportunity ; it is salvation. It is that which, once past, comes not again. It fixes the past. It moulds the future. Money cannot buy it. A dying queen may exclaim, " Millions of money for an inch of time," but the millions will not buy the inch. Money has no relation to it. To waste it costs no effort. We have only to wrap our talent in a napkin and sit still ; but to improve it requires both effort and wisdom, for it may be, and most often is, laboriously wasted.

"Gather up the fragments" of time, "that nothing be lost." This can be addressed only to those who are employing the greater portion of their time in some earnest work. He who floats loosely and aimlessly in society has no fragments of time, as related to a whole. It is all fragments. He himself is a fragment, lying useless, and his whole life requires to be recast. But whatever the great business of a man may be, however engrossing, there will always be some fragments of time that will remain ; and with most men these are so considerable, that the disposition made of them will greatly modify the results of life. The secret of doing much is to do a little at a time, but to persevere in doing it. A half an hour a day, in the service of an earnest purpose, has been sufficient for the acquisition of languages and the writing of books, and for laying the foundation of a lasting fame. Even the minute fragment required for drawing his waxed ends, was employed by

Roger Sherman in looking on his book open before him ;
and it was thus that he became a sage, and a signer of the
Declaration of Independence.   Let a professional man, or
any man, when he starts in life, have a side study, be it
History, or a Language, or Poetry, or any branch of Natural History, as Geology, and let him give to it the fragments of his time, and he will be surprised at his own acquisitions ; the whole tone of his thoughts and life will be
elevated, and the change of subject will be his best recrea-
tion.   Of such a pursuit of Mineralogy and Geology, we
have a striking instance in this vicinity.   And what is thus
true in literature and science, is still more so in religion,
and in all that relates to duty.   There is no time too brief
for an ejaculatory prayer.   When the countenance of Ne-
hemiah was sad for the desolations of Jerusalem, and the
king asked him, " What is thy request ? " there was time
between the question and the answer for him to pray " to
the God of heaven."   If the object of this world had been
to furnish opportunities for doing good, it could hardly
have been arranged better than it is ; and whoever has a
heart set upon that, will have no need that any fragments
of time he may gather up, should be lost.

But once more, you will expect me to say that this
principle applies also to property.

Owing to the undue estimate of wealth, this has indeed
been supposed to be the special field and domain of economy, and there are those who make it their chief business
to practice and to inculcate a small economy in this department.   Certainly the principle applies here as elsewhere.
Why should *any* property be lost ?   If it is worth the getting, why not the keeping ?   It is by saving, no less than by
getting, that accumulation comes ; and failure in this is
oftener from a want of economy than of enterprise.   Should
there then be accumulation ?   Certainly.   The right of

property is given by God. Property itself, that is, something accumulated and kept, is a necessity for society. It not only confers comfort and independence, but is a great and desirable power for good. It is a duty to give ; we are commanded to give ; but he who has nothing can give nothing. This is commonly thought a sufficient excuse. It may, or may not be. It is so, just as it is a sufficient excuse for begging, that a man has nothing to eat. But how came he to have nothing to eat ? How came the man to have nothing to give ? If there has been a want, either of industry, or of the strictest economy, it is not a sufficient excuse. Of the extent of this accumulation, with its temptations and dangers, I am not now to speak. Of that every man must judge for himself. But be it greater or less, there need be no hesitation in saying that any loss of property, any want of economy in spending it, any failure to save any portion of it, must be the result either of human imperfection or of sin.

But in this attention to minute things, this regard to fragments, is there not something of smallness and narrowness ; of a carefulness and painstaking not compatible with enjoyment ? Is there not something alien from the tone and temper of a high free and generous spirit ? That there are such associations, in connection with what is called enonomy, cannot be denied. But we must here make distinctions. There is that, if we call it economy at all, which must be called a wicked economy. It is that of the miser. He saves for the sake of saving, and so loses by his very keeping. The fragments were to be gathered up, not that they should be carried about in baskets and kept till they should be mouldy, for then they would have been lost by being kept ; but that, subsequently, and on the first fit occasion, they should be put to the use for which they were made.

There is, also, as I have said, a small economy—a careful parsimoniousness, not exactly miserliness, but bordering upon it. It is born of fear, has reference to self, and does not contemplate use, except for low and personal ends.

There is, again, an honorable economy, having for its end the gratification of the natural affections, opportunities for mental improvement, position in society, and all these in connection with the highest manhood and most perfect personal independence. For a parent to be economical, to the point of severe self-denial, for the education of a child ; for a young man to be thus economical for his own education ; for one accustomed or seeking to associate with the wealthy and the fashionable, to conform to no habit of expense that would require dishonesty or mean-ness in any direction, implies high qualities ; and the economy thus practiced is an honorable economy.

But besides these, there is what may be called a sub-lime economy. This is not confined to money, or property, but is in imitation of the method of God, and from a per-ception of its connection with beneficence. It includes the employment and expenditure of whatever would bear on human well-being, and its principle is, " *That nothing be lost.*" It sees that the water must be gathered in clouds before it can be poured out in rain ; that the reservoir must be filled before the city can be supplied ; that every where God gathers by little and little what he dispenses with a liberal hand, and thus, instead of being connected with smallness or narrowness, this economy becomes the very spring and fountain-head of generosity and liberality and beneficence. He who adopts this principle looks around him, and over the earth, and sees hunger to be fed, and nakedness to be clothed, and ignorance to be instructed, and vice to be reclaimed, and talent and worth to be encouraged, and institutions to be aided ; he hears the cry of heathen nations calling for the gospel ; and now a regard for the least thing that can work towards either, or all of these for which God is working, is dignified and consecrated by the principle that gave it birth. Now, nothing that can thus work is small to him. Of the cold water that he is bearing to the wounded and perishing on the battle-field of life, and which he knows to be far short of their necessities, he would not lose a drop. Now he works for God, and with God ; and he finds enlargement both of mind and of heart just in proportion as he is able to comprehend in his working plans, as God does in his, every instrumentality and means, however apparently insignificant and minute.

In what I have just said, it has been my wish to place before you one great element of all success, whether it be of that outward but delusive success, that belongs only to time, or of that inward and true success, that lays up its treasures in heaven. In connection with both, the principle applies, that nothing should be lost. This element of success is not the primitive, or the greatest. I have no wish to magnify it at the expense of the power of attainment and acquisition, but call your attention to it as equally indispensable with that, and because its character is often misapprehended, and its value not appreciated.

Between the two elements of success just mentioned, as between the great forces of nature, there is a tendency to opposition, and you will need to balance them carefully, if you would preserve the true course and orbit of life. With some the constitutional tendency is towards energy, attainment, acquisition ; and as the consciousness of power in this direction is greater, it is natural there should be a certain profusion and recklessness in expenditure. To the young and self-confident, their resources of time

of health, of energy, if not of money, seem exhaustless ;
and why should they care for loss? With others, the tendency is towards caution. They gain by saving. They
never either pay, or give, too much for anything. They
are in danger of withholding more than is meet, even when
it tendeth to poverty. Of these elements, if there must
be a preponderance of either, let it be of the first. But,
rightly viewed, these are not conflicting, but complemen-
tary elements. If there were no gathering, their could be
neither saving nor giving ; if there were no saving, there
could be no systematic, far-sighted, effective' use or dis-
tribution. Here, as everywhere, the example of our
Saviour is perfect. How grand the energy by which he
controlled the elements! How adequate, and more than
adequate, the provision for all that use required! And
yet how perfect the economy—an economy, you will be
careful to observe, that in no degree restricted use, but
simply provided against loss. Here we have the whole
principle. *Everything for use, nothing to be lost.* Why
should any thing, that can be used, be lost? How can
it be, but from recklessness, or weakness, or wickedness ?

You, my Beloved Friends, have rich endowments, a
rich inheritance, a capital of priceless worth, no part of
which ought to be lost. You have youth, and health, and
education, and freedom, personal, civil, and religious.
You inherit the past, and stand on the threshold of a
future that must be richer in thronging events and in
opportunities for good, than any past has been. Your
fathers inherited a continent that required to be subdued.
You, one that requires to be cultivated ; they inherited
the printing press worked by hand, and the stage coach,
and the sailing vessel ; you inherit the cylinder press

worked by steam, and the railroad car, and the steamship, and the electric telegraph. It was for them to lift up their eyes upon the varied forms of destitution and crime in our land, and upon the darkness and woes of heathendom, and to form the associations, and gain the knowledge necessary for effective working. It is for you to take these instrumentalities and work them. Work them with accelerated speed, and with mightier power. Meliorate the physical condition of man. Bring back a revolted world to its allegiance to God. And when you look at the magnitude of this work, is there anything, whether of time, or health, or money, or influence, or of capability in any direction, which you can afford to lose? No. Oh, no. In such a work every resource is needed; "Hold fast what thou hast;" for such a work, "Gather up the fragments, that nothing be lost."

But my friends, if it be the will of God that you should lose nothing of time, or health, or even of money, how much more must it be his will that you should not lose yourselves. This you can do. You can lose yourselves; and such a loss, you will observe, implies not merely deprivation, but all there is of suffering and of penalty under the moral laws of God. As the loss of health is sickness, and of light, darkness, so is the loss of hope, despair, and the loss of heaven is hell. You can throw yourselves away. You can become of no use in this universe except for a warning. You can lose your souls. Oh, what a loss is that! The perversion and degradation of every high and immortal power for an eternity! And shall this be true of any one of you? Will you be lost when One has come from heaven, travelling in the greatness of his strength, and with garments dyed in blood, on purpose to guide you home—home to a Father's house—to an eternal home? Will you not rather, on this day of interest, it may be of final decision, when all the world, and all choices are open before you, hear his voice saying, " Follow me." " For what shall it profit a man, if he shall gain the whole world, and *lose* his own soul? "

X.

GOD'S METHOD OF SOCIAL UNITY.

To whom coming as unto a living stone disallowed indeed of men but chosen of God, and precious, ye also, as lively stones, are built up a spiritual house. —1 Peter, ii. 4, 5.

IN building a house, materials of great diversity are brought into unity. They are placed in such relations as to be mutually subservient, and become one thing. This is what is done in all construction. It is what God has done in building this material universe. The process of this, as conducted by him, is expressly compared to the building of a house by man. "For," says the Apostle, "every house is builded by some man, but he that built all things is God."

As thus constructed, the universe is no mulitudinous mass of unrelated units baffling all comprehension. The separate beings and facts are, indeed, without number, and are infinitely diversified; but they may yet be partitioned off into divisions, assorted into groups, the ligament which binds each of these into unity may be distinctly traced, and each group, thus assorted and bound together, becomes the field of a separate science. And not only are the facts within each group related to each other, but the groups themselves. Not, as the ancients supposed, are the heavens, and the earth, and the regions beneath, constituted and governed each on different principles. The light from the farthest star is the same as that which comes from the sun, and which is struck from the flint; the particle of dust that floats in the air is governed by the same laws as the earth that floats in space and is enveloped by that air ; the spire of grass at our feet requires not only the sun and the rain, but all those laws of electricity, and magnetism, and cohesion, and affinity, by which the globe itself, and the solar system, and the far vaster stellar systems cohere and stand up together.   Not only, therefore, is there a unity of each science, but a unity of the sciences. The farther we investigate the more do we find of unity in the works of God, and nothing seems left to science but to accept that instinctive and universal conviction which has recorded itself in language, and which calls these works of God, so varied and so vast, a *uni-verse.*

With this constitution of the external universe, that of the mind is in harmony.   It is a necessity for it to seek to reduce its knowledge to unity.   Before science can begin, we must observe separate facts ; but as soon as these are observed, there is an effort to bring them into system, that is, into unity ; and when this is fully done, there is a completed science.   No man can observe a new and strange fact, without seeking to bring it into relation with facts already known and classfied.

But it is not solely as speculative that man desires, and is required, to reduce all things to unity.   As a practical being, it is his great business to do this.   As the beings and facts of nature are given to him, as speculative, that he may find their mutual relations, and thus their unity, so are the substances of nature given to him, as a practical being, that he may find their capabilities, and bring them into such relations of convergence and unity as shall subserve his purposes.   Like the facts and phenomena, these substances are given separately.   The air is given by itself, and the iron, and the fuel, and the fire, and the water, and all these are to be brought into such convergence and unity of action as to cause the locomotive and the steam-ship to be, and to speed them on their wondrous way. In all contrivances, from the simple lever to those marvelous combinations of machinery that seem endowed not only with hands, but with thought, there is always to be found a unity in the subservience of every part to the purpose of the designer, and it is this unity which he designs, to produce. As a creature made in the image of God, man not only finds in his works unity with reference to an end, but he wishes to produce such unity.

But this is not all. If we pass from matter to mind we find another, a spiritual universe, to which the first is subservient. We can scarcely avoid the conclusion, favored as it is by the Scriptures and by all analogy, that there is a spiritual universe corresponding in vastness and variety to the material one ; and if so, the great object of God, in the whole, must be such an arrangement and government of this as shall secure for it the highest social and spiritual unity. This, too, is favored by the Scriptures. Christians are to be built up a spiritual house. Christ prayed that they might all be one ; and the Apostle, glancing, it would seem, at that wider range of which we have spoken, says : " That in the dispensation of the fullness of times he might gather together in *one* all things in Christ, both which are in heaven, and which are on earth ; even in him."

And here, also, in this spiritual universe, man is not merely to find a unity produced by God ; he is also, and in this chiefly, to seek to produce unity.

In doing this, the first sphere of action for every man is his own spirit. Blessed is he who can bring into that, that unity which is at once peace and power. This is the first condition of all true rest and of all healthful activity.

The more complex man is ; the more incompatible are his desires ; the more deeply opposed are the flesh and the spirit ; the more needful, and the more beautiful is that unity which belongs to the original design of God, and which is brought in by one overmastering purpose subordinating all things to itself. In this is singleness of eye ; in this consistency, efficiency, a ground for self-respect, and for the respect of others :

But this unity of the individual spirit is not only a condition of individual peace and joy, but also of those bonds of peace by which individuals are united to each other. This brings us to a wider and more complex field, to that social and spiritual unity which we now propose to consider.

In this field the first and most perfect unity is to be found in the marriage union. In marriage, according to its original idea, there is the most perfect social unity known on earth. They twain become one flesh. It is based on a diversity in the whole being,—a diversity, not of opposition, but of correspondence, by which each supplements the other, and in which there is always the basis for the truest and deepest unity.

It is from such a unity that society springs, branching out into families, communities, and nations. Here, again, unity is needed not only within each family, community and nation, but also between families, communities, and nations. This is possible. Despite the isolations, the alienations, the enmities there are, it is the law, it is the only condition of social good, and it is the production of this that is the end of all constitutions, and legislation, and government. A solution of all social problems, those which have taxed the powers of man from the beginning, can end in nothing better than this. That the race of man should recognize its own unity in a spirit of brotherhood, overlooking no one having the attributes of man, and thus, under the government of God, become fitted for a unity with other races, trained in other planets, in other systems, related to us by the correspondence of diversity, they fitted to supplement us, as we them, gives us the grandest conception of a social system which it is possible for us to form. It is towards this that all true reformers look; as they approximate this, their end is attained ; as they find the principle of this, they find the principle of all real reforms.

It is of this complex social unity that the text speaks under the figure of a house built up of separate stones. "Ye are built up a spiritual house." And this unity men have sought, and still seek to secure, chiefly in two ways.

The first is by the balance of mutual interests and selfishnesses.

Interest and selfishness are not, like malignity, necessarily repellent. So far as two selfish persons are either necessary to each other from the conditions of their being, or can make use of each other, they can go on together ; and, by a skillful adjustment of checks and balances, much may be done to make it for the immediate interest of all to go on thus. Selfishness may do good to others, that others may do good to it ; it may lend to others, "hoping to receive as much again." It may, for its own sake, do much for the upbuilding and perfection of society; and with this as its controlling principle, together with the gregariousness common to man with the animals, society may exist and have a degree of unity. But with a governing selfishness, held in check, and known to be, solely by expediency, there must be constant distrust. Thus governed men will overstep the limits of right when they dare, and the individuals of society will resolve themselves into an armed neutrality, with a constant outlook for opportunities of safe aggression. Outward peace there may be, but it

will be from mutual dread, as when two prize-fighters sur-
vey each other, and each perfers to decline the contest. It
will be on the principle that a certain gun, supposed to be
very destructive, was named " the peacemaker." There
will be sought a balance of power like that so long made
the object of European politicians. Such a political balance required for its maintenance standing armies, and
navies, and fortifications, and constant watchfulness. And
such a balance in society will require the division of powers,
and a police, and courts, and prisons, and written contracts,
and securities. Such a unity may be better than none. It
is far better; but there must be something better than
this.

A second mode of producing unity among men is by
power, or pressure from without.

This involves the first, to some extent, and is superin-
duced upon it. It is the method adopted by all despotisms, whether of one man, of a few, or of many. The great
object of ambition has been to exercise the power of a des-
potic will over masses of men organized as armies, and
through these to hold in subjection, as one empire, vast
regions, peopled, it may be, by nations the most discordant. Such was the empire of Nebuchadnezzar, who sent
forth his decree "to every people, and nation, and language." Such was the Persian empire under Ahasuerus,
whose letters were sent " to the rulers of the provinces
which were from India to Ethiopia, a hundred and twenty
and seven provinces, unto every province according to the
writing thereof, and unto every people after their language."
Such was the empire of Alexander, that fell in pieces by its
own weight, as soon as his strong grasp upon it was relaxed.
Such, emphatically, was the Roman empire. Extending
from the African deserts to Britain, and from India to the
pillars of Hercules, it held in a forced unity nations utterly

diverse in language, and habits, and interests. It was a mere aggregation, a conglomerate, whose parts were held in position by Roman legions. Such, indeed, were the *republics* of antiquity, when they became extensive. Of the rights of man as such, they knew nothing : they did not extend citizenship with their conquests, but held their provinces in subjection, and so preserved unity by power. Such has been, and still is, to a great extent, the condition of Europe : much more of countries less enlightened. Different nationalities are forced together. Every where there is the pressure of power as an external force. The free play of affinities, whether laterally, or vertically, is checked ; and the spirit, if not the laws of caste, is rigidly maintained. Hence the unity, such as there is, being enforced, is unquiet ; not peaceful, spontaneous and fruitful.

In opposition to these methods, now tried so long that the world is weary, is that adopted by God, and beautifully indicated in the text, The figure in this passage is remarkable, as bringing into coalesence objects and qualities seemingly the most incompatible. A stone is passive. You may lift it, toss it, hurl it, smite it, lay it in a wall, and it will resist only in virtue of its inertia and cohesion A stone is dead—so dead, that when we would speak of the perfection and intensity of death in other things, we say of them that they are stone-dead. A stone is solid, permanent, a fit material to enter into structures that are to endure for ages. How opposite is all this to that vitality, and sensibility, and self-assertion, and transient character that belong to all organic and living things ! How opposite, especially, is it to spirituality. Nothing could be more opposite, and yet it is precisely in the blending of these opposites that the power and beauty of the figure are found. That the building should be of stone, was required to indicate its perpetuity ; for its turrets are to gleam forever in the light of eternity. That the stones should be living, was required to indicate their union, each in its place ; not by mechanical means, or outward pressure, but by *vital affinity.*

Here it is that we reach the peculiarity of this structure. It is that the materials are living, and are united by a vital affinity. If now we suppose this affinity to spring from that which is deepest and most essential in the materials, we shall have the whole method of God in producing social unity : we shall have that which *we* must adopt in seeking to produce it, if we are ever to succeed.

Of this method of union by vital affinity, there are two conditions. The first and indispensable one is, that the materials should be vitalized, or be alive. The second is, that they should be free to move in accordance with the laws of vitality.

What it is to be vitalized in mere matter, and how this is done, we know. It is to have life communicated to that which was dead ; and this is done by bringing the materials, not in masses, but particle by particle, into contact with that which already has vitality. It is done as by a leavening power, a kind of sacred contagion ; and when it is done, the materials are ready to be marshaled into their places, and to perform their functions under the vital laws.

So far the process is beautiful and typical, but the marshaling is perhaps more so. Here the second condition, that of freedom, comes in. In matter, fluidity is freedom. It is the freedom of the individual particle to move in any direction ; and strange as it may seem, that a fluid should be alive, yet it is, and the Scripture doctrine, that the blood " is the life thereof," is a philosophical necessity. Having then materials for the upbuilding of every part of the body, vitalized, and free, as held in solution, what is to be done? There are to be formed bone, muscle, tendon, brain, nerves, skin, hair, nails, the transparent humors of the eye, and its dark pigment. The materials are undistinguishable, and mixed in utter confusion. But now the affinity shows itself, and the miracle of bringing order out of chaos, as seen in the first creation, is repeated. Each particle goes ' to its own place, stands in its own lot, performs just the office it is fitted to perform ; and thus, to a body constantly changing in its matter, there is given permanence, and strength and beauty.

Of the process now mentioned all materials are not capable, but only food. It is the capability of this that makes them food. But whether capable of it or not, any substance not actually vitalized, or in a position to be so, is a foreign substance. As such it is either an encumbrance or an irritant, and is expelled by the vital force. This power of rejection and expulsion is no less essential than that of assimilation.

All this perfectly represents what occurs, or should occur, in the higher social region. Every particle thus vitalized becomes a living stone to build up a living house, and in thus helping to build the whole, its own place is found, and its appetency satisfied.

In passing to the higher spiritual region, if we find differences, it is only those required by the nature of the subject. We have here the same indispensible conditions of vitality and freedom, and the same expulsive power. But life here, in accordance with the usage of the Scriptures, and with all usage, is something more than life, and death is not merely its absence. Life here is consciousness sensibility, sympathy, affection. It is consent and harmony, and the more intense the life in one direction, the more perfect the death in another. To be alive to God is to have every faculty active and quick in apprehending his perfections, and in doing his will ; and one wholly in this state would be dead to sin. Its allurements would awaken no more response than an appeal to the senses of the dead. They would be viands set at the mouth of a tomb. On the other hand, no life is more intense than that of him who is "dead in trespasses and sins." He is so engrossed in his own selfish plans that no voice of the word, or providence, or Spirit of God, makes any impression upon him. Call as you may, there is no response. There is no voice, nor any that answers or regards. He is dead. In the same way men may be alive to the beauties of nature, or of art, to the behests of duty, the calls of compassion, the voice of their country; and they may be dead to all these. They may be wholly engrossed in business, or in pleasure. Men may be so alive to the wages of unrighteousness as to become, as the Apostle says, "trees twice dead, plucked up by the roots."

We say, then, that for a social structure, he is a living stone who is capable of being so inwrought into it as to add, and only add, to its strength and symmetry. This will imply that he be permeated by those ideas which are the life of the system, that he be plastic to its forces, and responsive to its instinctive wants. He must be an agent, and not an instrument. It is the characteristic of vital methods, as opposed to mechanical, that the movement is from within. The moment the interior appetency, and impulse, and choice, cease to be respected, there is social death; the idea of mutual subserviency through vital action, which is God's idea, is lost, and society, instead of moving like the heavens, becomes a crazy mechanism, whirling and crashing on with the blindness and unsteadiness of human passion and power.

Such is the idea of vitality in a social system. It implies a sympathy, a rational consent and harmony of the individual with the movements and ends of the system, that will lead him to seek and to keep, not office, but just that place for which he is best fitted.

The idea of freedom, figurative in matter, is literal here. It implies both the immediate absence of arbitrary power, and security against it. The lion must not only be sated for the moment, or accidentally sluggish, he must be caged. There must be no intervention of mere will, seeking, for a side and selfish purpose, to wield the masses as instruments or to prevent any living stone from finding its true place. The idea of freedom also implies the absence of any horizontal and petrified strata in society, as caste, or fixed classes, which would prevent a free movement, upwards or downwards, horizontally or obliquely. Such strata *may* exist without arbitrary power ; *it* may exist without them, but they naturally go together and mutually aid each other. Established orders are a frame-work to support the throne, and the throne concentrates power to guard these orders from the encroachments of each other, and of the people.

Of such a combination of concentrated power and established orders, great public works, and high civilization and refinement in the favored classes, are the natural result, while the lower classes are degraded. In such a form of society there may be much of beauty, and power, and beneficence. Once originated, it readily perpetuates itself, and becomes venerable. From this, with the vast wealth accumulated, public and private, though in few hands, and from the consequent magnificence, it appeals strongly to the imagination and tends to control the associations. Being born into it, children are overshadowed by it, and their associations are conformed to its order as they are to that of nature. Both seem to come from a power above them, and to belong almost equally to an order of things over which they have no control. Institutions, just those established, with their settled order, are every·

thing ; the individual is nothing.   There is no longer room
for an appeal to original rights and fitnesses.   The sphere
of choice and of action provided by God, and needed for
the best development of the life of all, becomes limited.
There is no fluidity, and for a man to pass up through the
orders of society by merit, is a marvel.   If he choose to
fall in with the prescribed course, well ; but if Bonaparte
is to rise from the lower strata of society to its top, it can
be only as the metallic vein is shot up through the earthy
strata by an underlying force that would convulse a continent.

Of the two great elements of social order now spoken
of, vitality and freedom, freedom has been most prominent
in the thoughts and in the speech of men.   Freedom has
been the battle-cry of the race.   For this heroes have fought.
Men seek scope, that is freedom, for the action of vitality,
but do not so readily feel the deficiency of that or seek its
increase.   This is natural, because the absence of freedom
is a restraint that is instantly felt, and naturally resisted ;
but the absence of vitality is insensibility, and the less life
a man has, of any kind, physical, intellectual, spiritual, the
less inclined will he be to struggle for more.

But while freedom is thus more prominent than vitality,
it is not at all in the same rank.   All good is from vitality.
Freedom is only the condition of its best exercise.   For a
good man, freedom is a good ; for a bad man, it is an evil.
Without vitality in the sense of the text, freedom becomes
anarchy.   With it, pervading the whole social system,
there will be essential freedom, whatever the outward
form of society may be.   If every stone in the house be
living, there will be nothing to originate mechanical
methods and obstructions ; vital laws will rule, and the
rule of these is freedom.

All that has now been said will apply to social unity

of any kind ; but that here spoken of is spiritual. " Ye
are built up a spiritual house." Let there be vitality and
freedom, and there may be unity after God's method ; but
its strength and value will be as the life from which it
springs. Spiritual unity must be from spiritual life, and
in these we find the sphere and method of God in his
grandest work.

Of spiritual unity the peculiarities are two. The first
is, that it springs from that life which is deepest.

Surely, if man is made in the image of God, that by
which he is thus made must be that which makes him man,
and so is his very being. If so, his natural affinities—
using the word natural in its highest sense—will be for
God and those who are like him. If so, as union with
God and those who are like him is essential to this life, it
must expel every interest, or life, or love, incompatible
with it. No love of father or mother may compete with it.
It will move on as the river towards the ocean. Not to
do this, would be to deny its own nature.

The second peculiarity of spiritual life, at least in
man, is, that Christ is, for him, both the source of vitality
and the centre of unity.

Without Christ, men are destitute of spiritual life.
They are "without God, and without hope." This is the
cardinal fact in the moral history of the world. The
recognition or non-recognition of this, will determine the
character of all speculative theologies, and also the character and results of all efforts for the good of man. This
fact the world do not admit ; and hence they disallow
Christ, both as a source of life and as the centre of unity.
He is "disallowed indeed of men, but chosen of God and
precious." It is on this that the whole method of God in
the restoration of man is based, and it is for the recognition of this by men, and their adoption of God's method

of vitality and unity, that the tardy and laboring and dis-
tracted times wait.   No partial reform will do ; no "coming man."   Every where men are divergent, repellent.
The bond of a common humanity has been found to be
but a bond of tow to bind the Samson of human selfishness and passion.   There must be a divine life, a divine
centre, a more than human bond.   This life is in Christ.
He is "the life."   This bond is from him.   In him are
condensed all human relationships, as of "brother and
sister and mother ; " and to these—higher and holier—
that of Saviour is added.   In him, as the second Adam ;
in his matchless character, human, yet divine ; in his
all-embracing and self-sacrificing love ; in him as the
champion of humanity in its weakness and guilt, able and
willing to bring succor in the hour of its direst need, and
to raise it up from the darkness and the dust of death,
there is every requisite for a centre of unity for the race,
so that "all things which are on earth," as well as "those
which are in heaven, may be gathered together in one,
even in him."   In this, in this only, is there an object
worthy of God.   He has created worlds, and families of
worlds, of mere matter, and given them a unity of unspeakable beauty and grandeur ; but without sensation or recognition, without enjoyment or praise, what would they be
worth?   Nothing.   No, the only work worthy of God is
one crowned by creatures made in his image, with their
vitality from him, and himself the centre of their unity—
unity in love, fitly represented by the marriage union.
This work, we believe, will correspond in its vastness to
that of the stellar hosts, and as far transcend them in
glory as mind transcends the inanimate clod.   It will
embrace all orders of rational intelligences, in all worlds ;
sin and its consequences will be eliminated, and it shall
stand in its glorious order forever.   The promised new

heavens and earth do not so much respect any new combinations and unity of matter, as of conscious agents; and
they will be such that all that has gone before in the works
of God will be as nothing. " For behold," says God, " I
create new heavens and a new earth ; and the former shall
not be remembered, nor come into mind. But be ye glad
and rejoice forever in that which I create ; for, behold, I
create Jerusalem a rejoicing and her people a joy."

It is of such a social system, my friends that you are
to fit yourselves to form a part; it is into such a system
that you are to seek to bring others. This will comprehend your whole duty. This you will best do, not by
ignoring or disregarding those lower social systems on
earth which God has ordained, but by filling your places
as living stones in them all. That you may do this rightly
I have wished, to furnish you both with a test of systems,
and with guiding principles.

First, then, it will follow, from what has been said, that
if you are either to fit yourselves for such a system, or to
aid in fitting others, an indispensable condition must be,
that you should be *alive*.

What can a dead man do ? In the first place, death
can enjoy nothing. And then, what place has a cold, unconscious, apathetic stone, where everything is vital, and
responsive, and eager to meet the wants of the whole ? It
is an obstruction not merely, but an offense, and cannot
be permanently suffered. So is it in the family; so in
the college—what is the use of a dead student? so in
the state ; so in the church ; so, emphatically, must it be
in heaven. With little vitality, such offenses may be endured, but the more intense the life, the more does it array
itself against all death, and seek to free itself from its contact. The very pavement of heaven would rise against the

5*

foot of the wicked; it would cast them out. "Without
are dogs." And what, again, can a dead man do in com-
municating life? Life comes from life. God is its author;
but, having originated it, it spreads from centres according
to laws, and those centres must be alive. In the spiritual,
as in the natural world, there is no spontaneous generation.
Would you communicate knowledge? You must have it.
So of life. Christianity does not spring up of itself; it
must be borne by the living preacher. Yes, by a *living*
preacher, and not by one that is dead.

If, then, you would enjoy any thing; if you would not
be an offense; if you would communicate any thing, you
must be alive.

You will also find, in what has been said, a test of all
social organizations. Of these, the present emergency requires that I should refer especially to those that are national, and to your duty to the government in which you
are to have a part.

Organizations express life, and react upon it. Of these,
some are better than others. It is not true, that, "that is
the best government which is best administered." That
government is the best, and is likely to be best administered, which is constructed most nearly after God's method.
That, accordingly, is the best government which combines
most perfectly vitality, freedom, and unity. We are wont
to think of the excellence of our government as from freedom. Not so, except as there is vitality back of the freedom, and as it leads to unity. Its excellence is that its
method is vital, and not mechanical. It is self-government,
working out, as by an instinct of life, the common good.
It is a common-wealth. It casts the character in the
mould of freedom, and becomes a great educating and for
motive power. It makes a radical difference whether the
people have a government distinct from themselves and

exercised over them, or whether they *are* the government, expressing their will through constitutional forms. In the one case the people will be recipients and instruments, receiving a provision made for them by those whose business it is to take care of them ; in the other they will be vital, and will perform a high function of vitality by which, if they perform it well, they must grow into a larger manhood. *If they perform it well!* Just here it is that the voice of patriotism, of oppressed humanity every where, that the voice of God reaches every young man, and especially every educated young man. You inherit a government more conformed to the methods of God than any other. There is in it more of freedom in all directions ; we trust there is also more of vitality, of unity, and of power to expel what would be destructive of its life. But this is yet to be tested, and the result will depend on the present generation of young men. There is no strength like that of unity from vitality and freedom. There is no beauty like it. Go forth, then, and do what you can in giving to the nation this strength and beauty. Be true to God's methods ; be true to the interests of freedom, and to the rights of man.

Again, as we have seen that vitality is the chief thing in order to social unity, it will follow that your highest aim will be to communicate that.

This was done by our Saviour. He had life in himself. He was the Life, and his great object was to give life to the world. For this he gave himself. This principle was original with him. It is distinctive. It is this, and this only, that has made his religion a power in the world, working like leaven. Overlooked by the world, " disallowed of men," it is yet demonstrably the only true principle of reform. If a living house is to be built, there must be living stones. *The difficulty in social structures is in the material.* If this nation is to fail, it will be from that.   Ambition, selfishness, human wisdom, take such materials as they find and use them as they may, often skillfully, for their own ends.   Christ says, begin with the materials.   "*Make the tree good.*"   Go to the ignorant, the vicious, the proud, the sensual, the selfish in every form,' and teach them that wisdom of God which consists, not in getting any thing, or in achieving any thing, but in *becoming* as little children before him.   Thus shall they enter, by love, into his kingdom, and into the heirship of all things. This is totally different from any achievement for admiration, or from any exercise of power, as by the great ones of the earth.   It is wholly alien from the spirit of the world, and yet from this only can there be renovation in society, or fruit unto life everlasting.   This will preclude all monkish seclusion, it will bring you heart to heart with your fellow-men, no matter who, so they be men, and will call for all you may have of life to communicate.   Your usefulness will not be as your talents, but as you may communicate vitality.   I rejoice, my friends, in the confidence that you will adopt this principle.   Apply it in your lives, unmoved by the sneers of skepticism, or by the success and self-complacency of the worldly wise.

Once more, in view of the discordance and divisions in the world, it will readily occur to you, from what has been said, how important it is that your centres of unity should be rightly chosen.

Both your influence and peace will depend much upon this.   Here your wisdom will be to choose only those which God has established.   God has established the family, and not communism ; the state, and not party ; the church, the one living, spiritual church, and not sects ; Christ and not popes, or theological doctors and teachers. The true ground of union is vitality with reference to a common centre ; and distant as it may seem, we hope and believe the time will come when men will every where swing away from centres false, artificial, divisive, and revolve only, with mutual attraction, around those that are God-appointed.

Finally, while I exhort you to enter, as a vital part, into every social unity instituted by God, the great question with you, as with us all, is whether you have come to Christ. " Unto whom coming." Have you come to him as unto a living stone, and so been made yourselves living as to be fit to become a part of that spiritual house which God is building? Christ is still " disallowed of men." The builders refused him. So do not you. You are building for eternity ; look well to your foundation. Christ is "chosen of God," and other foundation can no man lay. He is precious to him as " the Head-stone of the corner." " He is precious to them that believe." If you have not done so, come to him now, in this hour of transition, and of look-out upon the future, and he will be precious to you. Is it to be to any of you that your strength will be weakened in the way and that death will claim you early ? Christ will be precious, O how precious ! Are you to bear the responsibilities of life, and wage its battles till old age? Little do you know of your own weakness, and of the besetments and fierce struggles of the long way, if a divine Helper would not be precious to you. He will be precious to you in the final hour. When you shall walk through the valley of the shadow of death, his rod and his staff, they shall comfort you. And when the present order shall come to an end, and that building of God, whose stones are now preparing, shall go up without a sound of the axe or the hammer, till " the head-stone thereof shall be brought forth with shoutings," you shall be there, and cry, " Grace, grace, unto it."

XI.

ENLARGEMENT.

Now for a recompense in the same, (I speak as unto my children,) be ye also enlarged.—2 Corinthians, vi. 13.

THAT is a slow process by which enlargement comes to man in his apprehension of himself, and of his wider relations. At his birth he is often spoken of as a stranger. He is a stranger in a strange world—how strange!—but to no one is he a greater stranger than to himself. How little does the infant know or suspect of the capacities that are in him for apprehension, for joy and suffering, for varied emotion and passion, for action, and for an eternal duration. He is a point that is to enlarge into a capacity to reflect the universe, but that capacity is revealed only as he is brought face to face with that which is to act upon him, and upon which he is to act, and few men, if any, learn, during a life-time, their own capacities. Among the last things that a man comes to know thoroughly, is himself.

Then of the past, of the future, of things around him, what does he know? Of that endless duration that is back of him, he knows nothing. He does not know that there has been such a duration, much less what has taken place during its countless ages. Whether he is the first child of the first man, or the last in a succession of myriads of generations, he knows not. So of the space around him, and what is in it. To him, the walls that his eyes rest upon

₊ AUGUST 2, 1863.

are the limit of the universe, and those around him are all
the beings it contains. Of wide plains, and high mountains, and broad oceans, of an infinite space with its countless suns and systems, of the multitudes of men, and the
myriads of the heavenly hosts, he has no apprehension or
suspicion. So also of the great future. Shall all things
continue as they are forever? Shall the earth and the
things that are therein be burnt up? When will the mil-
lenium begin? Where will he be after myriads of ages?
These, and such as these, are questions that do not as yet
disturb him.

Now the business of education for this incipient being,
certainly its first business, is simply enlargement—enlargement in the apprehension of things past, and future, and
around him; and the comprehension of them so as to bring
them all into unity.

But to this enlargement there are great natural obstacles; and if man be left to himself, it must, whether we
regard the individual or the race, be slow. In part, it is
indeed spontaneous. The child, let alone, will grow up to
such apprehension and enlargement as will enable him to
meet his animal wants, and something more. But in its
relation to the human faculties, this universe is so constituted that enlargement soon ceases, unless there be voluntary, rational, persistent, and organized effort. From the
great number of objects around us, their complexity, the
magnitude of some and the minuteness of others; from the
subtlety of natural agents, the interaction of laws and the
long cycles of nature; and from the necessity of labor and
the brevity of life, it is clear that one individual, or one
generation, could do but little. How could the first man,
or the first generations of men, have known that the earth
is round, or that it revolves round the sun, or that its surface lies in strata, or have calculated an eclipse? How

could they have known the composition of bodies, and the subtle agents of chemistry ? Clearly man was placed here as in a school, and both the individual and the race were to be gradually educated into such an enlargement as to comprehend and use wisely the substances and forces around him, and to know something of his position, among the stars, and as related to other worlds.

Owing to the obstacles just mentioned, this process of enlargement could not have been rapid, but it might have been more so than it has been. Men are sluggish, and gravitate towards sensuality ; they fall into habits and routine, and run in ruts ; they carry the grain on one side of the horse, and a stone on the other because their fathers did. Notions indolently taken up gather about them a crust of antiquity that no one dares to break through. There is nothing that men have been so reluctant to do as to think. They would go on pilgrimages, hang on hooks, accept dogmas, bow down to power, but they have been slow to put forth their powers in an earnest effort after comprehension and enlargement.

And not indolence only, but pride and selfishness have arrayed and organized themselves against this enlargement. Once accepted, a dogma links itself with modes of thought and habits of association ; it becomes a part of the systems of the schools, or of religious teaching. Then pride comes in, and the will is up, and men contend, not for truth, but for victory. Often also a dogma is so inwoven with the structure of society, that if you overthrow it, men's occupation will be gone. Then interest takes the lead, and pride and passion fall in, and the whole guild of silversmiths, with whatever rabble they can collect, are full of wrath, and cry out, saying, " Great is Diana of the Ephesians." Again, knowledge is power. Ignorant men may be held in subjection, and used as instruments ; and whole classes, nay, the mass of mankind, have been so held of set purpose and by law, that those thus holding them might rule over them and avail themselves of their labor.

From these causes there has been little zeal for truth ; and men zealous for it, and especially those in advance of their age, have been persecuted. Leaders of the race, and those set for the advancement of truth, have been its worst enemies. Holding the key of knowledge, they have not entered in themselves, and them that were entering in, they have hindered. Seats of learning, the very fortresses erected to guard and advance truth, have turned their guns against her.

· But now there is a change. The bonds are relaxed. Henceforth no coming Galileo shall need to smite with his foot the floor of a dungeon when he says the earth moves. If not the summer, yet the spring-time of truth is come. The few are greatly enlarged, and the mass of humanity is quickened. A feeling that gropes for the light, is pervading it, a dim thought that it is coming out into enlargement. Always there has been a voice from every thing that could supply want, or gratify curiosity, or enlarge science, or adorn life, from the flower on the earth and the star in the heavens, saying, Be ye enlarged ; but now that voice is heard by the alert sense of very many. Now, too, it begins to be felt that truth is one. The different angles and walls of her temple are seen to belong to one building, and instead of scowls and reproaches, the workmen more often send greetings to each other, and feel that they are working together.

To this wide enlargement there are, as has been said, natural obstacles ; but there is also a tendency to it, and with right affections progress would be indefinite. From the first, the affections are complicated with the intellect, they react upon it as the brain upon the stomach, and when these are disordered and dwarfed, it is not possible that the general intellectual level should be high. Society will soon reach a point where it will become stationary, and will begin to go back. Hence the great thing needed is enlargement of the affections, and it is accordingly of this that the Apostle Paul speaks when he says. " O, ye Corinthians," "our mouth is open unto you, our *heart* is enlarged. Ye are not straitened in us, but ye are straitened in your own bowels. Now for a recompense in the same, (I speak as unto my children,) be ye also enlarged." Be enlarged in your affections. Give as you receive ; love as you are loved.

For the Apostle Paul to say this to the Corinthians, was a great thing—how great, we can understand only by going back to his position. Socially, the world was in a state of disintegration. Men were divided into clans tribes, nationalities, with diversities of language, customs, interests, that were constant grounds of alienation and of settled antipathies ; and, to human view, any common ground or centre of unity for the race was hopeless. Except in dreams of conquest and subjugation, the very idea of such unity did not exist. But of nations thus diverse and hostile, the Jews were the most exclusive, and the Apostle was not only a Jew, but had belonged to their straitest religious sect. As a Jew, his pride, and self-complacency, and zeal for Judaism, were boundless, and he looked upon Gentiles with contempt and aversion. Yet we here find him offering his fraternal regards, and warmest love, and intimate fellowship to Gentiles, and seeking theirs in return, and this without regard to the previous rank, or cultivation, or character of those Gentiles. Of some we know that their origin was low, and that their character had been vile. This too he did on a principle that would include all, for we hear him saying to other

Gentiles, "There is neither Jew nor Greek, there is neither bond nor free, there is neither male nor female; for ye are all one in Christ Jesus. And if ye be Christ's, then are ye Abraham's seed, and heirs according to the promise.

Now here was a moral miracle. I do not hesitate to say it. To one who has observed the tenacity of national pride and hate, and the virulance of religious bigotry, and who knows the state of feeling at that time in regard to women and slaves and barbarians, this transition from the extreme of narrowness to enlargement and absolute universality of affection, and to the recognition of all as entitled to common privileges, is as unaccountable on merely natural principles as any miracle of the New Testament. Now, the sympathies of this former bigot embraced the race. He knew no man after the flesh. To him every man was a *man*, made in the image of God, redeemed by Christ, exposed to the second death, but capable of being saved, and so he preached Christianity to all men alike, and received all men alike, for so must it be preached, and so must men be received, if it is to have its full power.

In adopting the above principle, the Apostle was simply faithful to the system he had espoused, which stood self-vindicated as from God by its recognition of man as man, and through that, by its fitness and tendency to become universal. Hence its leavening power. Did the Apostle preach at Rome? Why not in Spain also? If in Spain, why not in Britian and to our barbarous ancestors there? By ignoring every thing incidental, and seizing, as the material of its system and the ground of its regards upon humanity itself as it must exist under all modifications, it passed at once through all barriers of nationality, and clanship, and caste, and condition, and showed itself to have an assimulating, an organizing power that was capable of bringing all people into unity. This was the wonderful fact about it. As related to ultimate success it was the cardinal fact, and one not to be compromised. It is the fact that has made Christianity revolutionary from that day to this. If at times the giant has seemed to be quiet, as if pressed down by the mountains of human wickedness, it has only been to gather strength for the upheaval, and the earthquake. And so it will be, for in this fact is the principle of all true progress.

Marvellous then as this enlargement of the Apostle would appear on any other ground, it is yet perfectly natural when we look at him as a disciple of Christ both comprehending his system, and in sympathy with him. As in sympathy with Christ he could not do otherwise The example of Christ was the great miracle of love, both in its intensity and in its enlargement. In its intensity it was unto death, in its enlargement it was for the whole world. Receiving such a spirit of enlargement as this from the Master, how could there be in the diciple any thing of restriction or limitation? How could he refuse to preach Christ's gospel to any for whom He died? How could he refuse to receive any whom Christ received? No longer do we wonder when we find this former bigot and persecutor exulting in this universality, and saying so freely, and fully, and grandly, "Where there is neither Greek nor Jew, circumcision nor uncircumcision, Barbarian, Scythian, bond nor free; but Christ is all, and in all.

From this example of the Apostle, we readily see what that enlargement is of which he speaks. It is a coming out from all narrowness and restriction of nationality, or clanship, or sect, or caste, or local prejudice, or prejudice from color, and so apprehending the rights of man as God-

given, and his dignity and destiny as made in the image
of God, that we shall always feel towards every man, and
treat him as a man. This is no glittering generality, barren and impracticable. It is the great want and claim of
this age in which we live. It is the law of God. It is the
claim of humanity,

This enlargement, which is that of Christianity, some,
especially French writers, have sought to identify with
democracy ; but while Christianity is the only foundation
of a quiet and permanent democracy, they are yet rather
in contrast. Democracy respects political rights and relations ; Christianity respects all relations, and may exist
under all forms of government. Democracy looks chiefly
at rights ; Christianity at duties. Democracy respects
this world ; Christianity includes both worlds, but looks
chiefly at ultimate destiny. Democracy concedes rights,
but requires no enlargement of the affections ; Christianity
is, itself, in its very essence, an enlargement of the affections. Democracy is compatible with great individual
corruption within a nation, and with hostility and boundless ambition in the relations of nations to each other ;
Christianity involves individual integrity and good-will to
all. Democracy may be atheistic—men have sought to
make it so ; the very principle and foundation of Christianity and the enlargement it implies, is from the relation
of each to all as in the image of God, and so from their
common relation to him.

To the enlargement now spoken of there is not, as to
that of apprehension, any natural obstacle. Enlargement
of affection might, and should accompany that of the intellect as naturally as the heat of the sun accompanies its
light. But in this world it is not thus, and it is both sad
and amazing—if it were not so sad it would be amusing—
to trace the history of the world as it is related to this

want of enlargement. There is no conceivable differance by which men are separated from each other that has not been made a ground of alienation in affection and often of positive hostility.

> " Lands intersected by a narrow frith
> Abhor each other. Mountains interposed
> Make enemies of nations. "

A difference in name, nation, color, language, clan, occupation, residence, as in different towns, or even, at different ends of the same street, and especially a difference of belief and opinion, become the ground of alienations, divisions, and of settled, hereditary and unreasoning hate. Passions thus excited have been strong enough to override both humanity and self-interest. Often, as in families and clans, these passions have been intense and persistent in proportion as their range has been narrow ; often too as the point of difference has been frivolous, and and as the opponents resembled each other the more, except in the one point of difference.

Such differences must, of course, respect points that are capable of drawing in by association the deep feelings of our nature, and will have more power as those feelings are deeper.

Hence it is that, in this respect, religion has furnished so sad a chapter in the history of the world. When its grand beliefs, tending only to enlargement, are displaced by superstition, and those deep feelings in which true religion chiefly consists, concentrate themselves about trifles and forms, we might expect a narrowness more intense than any other, and a bigotry more unscrupulous and cruel. And so it has been, and is now. So great has been this narrowness that it has been impossible to caricature it, because the imagination could conceive of nothing more narrow. The Little-Endians and the Big-Endians of Swift, whose difference was on the question whether they should break their eggs at Easter at the little or the big end, were not a whit beyond the four-year-olds and the five-year-olds in Ireland, whose feuds have often led to murder, and between whom it became necessary for the bishop to interpose his authority. But more wonderful than this, we have seen, in our own country, large and intelligent bodies of Christians whose differences touched, and were conceded to touch, no vital point of Christianity, withholding all tokens of Christian communion and fellowship, and holding each other as heathen men and publicans ; and we have even heard prescribed, as the way of peace, the putting up of high fences and keeping them in good repair. What a work for the followers of Him who " broke down the middle wall of partition " between the Jews and the Gentiles, " having abolished in his flesh the enmity, even the law of commandments contained in ordinances "—that is in external rites and things unessential—" for to make in *himself* of twain, *one* new man, *so* making peace ! "

It is also impossible to conceive of bigotry more unscrupulous and cruel than there has been. In connection with no one of its elements, save that of religion, could human nature have either originated or endured such an institution as the Inquisition ; and the imagination may be drawn on in vain to exceed in its conceptions the horrid enginery that has been devised to do professedly the work of Christian love.

But as much ground as there is for discouragement in regard to this form of enlargement, yet here, too, the bonds are relaxed. Not alone is there light on the mountain tops, there is more of quickening warmth in the valleys, and here and there a deeper verdure. That the perfection of the world requires that the two forms of enlargement should go on together, we can see. But as there are in the way of this no natural obstacles, so neither is there for it, any law of progress, except as love naturally follows light, which all experience shows that in this world it does not in fact do. Hence, for such a training of the race as shall effect this enlargement, we must rely wholly on the special providence and grace of God.

The two points to be reached are—the one, that every man shall so respect manhood as to treat every other man as a man—the other, that every Christian shall so respect Christianhood, as to treat every Christian as a Christian. Manhood in man ; Christ in the Christian—these are to be the objects of our regard, and nothing selfish or sectarian, nothing local or accidental may prevent our enlargement to the full recognition of every right and claim which these would involve. It is not that the claims of self-interest rightly viewed, and of nearer relationship are to be disregarded. These have their place, primary, imperative, sacred ; but these claims are met with the broadest wisdom only when they are met in full compatibility with the claims of the widest enlargement. Towards these two points the movement has been slow. It is wonderful with what difficulty men have broken away from the narrowness of family, and clan, and tribe, and party, and caste, and sect, and nationality. But there has been movement. Feudalism melted into nationalities, often ill-assorted, and mere aggregates, but always with some increase of enlargement. Clanship, as in Scotland, that seemed to inhere as by some special mordant, has faded out. The Thugism of Ireland has well-nigh passed away. The French Emperor has kissed the English Queen, and the English and French have fought side by side. A new continent, this American continent, has been opened, where men might stand and see in the distance, and in a way to cause enlargement, arbitrary distinctions and conventionalities that had become chronic and hopeless, and where they might begin anew on a broader basis. To this continent and to this country have been swept, as by a vast diluvial current, English, and Irish, and Scotch, and French, and Germans, and Hollanders, and Swedes, and Jews ; and in the surging of free institutions they have been rolled together, and rounded, and smoothed. No experiment devised for the purpose could have been better adapted to promote enlargement.

And if we turn from nationalities and political relations to the church and to sects, there too there is movement. The cave whence Giant Pope formerly came out to seize pilgrims on the King's highway, has become his prison, where he is guarded by foreign soldiers, and must needs be defended from his own subjects. The Inquisition cannot be reproduced. Even Turks are converted to Christ, and avow it, and their heads remain on their shoulders. Nay, Turkey may well put Spain to the blush, for there the Bible may be freely sold and read. · In England there is progress. The intolerance of the Established Church is waning, and, both politically and socially, Dissenters are less under ban. And then there is one country where there is no alliance of church and state, and no civil disability, or liability to taxation, or social ban with a court to sanction it, on account of religious belief, or form of worship. If, to some of these things there are tendencies here ; if we are in danger, as we are, from ecclesiasticism ; if the old aristocratic leaven, driven from politics, tends to pass into the church ; there are also opposite tendencies, and we hope the spirit of enlargement will gain the mastery. It must gain it in the end.

Having thus seen what full enlargement would be I observe in the first place, that the Bible method of reach-

6

ing this is the reverse of that adopted by the world. The world seeks first intellectual enlargement. Its education is for that, and the ends secured through that. For enlargement of the heart it cares little, and supposes that will follow of course. But not thus can even a general enlightenment be reached. The interworkings and counteractions of selfishness would prevent that. Those who would gain such enlightenment must first seek a higher end, as he who would have all other things added must first seek the kingdom of God. Hence the method of the Bible is to begin with the heart. Any enlargement of the intellect without this it reckons as nothing. For the guidance of a moral being it is nothing. The doctrine of the Bible is, that " he that loveth his brother walketh in the light," but that " *he that hateth his brother is in darkness, and walketh in darkness, and knoweth not whither he goeth, because that darkness hath blinded his eyes.*" This doctrine the world has yet to learn. A general enlargement of intellect in any community can be reached only by bringing to bear upon the heart of that community the great motives of Christ's Gospel.

And now it has not escaped the observation of many, that the point of enlargement to which the providence of God is pressing us in this war, is the full recognition of the manhood of the negro in all its rights as a man. This point as fully as the laws of the Union would allow, was reached in this State, immediately after the Revolution. In the eye of the law the negro was placed on an equality with other men. From this no harm came, and if this point could be reached throughout the whole country to-morrow, our troubles would cease. When the black man shall be permitted to go where he pleases, to earn his own honest living in his own way, to enjoy all the natural rights of a man, and such civil rights as he is fitted for, the country will be quiet. We may not wish this ; probably we should not have ordered it so ; we may struggle against it. But this distinction of color and of race is from God ; these people are here by his appointment, and we are not to narrow ourselves by prejudice, and fear that the heavens will fall, if we apply impartially and fully those great principles of natural right which are surely from God, and which we have avowed before the world. It is these principles that are now in question, and it is the struggle between these and their opposites that is convulsing, and is yet to convulse the nations.

It is into that double enlargement of the intellect and the heart which has been presented in this Discourse, that I now invite you, to enter more fully. With the enlargement of your sphere of action, be ye also enlarged.

But, as you will have inferred already, my chief desire is that you should be enlarged in your hearts. There has been enlargement of heart towards you. You little know how you have been loved and cared for by parents and friends. There has been enlargement on the part of the public in providing for your education ; there has been enlargement towards you in the hearts of your teachers— and now what we ask you is, " For a recompense in the same." The best recompense of love is love in return, and the deeds which love prompts. What a recompense that is which you can make to your parents and friends ! How will your parents rejoice, how will your friends, to see you giving back love for love, care for care, and filling every enlarged sphere with an enlargement of intellect and of heart like that of the Apostle himself.

For this enlargement there is ample scope in this world ; but in that which is to come, O the illimitable enlargement of which you are capable ! O the wealth

which God has provided ! The wealth of this universe is
not in the things that may be possessed, though they be
gold and gems, though they be suns and systems ; nor yet
in the sciences that may be known, though they branch
out into infinity; but it is in the beings that may be
loved—God himself and his holy kingdom. Possessions,
knowledge, are but the pedestal to be crowned with love.
It is because there is excellence to be loved that heaven
is possible, and the possibilities of heaven itself are to be
measured by the possible enlargement of love.

At this point, however, perhaps a caution is needed.
The enlargement to which I call you is not to be confounded with what is sometimes called liberality. This is
a term under which, with the pretence of enlargement,
men often cover indifference to the truth, and, if the truth
be pressed, essential narrowness and even bitterness.
With such liberality, the enlargement to which I call you has
no affinity. It is its opposite. The more enlargement
there is, the more vivid the apprehension will be of the
beauty of truth, and of the dignity and excellence and
unutterable value of righteousness. You are called to an
enlargement of comprehension and of love like that of
Paul, with a corresponding opposition to all fundamental
error and essential wickedness. The enlargement to
which I call you is that of Christianity itself, which is at
once the most universal and catholic, and the most exclusive of all systems. If it had not been broad and catholic,
it would not have been fitted to include all nations ; if it
had not been exclusive, it would not have revolutionized
the world—it would not have had martyrs. Christ himself would not have died, if there had not been something
to stand up for, and to hold on to, with the whole energy
of our being. What this is we may know. God has not
shut men up to the alternative of the frigidity and imbec-

ility of indifference on the one hand or to a narrow and fierce bigotry on the other. No ; there is an open way of enlargement in comprehension, and in the love of God and of man, and in hating nothing that love and righteous-ness do not compel us to hate.

With this caution, the word that I would leave with you, that I ask you to carry with you through life, is *enlargement* —enlargement of intellect, enlargement of the heart, en-largement of the intellect through that of the heart.

From this combination there will naturally, but not necessarily follow, an enlargement of personal influence. To insure this there must be added, energy of will. With that added, your preparation for the work of life will be complete. Then, not only will you yourselves grow by the exertion of your own activities in the right direction—grow to be more like God, and so more truly human—but in the same proportion you will have an influence for good over others ! This is the object of a legitimate ambition ; and in this you will find, what so few have found, the point of coincidence between the highest ambition and the highest duty.

And now, my dear friends, in view of what has been done for you, of what is expected of you ; of the wants of a lost world ; in view of your capacities, and of the scope there is for them in the infinities that surround you ; in view of the call of God himself, and of Redeeming Love, I speak to you as unto my children, and I say to you, " Be ye also enlarged."

XII.

CHOICE AND SERVICE.

Choose you this day whom ye will serve.—Joshua, xxiv. 15.

PROBABLY Joshua is the most illustrious example on record of a great warrior who was also a thoroughly religious man. Chosen by God to bring Israel into the promised land, he had under him a people trained as no other had ever been. With the exception of Caleb the son of Jephunneh, not a man of them was over sixty years old. The faint-hearted and the murmurers of a former generation had perished, every one of them, from among them, and the nation, instinct with one life and one purpose, were ready to follow their leader. The faith of that leader never faltered, and with the single exception when there was an Achan in the camp, he led them to uniform victory. Having conquered the country, he divided to each tribe its inheritance, and for a time the land rested in quiet.

In this quiet the Israelites did not relapse into idolatry. They remained steadfast in their allegiance to God. That generation and the succeeding one received a higher testimony than any other that has been on the face of the earth. It is said, "And Israel served the Lord all the days of Joshua, and all the days of the elders that overlived Joshua, and which had known all the works of the Lord that he had done for Israel." Still, the heathen were not entirely

** JULY 31, 1864.

expelled ; the Israelites were the descendants of those who had made the golden calf at the foot of Sinai, and as the time for his death drew near, Joshua desired to do something to guard the people against that departure from the living God which was the only thing they had to fear.

Accordingly he "gathered all the tribes of Israel to Shechem, and called for the elders of Israel, and for their heads, and for their officers ; and they presented themselves before God." Then was seen one of the most solemn and imposing spectacles in the history of the nation. This leader, whose success had been so great, whose authority had never, like that of Moses, been questioned, now more than a hundred years old, stood before the assembled nation, and surrounded by its chief men, recounted to them what God had done for them, and required them to choose deliberately and solemnly the service of the God of their fathers ; or, if they would reject that, to choose whom they would serve. The question was to whom they would render supreme allegiance, and that question they were then to decide. This decision Joshua was careful should be made only with the fullest light. He not only told them what God had done, but also that he was a holy God, and the difficulty of his service on that account. They heard, they understood, and decided that they would serve the Lord. " And the people said unto Joshua, Nay, but we will serve the Lord." That was decisive of the history of that generation. So far as the choice was from the heart it decided the influence and destiny of every individual during the whole course of his being.

In this transaction with the Israelites one thing was required and another implied. It was required that they should choose their supreme object of affection and worship ; it was implied, that, having chosen, they would serve him. The choice was to be made once and forever ; the service was to be perpetual, involving volitions and acts constantly repeated. In this choice and these volitions the radical character of the Israelites found expression; in a similar choice and the consequent volitions our character will do the same, and on these our destiny will depend. Let us therefore look a little at these acts of choice and of volition, as they are in themselves; as related to each other; and to human character and well-being.

Taking then the act of choice, I observe, in the first place, that we *must* choose.

There are certain original and necessary forms of activity through which man knows himself. These are commonly said to be three—thinking, feeling, willing. In reality there are four, thinking, feeling, *choosing*, willing. These were never taught us. They are not the product of will. We do not think because we will to think, or choose because we will to choose, any more than we will because we will to will. We think and choose and will by a necessity of our nature immediately and directly when the occasion arises. These forms of activity we find originally in us, and a part of us; they go back with us to our first remembrance and conception of ourselves. If man did not find in himself each of these he would not be man. Free we may be in choosing, but not whether we will choose. This is so a condition of our being, that the very refusal to choose is itself choice.

And not only must man choose, he must also choose an object of supreme affection. A supreme object of worship, an object of worship at all, he need not choose, but of affection he must.

This belongs to the constitution of our nature. If a man were compelled to part with the objects of his affection one by one, as the master of a vessel is sometimes obliged to throw overboard his cargo, it must be that there would be a last thing to which he would cling. Without this our nature could have neither consistency nor dignity. In this the great masters of thought agree, and through it they account for the apparent anomalies of human conduct.

> " Search then the master passion—there alone
> The wild are constant and the cunning known."

As a river, if it be a river, despite backwater and eddies, must flow some whither, and as those eddies and the backwater are caused by the very current they seem to contradict, so must there be in man some current of affection, bearing within its sweep all others, and that would, if known, reconcile all seeming contradictions. In this too the Scriptures agree. It is only a statement in another form of the great doctrine announced by our Saviour, that in the moral sphere there can be no neutrality and no double service. " He that is not with me is against me." " Ye cannot serve God and mammon."

How far God so reveals himself to each man as he did to the Israelites that there must be a distinct acceptance or rejection of him, he only can know, but every being having a moral constitution must be either in harmony with, or in opposition to the great principles of his moral government, and thus virtually either choose or reject him.

To know what the supreme object thus chosen and the master passion is, is the capital point in the most difficult and valuable of all knowledge, the knowledge of ourselves. Not our capacities alone do we need to know, but the set and force of that current within us which is deepest. But what the object thus chosen is, or even that he does thus choose, a man may not distinctly state to himself, and it may come out into clear consciousness only as he is brought to a test. The covetous man may go on for

years amassing property; the upas tree of avarice may
grow till every generous affection is withered beneath it,
and yet no test may have been so applied as to compel him
to say to himself, " I am a miser." He may not even suspect it. If told the truth he may honestly, in one sense
honestly, as well as indignantly and reproachfully deny
it, and say with one of old, " Is thy servant a dog that he
should do this thing ? " A Christian may be in doubt
whether he loves God supremely. But let persecution
come and demand his property, and that will be one test;
let it demand his liberty, that will be another ; let it
demand his life to be given up through reproach and torture, and that will be a third and a final test. Then will
there be a felt ground of consistency and of dignity. The
ship will right itself in the storm, and with its prow toward
its haven, the fiercer the winds the faster will it be driven
thither.

But while we are thus necessitated to choose, and to
choose an object of supreme affection, the choice itself is
free. There is always in it an alternative. In this it differs from all that precedes it either in nature or in ourselves. Here it is indeed that we find the birth-place and
citadel of that great element and royal prerogative, Freedom, which underlies all moral action and accountability.
This it is which brings us into a moral and spiritual
sphere wholly out of and above that of mere nature. The
sphere of nature has for its characteristics uniformity and
necessity, but here is freedom. This element is typified
indeed, and foreshadowed in nature through all her forms
of unconscious life. Very beautiful it is to see a multi-
form life working spontaneously toward its ends. Wonderful is that selective power by which the root and leaf
of each vegetable, and the sense and digestive apparatus
of each animal, appropriate that which will build up the

9*

life of each, and reject all else. But here is no freedom. And the same may be said of all that precedes choice in our own life. We must previously have knowledge, but we know by necessity. No man can help knowing his own existence and acts of consciousness. We must previously have desire. Hunger and thirst, the desire for food and drink, are necessary; and there are hungerings and thirstings, appetencies and cravings so running through our whole nature that if we do not hunger and thirst after righteousness even, we cannot be filled. But here too the congruities are prearranged, and the desire is necessary. As such it has a wider range than choice. We desire many things which we do not and cannot choose. We desire wealth, position, power; we may desire the possession of the stars, or of universal dominion, but we can choose only that which is offered to our acceptance. There is in choice appropriation, and the thing chosen must be in such a relation to us that it may, in some sense, become our own.

But the peculiarity of an act of choice is that there is in it an alternative. This belongs to its definition. There is an overlooking of the whole ground, a comparison, and a felt power of turning either way. We must indeed choose, but we are under no necessity of choosing any one thing. When but a single object is offered us we may choose or reject it; when two are offered both of which we cannot have, as learning and ease, power and quiet, pleasure and virtue, we may choose between them. Thus, through the whole range of faculties which God has given us, we may choose which shall be brought into predominant activity; and through the whole range of objects which he has set before us, including himself, we may choose which we will appropriate as the source of nutriment to our inmost life.

In this act of choice, having thus an alternative, every man so stands forth to his own consciousness as free, that a conviction of his freedom must cling to that consciousness forevermore. The freedom is so a part of the act, and enters into the very conception of it, that men generally would as soon think of denying the act itself as of denying its freedom. No man can honestly deny it. Hence, as being known at once, and certainly, just as is the act itself, freedom can neither be proved nor disproved, but must be accepted on the immediate testimony of consciousness. A man might as well deny the fact that he exists, as to deny those characteristics of his being which enter into his conception of himself; and of these, freedom of choice is one. " We lay it down," says Dr. Archibald Alexander,* " as a first principle—from which we can no more depart than from the consciousness of existence—that MAN IS FREE ; and therefore stand ready to embrace whatever is fairly included in the definition of freedom." Let the few then impugn as they may this great element and fact of freedom, they can never lead the mass of men to disbelieve it. They can never really disbelieve it themselves, they can never practically discard it.

And this leads me to observe that as freedom finds in an act of choice its cradle, so does it also its citadel.

Interfere with a man in his outward acts, restrain him from passing the limits of a town, shut him up in a prison, fetter his limbs, and you are said to deprive him of his freedom. You do invade it in its outer sphere, and in the sense in which it is generally understood, but there is still a freedom which you do not and cannot touch. There is in choice an activity of the spirit that abides wholly within itself. It neither requires nor admits of means, or instru-

* Moral Science, p. 111.

mentalities, or outward agencies. Hence no power, human or div:ne, that does not change the essential nature of the spirit itself, can reach the prerogatives of this power. Here is the inner circle of freedom, its impregnable fortress. Within this, man is a crowned king. Here, though but a beggar, he may retire, and without his own consent, no man can take his diadem. Retaining the powers which make it what it is, nothing can prevent the spirit from choosing and willing, from loving and hating, and so nothing out of itself can prevent it from being loyal to duty and to God. But while we thus claim for man full powers of free agency, we also assert the power of God to govern free agents ; and the necessity of the Divine Spirit to quicken and regenerate those whose choice of evil is so exclusive and intense that they are " dead in trespasses and sins."

We thus see what choice is. But the Israelites were not only to choose, they were to serve. By distinct and separate acts of volition, or of will, they were to cause the choice thus made to find expression in all their outward life. Let us then, as was proposed, look at these acts of volition, and their relations to choice.

Almost universally, and by the leading philosophers, as Kant and Hamilton, choice and volition have been confounded under the common name of Will. As more immediately connected with action, volition has been made the more prominent, and obscurity and sad misapprehension have been the result. But not only are choice and volition, or an act of the will, not the same, they are totally different. To this I ask special attention.

And first, choice must precede volition. No man can intelligently will an act except with reference to some object previously chosen.

Secondly, choice, and not volition, is the primary seat

of freedom. In a sense we are free in our volitions. They are wholly within ourselves, they require no means or instrumentalities, and no earthly power can interfere with them ; but yet they must be in accordance with some choice that predominates at the time, and can be changed only by a change of the choice. But are not men compelled to will what they do not choose? Not strictly. By force unjustly used they are said to be compelled to will what they would not but for that, and this is slavery ; still the will will be in accordance with the choice on the whole, else a man could not become a martyr. A patriot, having chosen as his end, and with his whole heart, the good of his country, and while thus choosing, cannot will acts in known opposition to that good. He may die, but he cannot do that.

Again, choice and will respect different objects. In strictness, we never choose what we will, or will what we choose. The objects of choice are persons, things, ends. The object of volition is an act ; always an act. We choose God, we choose a friend, a house, a profession, an ultimate end, but we do not will these. To say that we will a house would be absurd. We choose health, we will exercise ; we choose learning, we will study ; we choose an apple that hangs with its fellows upon the bending bough, we will the act by which we pluck it.

And as the objects of choice are different from those of volition, so are its grounds. We choose the apple because it is good ; we choose a friend for his intrinsic qualities ; we choose an end as good in itself ; we choose God as infinitely excellent in himself, and as meeting through that excellency every capacity of our rational being.

Always we choose an object for something in itself— some beauty, some utility, some grace, some excellence, by which it awakens emotion or desire, and comes into some relation to our well-being. But an action we never will for anything in itself, but only as it is related to an end. An action tending to no end would be a folly, and one abstractly right without reference to an end, is inconceivable. We do indeed will actions as right, but we mean by that, sometimes simply their fitness to gain an end, and sometimes, also, that the end is good. If the end be good, and be chosen because it is good, the action will be morally right; if not, it will be right simply from its relation to the end. An act of choice is itself right when the true end for man is chosen, and the choice is made, not merely because it is right, but, as all choice must be, in view of some good in the end. Universally, then, it is true that we choose objects and ends because they are good, and will actions because they tend to secure such objects and ends.

Once more, in choice man is not executive, in volition he is.

We think, feel, choose, and though active in these, are not conscious of putting forth energy. Every one knows the difference between a mere choice, or even purpose, and that putting forth of energy, by which we attempt to realize our purpose. This gives a new element. Before, the man was contemplative, choosing an end, maturing plans ; now he is executive, working for an end. Choice and purpose are known in themselves, volition by its effects, and what these may be, experience only can reveal.

Thus at all points do we find a difference between choosing and serving, that is, of willing. Choice is primary—volition secondary; choice is directly free—volition indirectly; choice respects persons, objects, ends—volition acts ; choice is not executive—volition is ; choice too has the common relation of source to both willing and loving ; volition is not a source at all; choice fixes on ultimate ends and absolute value, which is a good and not a utility. The very idea of utility is excluded from this sphere. A System of Morals based on the choice of a supreme end as good in itself, cannot be one of utility. In choosing the supreme end appointed by God for the good there is in it, there can be no undue reference to self. If this had been seen, much misapprehension would have been saved. Ultimate ends we choose for the sake of an absolute value ; a utility is a relative value. It belongs to means and instrumentalities, to volitions and acts as related to ends.

We have now considered choice and volition as they are in themselves, and as related to each other. If any one should say that these points are too elementary, or, if you please, metaphysical, for an occasion like this, I should agree with him if their connection were less vital with human character and well-being. That connection it remains for us to consider.

And first, I observe that choice, free as we have seen it to be, is the radical element in rational love. In this is the difference between rational and instinctive love. I know that mere emotion has stolen the name of love, and that the impulsive affections have been made identical with the heart. I know that there are affinities, and attractions, and a magnetism between persons as well as things, that there are subtle and inexplicable influences by which individuals are strangely drawn together, and that under the domination of these they think they love. And so they may ; but not from these alone. So long as attractions are balanced by defects of character, or incongruities of temper, so long as there is a parleying between the better judgment and the feelings, and while as yet there is no ratifying choice, there is no rational love. Let this choice be withheld, and however emotion may eddy and surge, it is not love, and in time it will die away. But when the deliberate and full choice is made, the *heart* is given. Then objections become impertinent, imperfections disappear, and the full tide of emotion flows on, tranquil, it may be, but deepening and widening. Choice is not emotion, nor a part of it, but it opens and shuts the gate for its flow. It is the personality determining where it shall bestow those affections that are its life. It is the nucleus of a train that sets the spiritual heavens aglow. Emotion fluctuates ; it comes and goes with times and moods and health, but love is constant, and this is the constant part of love. It is principle as opposed to emotion. In these two—choice and emotion—it is that we find what is called in Scripture "the heart." "His heart is fixed," says the Psalmist. There is the choice and the principle. "Trusting in the Lord ;" there is the emotion. The heart is not the affections regarded simply as emotion ; it is not the will except as will and choice are confounded. It is the affections, including choice ; born of choice and nurtured by it. Hence, under moral government the heart may be rightly subjected, not only as emotion, to indirect regulation, but as choice, to direct and positive command. For God to say, "My son, give me thy heart," is wholly within his prerogative as a righteous moral Governor. This is a point of the utmost moment, and often but imperfectly apprehended.

Again, if choice be thus an element of love, I need hardly say that it must determine character.

This follows because the character is as the paramount love. If this be of money, the man is a miser, if of power, he is ambitious, if of God, he is a religious man. It is said by some that character depends on the governing purpose. It does proximately, but purpose depends upon choice. We first choose, then purpose. On this, too, depends disposition, so far as it is moral. A supreme choice is the permanent disposing by a man of himself, in a given direction. This is the trunk of that tree spoken of by our Saviour, when he said, " Make the tree good, and his fruit will be good." From this will flow a sap that will reach the remotest twig and leaf of outward expression, and give its flavor to every particle of the fruit. Such a choice will determine not only the disposition, but the subjects of thought, the habits of association, the whole furniture of the mind. Hence those expressions of the Bible, " the thoughts of the heart," " the imaginations of the heart," are perfectly philosophical. Thoughts, imaginations, fancies, castle-buildings, take their whole body and form from those choices and affections which *are* the heart. These come and go, but they swarm out as bees from the home of the affections, and there they settle again. So it is that " out of the heart proceed evil thoughts, murders, adulteries, fornications, thefts, false witness, blasphemies ; " and so it is that " out of *it* are the issues of life." But it is in these, as thus springing from the heart, that character is expressed, and hence it is that the heart, having its nucleus and salient point in choice, *is* the character.

But if character thus depends upon choice, then the connection of choice with human well-being opens at once upon us. Under a moral government—and if we are not under that we can have no hope of anything—if we are not under that there is no God—under a moral government character and destiny must correspond. Whatever apparent and temporary discrepancies there may be, ultimately they must correspond. That they should do this enters into the very conception of moral government. Settle it therefore, I pray you, once and forever, that as your character is, so will your destiny be. Whatever capacities there may be for enjoyment or for suffering in this strange being of ours, and God only knows what they are, they will be drawn out wholly in accordance with character. There shall be no inheritance of possessions, or felicity of outward condition, no river of life, or gate of pearl, or street of gold, there there shall be no serenity of peace, or fulness of joy, or height of rapture, or ecstasy of love; there shall be no hostile and vengeful element, no lake of fire, no gnawing worm, no remorse or despair, that will not depend upon character. It is by their bearing upon this that we are to test every claim made upon us in the name of religion for outward observance and self-denial; and we are to sweep away as superstitions all forms and observances that do not tend to the purification and elevation of character, because it is this alone that bears upon destiny. This is destiny.

We thus see the amazing import and responsibility attached to this prerogative of choice. As we are active and practical it is the one distinguishing prerogative of our being. Entering into it, not as that which we *may* do, but as that which we *must* do, it is so a part of our being that it cannot be separated from us, and that its responsibility cannot be shared by another. It is that by which we make ourselves known for what we are. It is by choice only that our proper personality, ourself, acts back upon the forces that act upon us. As an original primitive act, admitting no use of means, it requires no one to teach us how to choose; no one can teach us. If I am required to kindle a fire I can be taught how, because means must be used, and there must be a process; but I must think and choose before I can be taught how.

As a moral act the results of choice are immediate and inevitable because it is in that that morality is. Outward results and general consequences will depend on powers and agencies out of ourselves, but this is wholly between man and his God, and reacts upon the soul, leaving its own impress forever. To that impress all things outward will come to correspond, and thus it is that man decides his own destiny. His destiny is as his choice, and his choice is his own. In this, not alone in immortality—immortality without this would be but the duration of a thing—in this, crowned by immortality, is the grandeur of our being. All below us is driven to an end which it did not choose, by forces which it cannot control. But for us there are moments, oh, how solemn, when destiny trembles in the balance, and the preponderance of either scale is by our own choice. Do you deny this, ye who speak of the littleness and weakness of man, and of the power of circumstances? Ye who scoff at freedom, and sneer at human dignity, and mock at the strivings of a poor insect limited on all sides, and swept on by infinite forces, do ye deny this? Then do you deny that man is made in the image of God. You deny that he can serve him. You destroy the paternal relation of the Godhead, you blot out a brighter sun than that which rules these visible heavens. If God is to be served it must be by a free choice; by a free choice it must be if his service is to be rejected. Other service would do him no honor, other rejection would involve no guilt. Feeble as man is, and we admit his feebleness; limited as he is, and we admit the limitation, it has yet pleased God to endow him with the prerogative of choosing or rejecting Him and his service. Therefore do I call upon you, every one of you, to choose this day whom you will serve. I call upon you to choose God, the God in whom you live and move and have your being, the God who has made you, and redeemed you, and would sanctify you. Him I call upon you to choose and to serve as that service is revealed in the Gospel of his Son. " If the Lord be God, follow Him, and if Baal, then follow him."

Choice and *service*—these were demanded of the Israelites, these are demanded of you; these only. Choice and service—in these are the whole of life, and heeding practically the characteristics belonging to each, your life must be a success.

To choice belongs wisdom. Here, indeed, and in the choice of ends rather than of means, is the chief sphere of wisdom. The whole of wisdom is the choice and pursuit of the best ends by the best methods and means. But in the choice of methods and means to secure their ends " the children of this world are often wiser in their generation than the children of light." The difference is in their choice of ends. The ends of the children of this world are madness, and this, in the eye and language of the Bible, stamps them as fools.

But while wisdom belongs to choice, to service belong energy and firmness tempered by skill. You will be careful here not to mistake for energy a prevalent reckless and boastful tendency to " go ahead," or for firmness, a dogged obstinacy without candor. Indiscriminate antagonism is easy. Denunciation, indignant or sarcastic, coarse denunciation mistaking elegance for sin, is easy. By these a reputation as a reformer may be cheaply gained. But to be energetic and firm where principle demands it, and tolerant in all else, is not easy. It is not easy to abhor wickedness and oppose it with every energy, and at the same time to have the meekness and gentleness of Christ, becoming all things to all men for the truth's sake. The energy of patience, the most godlike of all, is not easy.

But while energy is to be tempered, it must still be *energy*, and, service being wisely chosen, failure in this is your chief danger. It is one thing to make a choice and adopt a principle, another to carry it out fully, wholly, entirely, giving it all its scope.   It is one thing to say, and to believe that "all men are born free and equal," and another to give to four millions of slaves all their rights. Here, I repeat it, is your danger.   Here it was that the Israelites failed.   Their choice was right ; their resolution was good ; they promised well, but they failed to take full possession of the promised land.   Will you fail "after the same example"?   Before you, as there was before them, there is a promised land; shall I not say there are promised lands, to be possessed ?   There is outward prosperity and honor ; there is the inward peace that comes from well-doing ; there is a country to be made united, peaceful, prosperous, free, wholly free ; there is that better time coming for which the whole world waits ; there is, above all, a promised land beyond the dark river.   All these are a promised land to you, and wait with more or less of dependence on your wisdom and energy.   They are no illusions.   Bright as any or all of them, except the first, may seem to you to-day, if you do your part, the reality will be brighter.   Always the realities of God transcend the imaginations of man.   "Eye hath not seen, nor ear heard, neither have entered into the heart of man the things that God hath prepared for them that love him."

Wisdom and energy—this is the watch-word that I would give you as you go down into the battle.   Do any of you say, we have not wisdom ?   I say to you, "If any man lack wisdom let him ask of God that giveth to all men liberally and upbraideth not, and it shall be given him." Do you say, we have not strength ?   I say to you, "Lo, He is strong," and "underneath are the everlasting arms."   Guided by his wisdom, strong in his strength, there may yet be for you struggle and suffering, the darkness and the storm. "The disciple is not above his Master." There may be weeping that shall endure for a night, but joy shall come in the morning. If the night cometh, so also the morning, "a morning without clouds," the morning of an eternal day.

XIII.

PROVIDENCE AND REVELATION.

GOD has always enforced the teachings of his word by his providence. When, however, as in these grand times in which we live, he does this signally, it becomes us "to give the more earnest heed." Especially does this become those who are just entering upon life, and who hope to control its wider and higher issues.

Among the great changes wrought within the last four years, is a wider and fuller recognition of a Divine Providence. So apt and critical have been the conjunctures throughout the war, so evident the purpose when events have lingered and when they have hastened, so convergent seeming opposites, that to very many who had been either thoughtless or skeptical, the hand of a personal God working out his high purposes through fixed laws and human agency has become visible. The mass of the people have had a growing conviction that God was dealing with this nation in a special manner, as with Israel of old, and shaping events for moral ends. Nor need it be thought strange, if, as the providence of God moves toward its consummation, the coincidence between it and his word should become more obtrusive ; if, more and more, there should be glimmerings through that veil, ere long to be lifted, which separates the visible from the invisible.

₊ JULY 30, 1865.

Hence I ask, on this occasion, the attention of this audience, and especially of the Graduating Class, to the summary by our Saviour of the second table of the Law, and to the enforcement of its teachings in our day by the Providence of God.

This summary will be found in the 22d chapter of Matthew and the 39th verse

"THOU SHALT LOVE THY NEIGHBOR AS THYSELF."

And here, with the lawyer willing to justify himself, we inquire, "And who is my neighbor?" "And Jesus answering said, A certain man went down from Jerusalem to Jericho, and fell among thieves, which stripped him of his raiment and wounded him, and departed leaving him half dead. And by chance there came down a certain priest that way ; and when he saw him he passed by on the other side. And likewise a Levite, when he was at the place, came and looked on him, and passed by on the other side. But a certain Samaritan as he journeyed came where he was, and when he saw him he had compassion on him, and went to him, and bound up his wounds, pouring in oil and wine, and set him on his own beast, and brought him to an inn and took care of him. And on the morrow, when he departed, he took out two pence and gave them to the host, and said unto him, Take care of him, and whatsoever thou spendest more, when I come again I will repay thee. Which now of these three, thinkest thou, was neighbor unto him that fell among the thieves ? And he said, he that showed mercy on him. Then said Jesus unto him, Go, and do thou likewise." The Samaritan is thy neighbor—the man with whom "the Jews had no dealings." The man of all others on the face of the earth farthest removed from you by national and religious prejudice is thy neighbor. In principle, and for us, the answer of

Christ is, that whoever, without regard to nation, or race, or color, or even to character, shares our common humanity, and can be reached by our sympathies and kind offices, is our neighbor.

Of this neighborhood the basis is to be found, not simply in a community of nature, but of *such* a nature. The key-note of the teachings of the Bible in regard to man, and of God's dealings with him, is to be found in the account of his creation. "So God created man in his own image, in the image of God created he him." Hence it is that this world is furnished and adorned as for a child. Hence the sacredness of human life, so early proclaimed : "Whoso sheddeth man's blood, by man shall his blood be shed ; *for in the image of God created he him.*" Hence brotherhood in Christ, and a common heirship with him of God. Hence the worth of that nature which makes rational love possible, and so furnishes a ground for the command of the text.

Seeing thus who our neighbor is, and the ground of the command of the text, we next inquire what is implied in, and what is meant by, loving our neighbor as ourselves.

I observe, then, that in loving our neighbor as ourselves, it is implied that we do and should love ourselves. Some seem to think it wrong to love ourselves. Not so the Bible. That gives the formula of human duty precisely right. "Thou shalt love the Lord thy God with all thy heart, and thy neighbor as thyself." This takes it for granted that we are to love ourselves, and that this love is to be the measure of our love to others. This is indeed the only possible starting point ; for if we had not in ourselves some consciousness of the worth of being as our own, we could have no regard for it in others, and so no rational love.

So much is implied in this love. What is meant ? Not

natural affection. The difference between natural and moral affection is that the one does not, and the other does, involve the element of a free and rational choice. Moral affection has its basis in a free and rational choice, and without such choice it cannot be. We love ourselves, according to the command of the text, when we choose for ourselves the end for which God made us, and are willing to sacrifice all things, even life, for its attainment. We also love others as ourselves when we choose for them the end for which God made them, and are willing, according to the spirit of Christ, and of martyrs and missionaries, to lay down our lives that they may attain that end.

Of this love the demand is not, as some say, simply to give others their rights. It is that, that first, but also more. It is in the family, self-sacrificing kindness ; in the State it is patriotism; in the world it is philanthropy, and in the church it is missionary zeal.

This law of God is styled in the Scriptures "the royal law." It is so. As a law for the regulation of society it is perfect ; that is, from its observance, and from that only, a perfect state of society would result. Let all the members of society be controlled by this law, and *co-operation* would take the place of *competition*. This would revolutionize society. There could be no intentional injury, and there would be a full and hearty co-operation by each for the welfare of all. Evils there might be from other sources, physical evils, but there is no institution, or form of government, or arrangement of political economy favorable to society that would not spring, as by a divine instinct and without effort, from such a love, and through it reach its highest efficiency. The reason of this is that love is wisdom. Always, love is wisdom and selfishness is folly. Practically, therefore, it is the same whether men are governed by wisdom or by love. Hence,

in all governmental and social arrangements, and in political economy, wisdom will consist in establishing and
sustaining those forms of government, those institutions
and methods of exchange with which love would most
naturally clothe itself, and through which it could best
work. Not that the form without the spirit can avail
anything. All history shows that it cannot. Nor, on
the other hand, that any form where the spirit is, is to be
blindly and rabidly attacked ; but as the spirit is invisible
and intangible, the struggle must be for forms. The long
battle for freedom, which is only another name for
society organized in the spirit of the text, has been for
its forms. And so it must be. The outward contest
must be for forms ; the thing needed is forms moulded
and vitalized by the spirit.

But to this spirit of love, thus beneficent, there is an
opposite. It is the spirit of selfishness, becoming when
opposed, domination and hate. Protean and pervasive,
this spirit has been everywhere ; but its great organic and
permanent forms of manifestation have been three :

In connection with government, it has shown itself as
despotism.

In connection with industry and social relations, as
caste ; and

In connection with races, as a *general antagonism.*

In connection with each of these, or with them in combination, this spirit has entrenched itself, it would almost
seem, impregnably. Availing itself of the necessity of
government and of labor, it has divided society into
permanent strata ; with surprising art it has balanced the
interests of class against class, and denying the possibility
of either government or industry under free forms, it has
for the most part, ruled the world. The people it has
despised and refused to trust because of their ignorance

and vice, and it has kept them in ignorance and vice lest they should become worthy of being respected and trusted.

Now what we claim is, that God has, in our day, by his providence, signally rebuked this spirit in each of its great organic forms. We claim that he has set the seal of his approbation to free forms of government and of social organization ; that he has vindicated the claims of simple humanity, and justified to its utmost limit the broad interpretation given by our Saviour to the word " neighbor."

First, then, we say that God has by his providence, not incidentally, but distinctly and signally, as with forecast and method and by a prearranged test, set the seal of his approbation to that free form of government, which, as giving men all their rights, is the natural outgrowth of the spirit of the text. Evidently he has been repeating, on a larger scale and under new conditions, the experiment that was tried and failed three thousand years ago. God then established for the Israelites a free commonwealth. Under himself this was a government by the people, for the people. When they desired a king, he regarded it as a rejection of himself, and foretold the servitude that would follow. "They have not," said he to Samuel, "rejected thee, but they have rejected me, that I should not reign over them." A commonwealth is virtually the reign of God, because it is possible only as the laws of God are voluntarily accepted up to that point which will give it stability. But the people were unfit for freedom. Servitude followed, and from that time till this freedom has been militant. It has been regarded askance, and persecuted as opposed to Law and Order. Law and Order ! Names venerable and sacred ! Ordained of God ! and yet of no avail except as guards and channels of a rational freedom.

For such a freedom—a freedom not to do wrong, but to enjoy every right—there was no congenial home in the old world. Kingcraft, priestcraft, feudalism, caste, had everywhere entwined their roots, and no garden of freedom could be planted where offshoots from these were not ready to spring up. Then it was that God lifted this western continent above the horizon, and brought hither those whose central idea was a religious commonwealth. To that movement, having its remote origin in Judea, but for us in the Mayflower, attention was more and more drawn, because it came to be felt that the experiment of liberty for the world was to be made here. If not here, where ? Here it had a fair beginning. Here was a free Christianity. The complications and impediments of the old world had been left behind. If men could not have here a government of the people strong enough for security and not too strong for liberty, where could they ? Then came the long colonial probation, the Revolution, the Union. This seemed a success, but till the rebellion, neither we, nor those across the water who wished us well, nor those who feared and hated us, had ceased to call our government an experiment. It was that,—made so mainly through malign influences, which, it did seem, need not have come in, but which were in and had to be accepted.

If now it had been the purpose of God to apply, at this juncture, a decisive test to our government, I ask whether one more perfect could have been conceived. Is there an element of stress and pressure that could be brought to bear on any government that was not brought to bear upon ours. Confessedly there was a stress upon it which no other government could have borne. Upon a people, all whose habits and interests and tastes were those of peace, there was suddenly sprung a war, and not merely that, but a civil war, and one unprecedented in its gigantic proportions. Then, at a moment, and under circumstances of the greatest disadvantage, came the call for men, and they went. It came for more, and more, "six hundred thousand more;" and the men were ready. Next, and to a people always charged with loving money overmuch, came the call for money ; and the money was ready. Taxes came in new forms, but not only were they paid, the people were clamorous for them. Money was poured out like water, and as never before, for bounties, as a loan to the government, for the Sanitary and Christian Commissions, for the refugees and the freedmen. Meantime battles were disastrous; faint-heartedness and even treason were not wanting at the North ; our English friends pronounced our cause hopeless, and did what they could to make it so ; homes were desolated ; the wounded and maimed walked our streets, and the sickening wail of exposure and starvation came up from Southern prisons. In the midst of all this came a new and unheard-of trial—the popular election of a chief-magistrate by a great nation in time of civil war. How solemn, how grand, how quiet, how decisive was that day ! It was the noblest triumph of the war—its turning-point— the turning-point in the destiny of the country. Then came that second Inaugural, and the final campaign. After four years of hope deferred, President Lincoln walked the streets of Richmond, and the old flag was replaced upon Sumter.

And was not this enough ? No. The very day that flag was raised, the Head of the nation, beloved, revered, trusted, rested on in that critical moment of transition, was smitten down by assassination. This was the final trial. Was a greater possible ? In most nations such an event would have been the signal for convulsions, if not for a revolution. Here, with the exception of the universal grief and indignation, everything went on as usual. The government did not reel for a moment. No interest received a shock. Vast as was the country, heterogeneous as was the population, yet so organized and compacted had the institutions of freedom become that no one man could be essential to them. The world had seen nothing like this. The experiment of freedom was made; it was an experiment no longer.

We now pass to caste, or permanent classes, the second organic form in which the spirit opposed to that of the text has shown itself.

The spirit of the text requires that every man shall be regarded for what he is as a man, and that no one shall be debarred by artificial and arbitrary arrangements from any employment or position. But in some countries, as in India, besides a permanent governing class, society has been so organized with reference to all occupations as to hold the laboring classes in complete subjection for ages. In most countries in Europe, and particularly in England, much of this runs through the structure of society. This, free institutions cannot allow in form, but the spirit of it lingered in our society, and was fast becoming a ruling element at the South. Moreover there grow up in artificial society distinctions from wealth, culture, manners, conventionalism, that by an infusion of the same spirit, interfere with a broad and fair recognition of simple manhood in whatever form it may appear. It was to correct this narrowing tendency and give humanity as such its true place, that Christ came as he did, clothed with that only. He was "found" simply "in fashion as *man*"; and that fact has done, and will do, more to break up this spirit than all things else.

Not a little had this spirit to do with fostering the rebellion, both at the South and at the North. That word "mudsills" meant much. If Abraham Lincoln was not one of these, he had been. Humble in his origin, in his early occupations, associations and advantages, he was ungainly in person, awkward in manners, and homely in speech. He had no elegance of literature, no foreign travel, no arts of diplomacy, no drawing-room accomplishments. If there was ever a man who came up out of the soil and had the odor of it, it was he. He had nothing splendid or striking about him, and it was especially said that he lacked the heroic element. Unspeakable was the contempt with which he was regarded in aristocratic and fashionable circles. There were whole classes at the South, and many individuals at the North, who could not abide institutions that could bring such a man into such a position. Their taste was outraged. He would disgrace us in the eyes of those who had seen foreign courts.

How, now, might this narrow and supercilious spirit be providentially and most effectively rebuked? How could it be but by taking just such a man, and despite these imperfections and disadvantages, which we confess and proclaim them to be, by lifting him up into our political heavens, revealing gradually as he should rise an orb of manhood so grand and so bright that these spots should disappear, and till he should take his place in the hearts of his countrymen and in the eyes of the world by the side of Washington himself? This has been done. Made President of the United States at the most critical period of our history, by his thorough honesty, by his singleness of purpose to uphold the Constitution and save the Union, by a common sense that became to him an instinct of statesmanship, by the even balance of his conservative and progressive tendencies, caution predominating; by his firmness in holding his positions when he made those grand steps onward ; by the simplicity of his character, free from all affectation and pretence and egotism ; by the fitness and weight of his words on great occasions ; by his gentleness and tenderness ; by his reverent recognition of God and of Christianity, he won his way to the hearts of the people as no other man had.　On his second nomination the old feeling lingered.　Many opposed him.　More would have done so if they could with hope.　But the instinct of the people was right.　Widows and mothers blessed him.　Three millions of people hailed him as their emancipator.　The nation trusted him wholly.　They rested on him as with a filial feeling, and when he died the continent from the Atlantic to the Pacific was draped in such a mourning as the sun had never looked down upon. The lesson of such an elevation, and the elements of just such a character, were needed in the new life of the nation. Henceforth his character will blend with that of Washington in its moulding influence on the times to come.

Nor in all this do we see anything that could lead us to undervalue culture, or that would encourage any manifestation of coarseness.　Abraham Lincoln had nothing of this.　We see simply the diffusive power of culture under free institutions, opening up to the humblest, avenues to distinction ; and an assertion of the paramount worth of those sterling qualities that belong to a true manhood as compared with all that is artificial and adventitious.　This paramount worth it is that God has providentially vindicated, together with the right of all who possess it to means for its increase and a fair opportunity for its recognition.

We next consider the third form in which the spirit opposed to that of the text has manifested itself.　This has been in connection with races.

The division of men of the same race into permanent governing and laboring classes is artificial and horizontal ; the division into races is natural and vertical. How far, or whether at all, such a division should be a bar to inter-marriage, or to any form of social intercourse, does not now concern us. Other races are our neighbor, and no less than our own, are to be loved as ourselves. We are bound to give them every right, and to seek their good. But instead of this, difference of race has been the occasion of prejudice, contempt, oppression, and of the most bitter and long-continued hostilities. But for this the English and French would not have been called natu-ral enemies. But for this the nationalities of Europe might coalesce. The great wars have been those of races.

In this country we had made, in this, a great step on-ward. Not only all religions, but, with a single exception, all nationalities and races were received on an equal foot-ing. But that exception was so flagrant, and so opposed to our avowed principles, as to draw to it universal atten-tion. Nor was race alone in question. There was color ; and both were combined with caste intensified into the form of chattel slavery. Here, then, was a fortress with a triple line of defence. The institution, too, had prestige as transmitted. It was so incorporated with the industry and supposed interests of the South ; was so allied to the spirit of caste both abroad and at the North ; was so supported by prejudice and pride and indolence ; was so an element of politics, and so claimed by the churches as a divine institution, that its removal seemed hopeless. Ah! if the rights of the black man had never been violated, how simple the problems of our society would have been. If, having been violated, we had heeded the law of the text, how facile and bloodless the remedy !

But no ; there stood the fortress growing more and more defiant and insolent.

But if the hand of God had been unmistakable in rebuking the spirit opposed to that of the text in the forms already mentioned, it has been still more so in this. Not more conspicuous was it in leading the children of Israel out of Egypt. The destruction of slavery within four years is a moral miracle. Many present will remember when the first haze from this sea of death began to spread itself in our political sky, and how from that time the heavens continued to grow darker. Compromise availed nothing. Attempted suppression of petitions and of discussion availed nothing. The negro was passive, quietly at work among the rice and the cotton, the sugar and the tobacco, but he was everywhere. You all remember how inevitable he became. Was there a political or ecclesiastical convention anywhere from Maine to Texas, he was there. No threats and no coaxing could keep him out. He was in every railroad car and steamboat, and barroom. Were two excited men talking at the corner of the street, you might be sure he was there. It was he that put the President in the White House, and the Speaker of the House of Representatives in his chair. He unsettled ministers, broke up churches, perplexed the action of religious societies, and rent asunder great denominations of Christians. He was in the struggles of Kansas, and when ruffianism and treason showed themselves in the Senate Chamber he was not far off.

Then came the first gun, the great uprising, the tramp of armed men, the 19th of April, the *War*. Nobody wanted it, everybody dreaded it, but majestic, resistless, as when God flings out the banner of the storm and bids it move, it swept on. No man guided it, no man could foretell its duration or issues. So tumultuous and perplexed were the movements, that the avowed and wise policy of the President was to have no policy, but simply an end sought as wisdom might be given moment by moment. It came to that, that all that men knew was that there was nothing to do but to fight on. And they did fight. And Oh! the agony of those days! "We waited for light, but behold obscurity; for brightness, but we walked in darkness." We cried out, "O, thou sword of the Lord, how long will it be ere thou be quiet; put thyself up into thy scabbard, rest and be still." But the voice came, "How can it be quiet seeing the Lord hath given it a charge?" And what that charge was, those who watched began after a time to discover. It was, first, to lift the negro up into manhood by bringing him into line with the white man in fighting the battles of freedom. We all know how this was resisted and scoffed at. It could not be. But the pressure did not lift; it waxed heavier and heavier and it was done. The negro fought and was welcomed. A second charge was to make the Proclamation of Emancipation, ridiculed as the Pope's bull against the comet, to make that as the breath of the Almighty to sweep away slavery. That was done. Again, the charge was to bring the South, the chivalry, to recognize by public act the manhood of the negro by making him a soldier, and by confessing the dependence of their cause upon him. This was all; it was enough. When this was done, the war ceased.

And now, I put it to you, if the antagonism of races, intensified by caste and by color, was to be providentially rebuked, could it have been done more signally or more effectually?

Of the three forms of providential testimony now presented, each is distinct and emphatic. There is another, and carried out too with the same completeness. Slavery may stand as the type and culmination of all oppressive systems, and the testimony consists in a manifestation of its legitimate and matured fruits.

Till our armies went South, and Southern prisoners came North, there was but a slight impression among us of the general ignorance under such a system—of the number who could not read or sign their names. But for this ignorance there could have been no rebellion. There had been no adequate conception of the want of thrift and general behindhandedness, nor of the pervading spirit, at once of license and of despotism. What were called the abuses of the system were more frequent and foul than had been supposed. But these are little, compared with the spirit of the system as revealed, First, by atrocities in the treatment of Southern Union men, not exceeded by anything in the Sepoy rebellion ; second, by the massacre at Fort Pillow, intended to be the inauguration of a policy; third, by preparations to blow up Libby prison ; fourth, by the deliberate, systematic, long continued exposure, neglect and starvation of Union prisoners ; and finally, by the assassination of the President. These things we do not charge to all the people of the South. They are like other men. Many are better than their system. But we do charge them to the spirit of the system ; and we say that by these exposures and revelations, culminating as they did in a way to send a thrill of horror through the civilized world, God has pilloried the system before the nations, and all that has affinity with it.

That there were atrocities on our side we do not deny They are incident to war. But we do deny anything that can be at all an offset to such a record. It is to be said further on the part of the North that the war was carried on here chiefly without proscription, and that in connection with it there were the Sanitary and Christian Commissions, that furnished by voluntary contribution millions for the aid of wounded and sick soldiers, to be applied equally, so far as might be, to friend and foe. Any thing like these, in connection with war, no institutions or form of government had ever before developed.

I have thus presented four simultaneous processes indicating a providential testimony in favor of free institutions and of equal rights, both for all classes of the same race and for all races. If any one of these had been contrived by man for this express purpose, could it have been more elaborate, I had almost said artificial and dramatic? But when we see them combined as these have been, all bearing virtually on this one point of loving our neighbor as ourselves, and in connection with events that have so lifted them up to the gaze of the world, we cannot doubt the presence of a divine hand. It is the providence of God enforcing his word.

Possibly we may now find some explanation of the presence and condition of the negro in this land. Who has not wondered that these have been permitted? Who has not felt irritated that there should be such an obstacle to the facile working of our principles and institutions? But in no other way could the broad requisitions of the gospel have been so interpreted to us, and so enforced upon us. Race, color, caste, interest—all were needed for the fullest possible test of those requisitions. The negro in Africa it would have been an easy thing to love as ourselves. But to take him by the hand here, and lift him up into the enjoyment in all respects of equal rights with ourselves is quite another thing. This we were not prepared to do, and it was needful that this very race, the farthest of all removed from us in physical, and if you please, in mental characteristics, should so become passively an obstruction and a clog in the working of our political and ecclesiastical machinery, as to compel us to see the difference between an abstract profession of principles and their practical application. We needed to learn what that meaneth, " I will have mercy and not sacrifice," and to be made to know how *any* failure to carry out the principle of the text must work its own retribution. May the future show that this nation has learned the lesson thus taught of God. If not, we may be sure that retribution will come.

In view of the providences above-mentioned as bearing on the text, let me inquire of you, my Dear Friends of the Graduating Class, whether the second table of the law has its true relative place in your minds. Has it in the mind of the religious public of this land ? That place it has not always had. There has been a one-sided piety. Duties toward God have been emphasized while those towards men have been slighted. There has been something calling itself piety that has been dissociated, not merely from beneficence, but from kindliness and honor, and a high morality. Of all caricatures of the religion of Christ none is more repulsive than a combination of high pretension to piety with a narrowness and meanness bordering on dishonesty. From such a type of piety the natural recoil has been to mere philanthropy. This, if less repulsive, is hardly less mischievous. Having no root in the love of God, it runs into sentimentalism and self-seeking and even into malignity. There is nothing sourer than a soured philanthropist. The second table of the law has no power without the first. That must stand in its grand pre-eminence. Its summary is, and must be, " the first and great commandment." But the second is like unto it, and every failure to carry out its principles fully, is a failure in one of the highest forms of a rational piety.

Let me, then, especially commend to you at this time the love of your fellow-men. Take for your motto, LOVE IS WISDOM. Always love is wisdom. Rational love is the central, plastic, unconsciously organizing and adjusting force of a rational society, as natural law and instinct are of the inanimate and animal creation. Hold on, I entreat you, to this. Abide steadfast in it, and you shall be the men needed for these times. You shall work with the providence of God.

It has, my friends, been one result of our studies the past year to bring the teachings of the human constitution into harmony with the revealed law of God. To-day I close my instructions to you by seeking to show you the harmony of the Providence of God with the second table of that law. In their relations to the well-being of the individual, and of society, the two tables are very different. For the individual, the great good must be from conformity to the first table, that is, from love to God. That fits us for heaven. But for the community, that good must be from conformity to the second table, that is, from love to man. Whether God providentially favors piety, as such, may be doubted. It was, in the time of Job, and has been since. But in giving men rights he has pledged himself to favor those forms of society in which such rights are conceded. This he does in the long lines of his providence, because natural rights tend to their own vindication and enjoyment with the constancy of natural law, and till they are conceded society cannot be in a state of stable equilibrium. Whatever may be said of the first table of the law, I hold it to be demonstrable that the second table is the only law of a stable society. It is radical. There is in it the intensest radicalism. The very essence of it is to give to every human being his rights—*To every human being*. What more can

radicalism ask? It is also conservative. There is in it
the intensest conservatism; for to give to every one his rights
is the work of righteousness, and " The work of righteousness is peace, and the effect of righteousness, quietness and
assurance forever." When society shall be established on
a right basis, and every man shall have his rights, conservatism will be the true doctrine, or rather radicalism and
conservatism will be identified. Then, too, in the peace
and prosperity that shall follow, will be found a perfect
coincidence between the word and the providence of God.
Of that coincidence do not you doubt. Labor for it. It
must come. God is *not* on the side of the strongest battalions. He is on the side of the oppressed. The rights
that he has given he will vindicate.

This coincidence of Providence with Revelation, is
the great lesson of history read in the world's unrest.
That is the long, silent protest of God against the violation
of his fundamental social law. It is more distinct and
emphatic now than in former times. The march of Providence is slow. Its early lessons are dim. There is no
convergence. But the times in which we live feel the
quickening impulse of an approaching consummation.
Events converge and hasten. Mighty physical agencies
are wheeled into line ; ocean depths are a highway for
thought ; providences reveal a divine hand ; a deeper
sense both of rights and of responsibilities is leavening the
masses ; the thunderstorm of a war has cleared the moral
atmosphere ; slavery is swept away as by the breath of
God ; " God is marching on." Fall in, my friends, fall
in !

It is to do this, to work with and for God, that you go
from us. You go with our prayers and blessing. For me
it has been a great satisfaction to tread with you some of
the highest fields of thought. The truths we have reached,

and the spirit of our studies, will abide with you.   Nor
will the bond between us, formed by communion in those
truths, and not by that alone, be soon sundered.   But
now, we part.   The staff is in your own hands.   Before
you is the upward and limitless way.   Move on.

The four years of your college course have been
almost synchronous with those of the war.   All honor to
the six of your present number, to the fourteen in all, who
have taken a part in this.   Of these, one was killed in
battle, one died at Andersonville, one in camp of fever,
and two were wounded.   These years have opened a new
era to the country and to the world.   As years of solemn
feeling and of deep excitement in regard to great principles
they should have toned you up—I trust they have—to a
deeper sense of responsibility, to greater earnestness, to a
higher manhood.   All these you will need, for into your
keeping will go these institutions that have been bought
with so much of blood and treasure, and woe to you if you
do not do your part in carrying on to its completion that
which has been so grandly begun.   Such a trust no
preceding generation has ever received.

Nor has the excitement and solemn feeling during
your course respected solely human government and the
interests of time.   Your attention has also been drawn
to the great principles of the divine government, and
to their bearing upon you as the subjects of a spiritual and
an eternal kingdom.   In view of these, many of you have
professed to enter upon that nobler warfare of all time, for
the establishment, universally and forever, of the principles
of freedom and of righteousness.   This is the true arena of
human labor and conflict.   Into this I welcome you.
Into this the church of God welcomes you.   She needs
standard bearers.   Upon what you shall do in this arena,
a great cloud of witnesses will look down.   " Run, then,

with patience, the race that is set before you, looking
unto Jesus ;' and when the goal shall be reached, may
each one of you, " crowned with victory," be permitted, at
his feet,. to " lay your laurels down."

XIV.

THE BIBLE AND PANTHEISM.

Behold I stand at the door and knock ; if any man hear my voice and open the door, I will come in to him and will sup with him, and he with me.—Revelation, iii. 20.

EVERYTHING which God has made he treats according to the nature he has given it. Willing it to be, he respects its essential attributes, and concedes to it its own sphere. This he must do or each thing would either cease to be, or to be that thing. Take the smallest particle of matter. It enters into the conception and definition of this that it occupies space. This prerogative it must assert and vindicate to itself or cease to be. A crystal ground to powder would cease to be a crystal, and in thus grinding it its nature as a crystal would be wholly ignored.

But in governing matter God does not thus ignore any essential property. All physical problems he works out under physical conditions, and it would be an imputation upon his wisdom to suppose that mere omnipotence must be called in to break down those conditions in order to the successful working of such problems. It belongs to our conception of the divine perfection that God should be able to govern his physical universe in accordance with the properties which he has himself bestowed. Accordingly, if we ascertain the essential properties of any material thing with which God begins to deal, we shall find that it will be through those properties, and not by ignoring or destroying them, that he will work out his purposes.

₄ JULY 29, 1866.

And what is thus true of matter that has properties, is also true of persons that have will and freedom and rights. Here the problems are higher. Grand and complex as are the problems connected with matter, taking hold as they do on infinity and eternity, unsolved, and apparently unsolvable by science, they are as nothing compared with those that arise in the government of beings conscious, free and responsible. And if, in solving physical problems God always works under the physical conditions implied in the nature he has given, we may be sure that in solving moral problems he will not disregard any right, nor trench on any original endowment or prerogative on which such right is based. We may be sure that here too his purposes will be wrought out through the fullest exercise of those very prerogatives and endowments in which the problems originated.

Does God then govern man as responsible? Is responsibility the one element without which moral government could not be? Then we have only to ascertain what the conditions of responsibility are, and we may be sure that they will be held inviolate by Him.

And here we say that the one condition of responsibility is the power of rational choice. I do not say freedom, because that is ambiguous. Freedom is a condition, but that is involved in this power of choice. This is the central power in our personality, the point of moral responsibility. In this, all processes of the soul that precede it and pass into outward activity culminate. All that precedes this is spontaneous, irresponsible, subjective. All that succeeds this is but its projection into outward act, and its being mirrored there. In a true life, in all moral life as God sees it, the outward act is but the reflection and image of the inward choice. Without this power we cannot conceive that a moral nature should be brought into activity. We may, and must be constantly affected by events, as the rising of the sun, that have no relation to our choice, but we cannot feel responsible for them ; and if God begins to govern us as responsible, we should, as has been said, anticipate with certainty that no crisis or emergency could arise in which he would not hold every condition of responsibility sacred. The point of harmony between the divine omnipotence and the divine wisdom is that the omnipotence creates the conditions of every problem, physical and moral, and that the wisdom works within and under those conditions.

Under human government each man has his own sphere to which he has a right. It is a maxim of English law that a man's house is his castle. Within this nor curiosity, nor caprice, nor malice may intrude. Unless in the interest of the state, and armed with the authority of law, no one may enter unbidden. This is his home, it is his own. Bating crime, he has a right to do in it as he pleases. He has a right to its exclusion and privacy, and if any one would enter, he must stand at the door and knock.

And so under divine government, there is a deeper and more intimate sphere of the thoughts and affections and sympathies and choices. This is the true sanctuary of our nature, where are celebrated the nuptials of the soul with its chosen good, and which is known only to the man himself and to God. Into this even God himself does not come except with freest consent. When he would enter here, he does not merge the attributes of the Moral Governor in those of the Creator and Proprietor, but respecting the constitution he has given, he says, " Behold I stand at the door and knock : if any man hear my voice, and open the door, I will come in to him, and will sup with him, and he with me."

What then have we here ? Have we not a prerogative that makes man independent of God ? So it seems to

some, and hence they hesitate to claim for it the entireness implied. Let us then inquire after those limitations
and conditions by which this prerogative is harmonized
with divine government.

And first. The power of choice is limited by endowments and capacities. A brute cannot choose between
books, or statues, or pictures, or steam-engines, because
it has no capacity to know them as such. A man cannot
choose between walking and flying. One born blind cannot choose between sight and touch. But capacities and
endowments, both in kind and degree, are wholly in the
hand of God.

Again, with given capacities there is a limitation to
choice in the objects presented. These as adapted to
man, it was for God to create or not as it pleased him.
In providing for physical wants and gratifications he might
have held forever the orange and the melon and the peach
in his creative capacity. The present variety is solely of
his goodness. And so the objects and range of the desires
and affections were provided and meted out by him. For
the race, and on the whole, God may have created objects
suited to meet every want, and to draw out every capacity. No doubt he has, but the limitation of choice through
the objects presented is specially noticeable in his dealings with individuals. From birth, sex, education, health,
the structure of society, the objects within the scope of
individual choice are greatly limited and infinitely diversified. The objects of desire are numberless, of choice but
few, Who of us has had it presented to his choice whether
he would be President of the United States, or be worth a
million of dollars? Capacities and opportunities seem
thrown together promiscuously. Capacity often lacks opportunity, opportunity waits for capacity. All this God
orders as seemeth him good. In this is much of his pro-

6*

vidential discipline, and through it his creatures are governed.

Again, choice is limited not only by capacity and the objects presented, but also by the time within which they are presented. Sometimes the time is long. "The long-suffering of God waited in the days of Noah," a hundred and twenty years. Sometimes the opportunity is given but for one bright moment and passes forever. In the history of every life and in relation to every interest, there are periods within which the choice must be made on which those interests turn. There comes a last and decisive moment. After that the offer is withdrawn ; the door is shut ; the harvest is past ; the opportunity is gone, and will return no more. This element of time God holds in his sovereign hand, abbreviating or extending as he pleases the period of choice.

Capacities, objects, time—controlling these God hedges choice within certain limits. Still, if we admit of plenary freedom within those limits, it may be said that we have an element if not irreducible under the divine government, yet capable of so setting itself against the will of God that that will shall not be done. And so we have; and the will of God is not done. If that will were done, there would be no sin ; if that will were done, why did our Saviour command us to pray that it might be done ? It is the one great characteristic of this world, controlling all its moral and physical phenomena, that the will of God is not done in it. For what did Christ come, for what do his ministers labor, and the church pray, and the Holy Spirit strive, but that the will of God may be done ? No, my hearers, the will of God is not done.

But if not, how is he omnipotent? Is it not said that "he doeth according to his will in the army of heaven, and among the inhabitants of the earth"? Here we need the distinction, made on a former occasion, between choice and volition, or between will as choice and will as volition. The choice of God is free, his volition is omnipotent. As volition, the will of God is always done, as choice it is not His choice is indicated by his commands. If these do not indicate choice there is no meaning in words, there is no sincerity in God. The opposite doctrine would be monstrous. No man will dare to say that there is not indicated by his commands a choice of God which the Bible calls will. But choice in itself, or as expressed in command, has no efficiency. It abides in the mind choosing, and a choice in the mind of God has no more efficiency beyond himself than a choice in any other mind. The choice of man, followed by his volition, originates that future for which he is responsible ; and the choice of God, followed by his volition, and only then, originates that future for which, so far as we may apply the term to Him, He is responsible. Omnipotence pertains to the volition of God, freedom to his choice. To the volition of man, omnipotence does not pertain, but to his choice freedom does. Omnipotence may create a being with the power of rational choice, and fix the conditions under which choice may be made ; but it must then stand in abeyance while that being is governed by laws to which omnipotence has no relation. It is not implied in an infinite attribute that it can perform contradictions. Omniscience cannot know the number of square feet in infinite space. Omnipotence cannot give solidity to thought or to time. By definition where a hill is, a valley cannot be ; and so, where omnipotent will is exerted as volition, finite choice cannot be. If we make the ocean fluid by definition, then God cannot govern it by congealing it into ice by his omnipotence, for it would no longer be the ocean. And he does not so govern it. No. He respects that condition of fluidity by which it is the ocean. He permits it to heave and toss, and assay its utmost; he lets its billows assault the heavens, and wreck navies, and thunder upon the shore; and it is then, at the very moment when the tempest is wildest, and those billows are mightiest that he says, " hitherto shalt thou come but no farther, and here shall thy proud waves be stayed." And so, respecting perfectly that power of rational choice which makes him man, does He govern man. "*He stilleth the noise of the seas, and the tumult of the people.*" It is the glory of his government, not that this earth and these heavens are marshalled by omnipotence in an order that is faultless, but that he so governs a universe of free intelligences without trenching upon their freedom, that the glory of the physical heavens shall be as nothing compared with that moral glory which shall illustrate forever in results of unspeakable beauty and joy, his wisdom, his justice and his grace.

But can such results be reached by God through the choice of his creatures with no control by him except through the above limitations? No. Whatever may have been true originally, we fail to reach through these limitations, a full conception of the dependence of a *sinner* upon God.

As a sinner, man must be wholly dependent upon God for forgiveness. Forgiveness is God's act, and must rest with him. Grace must be free, or it would not be grace, and as free, it must be sovereign.

As a sinner *dead in trespasses and sins*, man must also be dependent on God for quickening. His death is not one of mere negation requiring omnipotence to originate a new mode of being, but a death of chosen and intense activity in trespassing and sinning. So intense is this death, so absorbing the activity in it, that left to itself it would go on forever. Hence the necessity of positive interposition

on the part of God, and, in connection with that, of the
doctrines of grace. Hence the necessity that Christ should
stand at the door and knock.

What then is this knocking? In its broadest sense it
consists of every influence that addresses man's higher nature and tends to bring him into right relations to God.
Christianity is a great redemptive and remedial system.
Under it not only is a way of salvation opened for those who
may, of their own accord, choose to enter, but there is also
provided a system of means and influences to bring men to
enter into that way. It is, indeed, for this that the world
stands. The end of this world is not, as some seem to
think, progress—the boasted and hackneyed progress of
this age—progress, and an ultimate state of high civilization, or even of millennial perfection and glory for that
portion of the race that may then live. No. Christianity respects the whole race with its myriads from the beginning, and its object is to bring together in one permanent community, and with surroundings corresponding with
their moral character, all who have affinity with each other
through the love of God. To this end God weaves the
bright lines of his beneficence into the web of his providence. Suffering all nations to walk in their own ways, he
yet does not leave himself without witness in that he does
good and gives them rain from heaven and fruitful seasons,
filling their hearts with food and gladness. To this end he
revealed himself to patriarchs and prophets. To this end
Christ came, and taught, and suffered, and died, and rose
again. To this end the Holy Spirit, in his powerful and
special influences, is given. And now, throughout this
whole system, whether under what is called providence or
grace, whatever ought to appeal to the moral nature of
man, and, with his co-operation, would lead or fit him to
be a member of the great family of God, is God's voice, as,

in the person of Christ, and under a mediatorial system, he stands at the door of man's heart and knocks.

In the call implied in this knocking two things are required, just those that respect the two great crises in the spiritual history of every Christian. One is that he should hear the voice of the Saviour; the other that he should open the door.

For the most part men are engrossed in the things of time. So intense and exclusive is their devotion to them that their insensibility to the things of the Spirit is, as I have said, characterized by inspiration as death. Seeing they see not, and hearing they hear not. Now it is an era in any life when this engrossment and limitation of thought are broken up and the powers of the world to come assert their claims. Before, the man saw only the river on which he seemed to be sailing; now he sees the ocean, and feels the ground-swell of a mightier movement than that of time. Now the Saviour knocks, and hearing, he hears. He hears his voice.

And now comes the second great crisis in his spiritual history. Can he, will he open the door?

That he can in the proper sense of that word is implied in the fact that Christ knocks. If he do indeed knock, then to argue the question of ability is an impeachment of his sincerity.

But if he can, and do not choose to do it, can God so knock as to bring him thus to choose? Can God, without infringing upon the prerogatives of choice, cause all choices to be coincident with his? We think he can. The term omnipotence we do not regard as applicable here, because moral results must be reached by moral causes, and within the sphere of freedom; but yet we do not believe that God has let loose a power which is either in itself, or in its results, beyond his prevision and control.

We prefer to say that the limit of his interposition has been from the beginning, and is now, not the limit of his resources. but one imposed by his infinite wisdom.   What do we know of the possible modes of interaction between spirit and spirit?   Between the Infinite spirit and finite spirits? What do we mean by the drawings of divine love—the drawing of the Father?   What by the power of the Holy Ghost ;   These cannot be physical.   Omnipotence cannot be predicated of them, and yet, if God so please, they may be made as adequate within their sphere as omnipotence in its sphere.   God can come to his creatures, and can manifest himself to them and in them ineffably.   He can work in them " *to will* " as well as "to do," and yet such working may not be, it is not a limitation of freedom ; it is its purification and exaltation to that point where it reaches the certainty and the security of heaven.   It may be effectual, and yet of all that pertains to it God may be able to say, " Behold I stand at the door and knock."

You are entering now life at a period when the thought of the world, so far as it separates itself from the Bible, tends towards pantheism.   Modern infidelity has various names and forms, but the substance is that ; and under whatever form, it is sure to chill and dwarf man, and disintegrate society.   Of old, with the uniformities of nature unknown, and her forces unsubdued, pantheism was impossible.   The tendency then was to polytheism, and idolatry, and superstition.   But as science advanced, and that sense of uniformity which has been called the scientific instinct, prevailed, pantheism became possible.   Going in the direction opposite to polytheism, and not accepting one personal God, this is the last term which, a mind alien from God can reach, and which, without the Bible, it is sure to reach.   Polytheism, idolatry, superstition, on the one hand ; or pantheism on the other, I regard as inevit-

able for man without the direct revelation and recognition
of a personal God. Against both these the Bible guards
equally and marvellously. Its denunciations of idolatry
could not be more contemptuous and terrific ; its antagonism to pantheism and all affinity with it, could not be
more absolute. During the height and pressure of the first
tendency it was the Bible alone that preserved in the world
the knowedge of the One God, with such attributes as to
make him a worthy object of worship ; and it is the Bible
alone that now holds men back from pantheism.

Of pantheism as a system the mass of the people as
yet know nothing, and for it they care nothing ; but,
through conversation, the press, the lecture, the tendency
reaches them, coming in like a mist, and affecting, chilling, deoxydizing their whole atmosphere of thought. It
comes in two forms, with different origin, but similar result.
Beginning at the lowest point and working up, the pantheism of Natural Science is reached, which attributes all
things to principles, and laws, and to *development*. Of this
man is the highest result and expression. This is the
heathenism of science, and is just as much opposed to the
religion and God of the Bible as the polytheism of old, or
as fetichism is now. Beginning, on the other hand, with
God, and working down, a metaphysical, or theological
pantheism is reached, that, either from the difficulty of
conceiving of creation, or under the guise of exalting God,
merges all things in him. It makes God virtually the only
being, and his will the only will. But it matters little
whether you make God everything, or everything God ;
whether you destroy the freedom of something called God
in exalting man, or the freedom of man in exalting God.
In either case, instead of freedom, with responsibility, and
moral government, the majesty of a personal God, the
beauty of holiness and the joy of willing obedience, you

have a system of blind tendencies and dead uniformities; or, under the name of will, of an iron and remorseless fatalism.

Against both these you are to be guarded, against both to guard others, and both your shield and weapon will be found in that revelation which God makes of himself in Christ, and in the attitude towards man which he assumes when he says. "Behold *I*—." Ah, that word *I*, that little word! Nature does not know it. Except through man, pantheism does not know it; in its high sense fatalism does not know it; positiveism does not know it. Behold I—. Who? "Immanuel, God with us." Not from works now, not from laws, blind laws bringing all things alike to all, not by inferences do we know God; but, both condescending to our weakness, and meeting our wants, He stands before us, "God manifest in the flesh." This is the highest expression of personality which it is possible God should give. This will hold men to their moorings when nothing else could. If God has appeared "in fashion as a man" and spoken to us, to doubt his personality is no longer possible. Thus has he appeared and spoken.

And not only has he thus affirmed his own personality, but in saying, "Behold I *stand at the door and knock*," he recognizes the distinct personality of others, and all the conditions of responsibility. Everywhere the Bible asserts the distinct personality and supremacy of God; everywhere the separate agency and responsibility of man. These are the truths to be received. Settle as you please, or not at all, let others settle as they please, or not at all, the questions that grow out of a transmitted life, of an inherited nature, of the relations of spirit to matter, and of the finite to the infinite, questions about which the Bible never troubles itself at all, but hold you fast to a personal God, a Father in heaven, and to his supremacy; and also to a realm of freedom and supernatural power wide as his works, and as much grander than they as spirit is higher than matter. You cannot reconcile the two? Then let the legitimate supremacy of the practical nature assert itself, and with entire faith act on both. This must you often do in life. Often, with limited capacity, must your whole rational nature demand that you should act upon facts well authenticated, though seemingly discrepant, without waiting to reconcile them.

Finding rest then either in full comprehension, or in rational faith, with such a God above you, with a cloud of witnesses around you, with your freedom of choice respected even by omnipotent power, with the love that is in Christ taking in its higher sphere, the place of omnipotence in that which is lower, your whole nature is met. It only remains for you to choose for yourselves what guidance and companionship you will have. What I desire for you all, the one thing, is the guidance and companionship of Him who offers himself to you. "If *any man* hear my voice." You, my friends, need not, you cannot fight the battles that are before you—the battles of life, and the battles with death,—alone. It is the one great fact of our human life that its Giver and Lord offers himself to us in a form in which we can apprehend him not merely for redemption, but for help and guidance, for companionship and sympathy. In taking our nature upon him he has come near to us; having been tempted he knows how to succor us; in him "are hid," for us "all the treasures of wisdom and knowledge." And now as you look out upon life, full of interests so precious, and forward to the future life, with issues so momentous, He, the Saviour

of men, offers himself to you.   With infinite tenderness he
stands at the door of your hearts and knocks.   O, open
the door.   Open it fully.   In this is all your wisdom.
Open the door, and he will come in to you, and will sup
with you, and you with Him.

XV.

ON LIBERALITY IN RELIGIOUS BELIEF.

If there come any unto you and bring not this doctrine, receive him not in your house, neither bid him God-speed ; for he that biddeth him God-speed is partaker of his evil deeds.—2 John, 10, 11.

IS it possible that this passage was written by the beloved, and the loving Apostle John ? Is it he whose Epistles so commend and command love, who exhorts a kind-hearted woman disposed to hospitality to close her doors against men simply on account of the doctrine they bring ? Not on account of their character, or their life, but on account of their doctrine ! Yes, their doctrine ! ! How strange ! Was it that he was a Jew, and had but recently emerged from a system avowedly narrow and exclusive, and did not as yet comprehend the breadth and freedom into which Christianity was ultimately to expand ? Did the new wine of that freer and more liberal system which Christ brought, find in him an old bottle ? True, the doctrine to which he refers " was the doctrine of Christ." It involved the validity of His claims, and seemed to be in peril. " For," says he, " many deceivers are entered into the world who confess not that Jesus Christ is come in the flesh. This is a deceiver and an anti-Christ. . . . Whosoever transgresseth, and abideth not in the doctrine of Christ, hath not God. He that abideth in the doctrine of Christ, he hath both the Father and the Son." It is true, too, that the customs of society, the relations of parties, and

⁎ JULY 28, 1867.

the import of such acts were different then.   Still, making every allowance, if we judge from this passage and its connections, the Apostle John did not belong to "the broad church."

Freedom, liberality, breadth, liberal Christianity, broad church ; narrowness, illiberality, bigotry, superstition, or, to concentrate all in one word, orthodoxy,—these are the terms that we hear bandied on every side, and we would gladly know their import.

These terms are applied to men on the ground of their belief—not their belief on all subjects, but

First, as they believe less or more in the existence and agency of invisible personal beings, including God.

Secondly, As they believe less or more in the importance of religious truth.

And thirdly, As they believe in conditions of salvation that requires a life of less or greater strictness, and that thus include a smaller or larger number.

First, then, men are said to be liberal and broad as they believe little in invisible personal agency ; and to be narrow and superstitious as they believe more in such agency.

Of belief in such agency we have had, and still have, every shade from the drivelling superstition of African Fetishism to a blank atheism.   In a state of ignorance and barbarism, men attribute to personal agency many of those movements and changes in nature which, as society advances, are resolved into the operation of general laws, implying but a single agent.   The supernatural agency thus believed in is multifarious, capricious, with more of malignity than of good-will, often wholly malignant, and is made by artful men a means of terror, or subjection, and of degradation to the people.   There have been no despotisms like those based on superstition, and no lower deep of degradation than that caused by it, unless it be the degradation of a sensual and bloody infidelity caused by its rebound.

It is in this belief in the supernatural connected with fear and with irrational and debasing practices from that that we find the essence of superstition. Superstition is not, as is said by Charles Kingsley in a recent lecture on that subject, " the fear of the unknown." It is the fear of the *supernatural* in the unknown. Take away from superstition the element of the supernatural, and the residuum is simply error. To dislodge this fear as a cause of degradation to the masses, it does not appear that anything but Christianity can avail, and even that has not been able to do it fully as yet in any country. It is surprising how many superstitions still linger even in the most enlightened parts of Christendom, showing the natural and ineradicable affinity of man for the supernatural, and the certainty of a region, somewhere, and in some form, corresponding to that affinity.

But relatively, since the coming of Christ,--

> " The Oracles are dumb ;
> No voice or hideous hum
> Runs through the arched roof in words deceiving."
> " Peor and Baalim
> Forsake their temples dim."
> " Nor is Osiris seen.
> In Memphian grove or green."

Wherever the Bible is fully received, the brood of superstition is dispersed.

> " The flocking shadows pale
> Troop to the infernal jail."

Through the light and impulse given by Christianity, science has taken the place of superstition, and men have thus reached a position that has enabled them to go beyond the limits allowed by Christianity, and to repudiate that without which no such science had been possible.

In this whole movement there have been marked points of transition.   There has been the transition from heathenism to Christianity.   This involved no denial of supernatural personal agency, but a change from a belief in the "gods many and the lords many" of that system, to a belief in the one living and true God, and in the system of revelation and redemption made known in the Bible.

Then there is the transition from a belief in God as revealed in the Bible to deism.   Deism acknowledges God.   It may, or may not, believe in providence; but it knows of no revelation except through nature, and denies that personal interposition ever comes in to change her uniformities.

From deism there is a transition to pantheism, and from pantheism—though it may not be easy to see the difference—to absolute atheism.   According to either of these systems both revelation and miracles are impossible and absurd.

According to Comte, the apostle of positivism, these transitions, and the necessary steps of the human mind towards its enlargement, are from supernatural agency to metaphysical causation, and from that to positivism.   Positivism knows nothing of God.   It regards as illegitimate all investigations concerning causes, efficient or final; and would confine philosophy to a knowledge of facts and their order.

Now it is to be observed that at each of these steps those who make them, or opproximate towards them, claim that they become more liberal and broad, and look upon those they leave behind as narrow and superstitious.   If those thus left hold to their views strongly, they call them bigoted.   Those, on the other hand, who retain their position, call the party of movement latitudinarians, infidels, heretics.   These terms, whether used for commendation or reproach, thus become wholly relative.   To a believer in revelation, a deist is an infidel; to the atheist, or pantheist, he is still in trammels, limited, narrow ; and it is the atheist alone who has come out into perfect freedom and enlargement.

I have said that these terms are applied on the ground of a belief or disbelief in supernatural agency.   This is true ; but it is to be observed that when this belief is so held as to lose its hold upon the conscience and its control of conduct the intense meaning that belonged to the terms originally, especially those of reproach, is discharged.   They so fade out as to be used with indifference, or in jest, and it is practically regarded, as it really is, of little consequence what a man believes.

And this leads me to observe, in the second place, that the terms mentioned are applied to men as they believe less or more in the importance of religious truth, and so are less or more strenuous respecting it.

We here find an anomaly.   On other practical subjects men regard the truth as vital.   Truth is but an expression of the actual state of things, and if men do not act in accordance with that they fail.   Who goes to California for gold except as he is assured of the truth that gold is there ?   The Bible, too, attaches great importance to truth.   It says: " Buy the truth and sell it not."   " Contend earnestly for the faith once delivered to the saints."   It makes truth the means of sanctification : " Sanctify them through thy truth ;" It makes salvation depend on belief: " He that believeth shall be saved."   " He that believeth not shall be damned."   And yet it is not, perhaps, strange that the idea of liberality should attach itself to a light estimate of religious truth.

For what do we see ?   We see a belief in dogmas made a substitute for a Christian life,—loud profession and high orthodoxy in connection with lax and questionable moral- ity.   We see dogmas maintained with bitterness, and by means subversive of all the principles of the Gospel.   We see in most countries a belief in them connected with a settled order of things, and so with power and place.   We see how numerous and slight the points are—some of doc- trine, some of dicipline, extending even to ecclesiastical millinery—on the ground of which men divide and become hostile sects.   We see points of difference magnified, and feeling concerning them intense, as they are of less im- portance.   We become, perhaps, confused by the diversity and clamor ; and it cannot be thought strange if these exhibitions of weakness and of wickedness should cause a rebound in the opposite direction.   They have caused this ; and here, as before, the utmost extreme claims for itself the greatest liberality.   One cardinal proposition, and but one, those who make this claim do hold to.   It is that religious belief, articles of faith, creeds, are of no con- sequence provided the life be right.

> " For forms and creeds let graceless bigots fight,
>   He can't be wrong whose life is in the right."

This they hold ; and as a corollary they hold that those who do not believe it are narrow and bigoted, and not fit to belong to the broad church.   It is, indeed, questionable whether they are fit to belong to this nineteenth century.

But in the third place, the terms in question are applied to men as they believe in conditions of salvation that require a life of less or greater strictness, and that

7

will thus include a smaller or larger number. It is as thus applied that these terms excite the most intense feeling.

Some believe that all men will be saved do what they may. They believe in self-indulgence till the world is exhausted, and in suicide then as the shortest road to heaven. These are as liberal and broad in their sphere as the atheist is in his. Between this point and the fastings, the flagellations, the hair shirts of monasticism, or the precise bead-telling and genuflexions of lighter forms of superstition, there is every variety both of view and of practice.

In the early stages of all religious movements, whether dispensations, reformations, or the origin of sects, the tendency is to a definite belief and strict practice. But in time the force of the original movement dies out. " The letter that killeth " displaces " the spirit that giveth life." Forms stiffen into formalism, and under this there will lurk, first indifference, then infidelity, and then contempt. After this no human power can renew the movement. For human systems, decay is death ; while in God's system, apparent decay is simply winter. But during such a process of relaxation, men who had seemed molten together, separate, and re-combine as by elective affinity. As some become rich and self-indulgent, and more desirous of the fashions and gaieties of the world, they gravitate towards certain denominations ; and denominations themselves, as the Quakers and Methodists within the last two generations, become greatly modified. As such changes go on, the more strict lament the degeneracy of the times, while those thought to be degenerate regard themselves as coming into greater freedom and enlargement. They have become more liberal, and look back upon their former state as one of narrowness, or superstition, or bigotry. Perhaps they remain with the denomination in which they were born, but they will more likely take or make an occasion to pass into one where the general standard is more lax.

In this state of things, with lines not sharply drawn, with indefinite standards, with customs objected to and denounced, not as sinful in themselves, but on account of their associations and liabilities to abuse, we hear the terms in question applied quite promiscuously, and often with intense feeling. One man regards his own standard as scriptural and rational ; that of his neighbor as lax and worldly. His neighbor regards his own standard as en-lightened and liberal, and that of *his* neighbor as narrow and bigoted. He thinks him over-scrupulous and that he makes Christ's yoke heavier than Christ himself made it.

We have thus three spheres and standards of liberality. In the first the relation of man and of nature to super-natural agency is immediately in question ; in the second it is the relation of a belief in truth to practice that is in question ; and in the third it is the relation of the practical life to the spirit of Christianity and to the moral govern-ment of God. But while the questions are thus apparently different, their central point is the same. They all find their unity and interest in the relation of the human will to supernatural control. Eliminate but this one idea, and the crested waves of these controversies will subside to the merest ripple ; and the terms that may be used, how-ever intense in form, will be charged with no divisive elements. The real questions are, the existence of a holy God claiming control over the human will, and the extent of the control thus claimed.

Is there then any criterion of liberality in these several spheres? May we know where narrowness ends on the one side, and laxness begins on the other ?

And first, what is our criterion in the sphere of belief

respecting supernatural agency, involving a belief in efficient causation and in final causes or ends intelligently proposed and pursued in nature? If we begin with Fetishism and pass up, resolving phenomena that had been attributed to spiritual agency into general laws, where shall we stop?

We must stop at the point where negation begins to affect the sum and grandeur of being. This is the criterion. In passing up from Fetishism we do indeed constantly deny, but we also constantly affirm. As we diminish the number of supernatural agents we increase their greatness, till we resolve all natural laws and forces directly or indirectly into the will of the one infinite God. If now we clothe Him in our conceptions with perfect moral attributes, we have the highest conceivable sum and mode of being. This is the condition, and the only condition, of the perfect working and indefinite progress of the human faculties. Here we reach the point of the liberality without narrowness and without laxness. Beyond this we pass into negation and tenuity.

The criterion is one not merely to be seen by the intellect, but to be felt as a condition of growth. The condition of indefinite growth in intellect is thoughts of God still unfathomed; and the condition of growth in the moral nature is a recognized goodness in God that transcends ours. Man cannot live in negations. If he could reach a point where the imagination even could transcend the possibilities of being, he would begin to be dwarfed. As in passing upwards we reach a point where breathing becomes less effective from the thinness of the atmosphere, so the moment we begin to deny intelligent will to God, or to impair his moral attributes, or to limit his control over the universe by anything but the conditions which he has himself imposed, we come into a mental atmosphere of less vitality. All history shows that from that point constructive power wanes, and moral torpor begins.

What we say then is, that our criterion here must be the condition of highest activity and fullest growth for the human powers; that that condition is the complement and perfection of being as recognized in an infinite and personal God ; and that for man to apply terms of commendation to virtual negations that must stifle his own life and dwarf his own growth is to call evil good.

But secondly, what is the criterion of liberality in regard to the importance of religious truth?

It is here virtually the same as before. Truth is of importance only as it ministers to life, and as it is the only thing that can thus minister. What we claim for truth in the religious sphere, is the same that we claim for it elsewhere—just that and no more. Everywhere it is the basis of all rational action, the very light in which man must walk if he would not stumble. Men hold truth that is not acted upon. There is much that cannot be the basis of action, and that which may, and should be, is often held, or rather imprisoned, in indolence and unrighteousness. Be its adaptions what they may, let any truth lie in the mind undigested, unassimilated, giving no impulse or guidance, and it might as well not be there. Still, whatever rational action there may be, is, and must be based on the belief of something as true. Men do something because they believe something ; and in religion no less than in other things they must believe in order to do, unless, indeed, we resolve the religious life into that mere muddle of unintelligent feeling called mysticism. Men may believe in God and not worship him, but they cannot worship him unless they believe in him. Unless they believe that " Christ has come in the flesh," they cannot follow him. Unless they believe in a moral government, they cannot fear to sin ;

nor can they "flee from the wrath to come," unless they believe that there is a coming wrath. A man may conduct his secular business with a degree of success under some misapprehension of the facts on which it is based, but if he misconceive them wholly he must fail; and a man who wholly denies or perverts the facts on which a religious life is based, must fail in that. But in either case the more perfectly the truth is seen, that is, all truth that can bear upon results, the more the man acts in his true element as a man, and the more sure he is of success.

We believe then in no weak liberality, or pretence of breadth that would ignore the vital connection of truth with life; and our criterion here, the point of liberality without narrowness and without laxity, is *such a belief in all religious truth as shall be the condition of the highest life.*

But we are here met by another despairing and debilitating assertion. We are told that the human mind has not the power to separate the truth that is essential and vital from that which is not.

If by this it be meant that the human mind cannot know how little truth a man may believe and yet be saved, it is true. Nor are we required to know this. It is not our business to judge men, but systems, and neither liberality nor charity can require us to confound these, or to fail to discriminate them by sharp lines. Charity may make large allowance, but may not require us to confound things that differ. It may believe that a Mohammedan, or a Deist, may have truth enough to save him, but it cannot deny the power and the right to say that neither Mohammedanism nor Deism is Christianity. And so, if among those who call themselves Christians, any profess a Christianity that has no redemption in it; and if, on the best comparison he can make of it with the New Testament, any man shall conclude that that is not Christianity;

it is no more a want of charity to say so, than it is for a chemist, after testing it, to say that an acid is not an alkali. Let men use their intellects freely, fairly, modestly, and yet with a confidence that shall honor God, as implying that the faculty he has given for the discovery of truth is neither impotent nor delusive ; let them thus decide what Christianity is, and then receive to Christian fellowship those who accept what they conceive to be its essential doctrines, and who show that they submit their hearts to its claims. If, in doing this, some should include doctrines not essential to Christianity, it is to be imputed, not to a want of charity or liberality, but to the imperfection of human judgment.

Our criterion here will then require us not only to hold to the vital connection of truth with life, but to the power of man to separate the truths that are essential, not to the salvation of an individual man as he may be dealt with by the Spirit of God, but to Christianity as distinguished from any other system. In such a belief there is no narrowness. In anything beyond this there is laxity and feebleness.

But thirdly, we inquire for the criterion of liberality in respect of conduct.

The criterion of liberality in belief as respects conduct must refer, either to the law which is the standard of conduct, or to the results of transgressions.

If we suppose a being morally perfect, the standard of his conduct must be a perfect moral law. Such a law is required both as an expression of the moral character of God, and as a condition of the moral perfection of his creatures. It is the fountain of order, the guardian of rights, the only impregnable basis of security for the universe. Can it then be asked in the interest of anything claiming to be liberality, that the perfection of such a law shall be impaired? Ask rather that the brightness of the sun should be dimmed. Ask that God should abdicate his throne. If, as we have seen, liberality can have nothing to do in impairing the rights and prerogatives of intellect in its relation to truth, much less may it obliterate moral distinctions and lower the standard of moral action.

But the real question respects conduct under a law trangressed, with a possibility still remaining of forgiveness and restoration to full obedience. The question for every man, the one question on which his destiny turns, is whether he shall ever be brought into full harmony with a perfect moral law?

The law remaining, this must be so ; and being so, the principle here is obvious.   It is that *nothing can be allowed in conduct, whether in principle or in outward form, that would prevent the speediest possible restoration of ourselves or others to a full obedience.*

But is not God merciful? Does he not wish his creatures to be happy? Yes ; but " shall we continue in sin that grace may abound? God forbid." Little do they know of God's mercy who speak of it in such a connection. There is in it a depth and tenderness of which they have no conception. But then its first element is a regard for law, and any act of seeming mercy that would, in the slightest degree, impair the power of law, would not be mercy, but an act of indifference or of weakness. These, indifference and weakness, especially the former, are constantly confounded with mercy, but no contrast could be greater. Mercy is not compassion ; it is not simply benevolence. It is favor shown in accordance with the honor of the law to the guilty whose punishment is demanded by the law ; and the weakness and indifference that are in it find their measure in the agony of the garden and the death-cry of the cross. What Christ did, is the measure at once of the value of the law and of the depth of love there is in the divine mercy. Yes, God is merciful ; so merciful that he gave his Son for us, but not so merciful that he will pardon one sin except through Him. It is on mercy thus shown, revealing at once a love unutterable and a firmness unalterable, that we rely for quickening the consciences of men and bringing them up to new obedience ; and God forbid that we should give a fair name to anything that would weaken their sense of its need, or diminish its power. Yes, God desires the happiness of his creatures ; and therefore sets himself with the whole force of his nature against trangression. He has provided for every inlet of pleasure, and for every spontaneity of joy ; but these can be permanent only for those who have never wandered from the inclosure of his law, or who have been brought back by One who has sought them with weary and bleeding feet upon the dark mountains.

Let men but draw the inspiration of their lives from such an apprehension of the cross of Christ, thus coming into full sympathy with mercy in its end as restoring them to obedience, and they will easily dispose of many questions regarding conduct which perplex those who discuss them on a lower plane. On the one side there is a tendency to austerity and to forms in a legal or a superstitious spirit ; and on the other to ignore the inherent and essential law of self-denial, and the fact that a Christian is not of this world even as Christ was not of this world. But he who has it for his end to be conformed to a spiritual law, will not rest in any physical suffering or outward form ; nor, on the other hand, will he either make amusements, now so much spoken of, an essential part of his life, or rail at them. The question with him will be where his heart is, whither he is tending, and he will find both liberty and liberality under the great law of Christian self-denial,

7*

that permits a man to do anything which will not hinder
his restoration to moral soundness in the sight of God.
Yes, my friends, *you may do anything which will not counter-
work in yourselves or others the work which Christ came to do.*
In this is liberty, and any liberality that would go beyond
this is license.

Thus are our criteria all practical.   They are simply
the conditions requisite for the highest mental and moral
efficiency.   Take away anything from the sum or the excellence of being, or from the value of truth, or from the
power of the mind to attain it, and by the very laws of
mind you put it under conditions less favorable for mental
robustness and efficiency.   And so, if you lower the standard of moral law ; or take from the conditions of mercy
their legal element ; especially if any indulgence be allowed that for *you* dims the light, or impairs the power of a
self-denying, humble, prayerful, spiritual life, you preclude
the possibility of the highest moral efficiency.   But it is in
and through moral perfection that man finds his true end,
and no liberality that would lower the tone of this can be
admitted.

To some it may appear that the criteria proposed are
not legitimate, because they do not respect directly what
is true, but infer truth from that which is best adapted to
perfect man.   But such an inference will be least distrust-
ed by those who know most of the works of God.   If we
may not make it, the desire for truth and goodness will
thwart that for perfection, and there is, in the constitution
of man, a contradiction found nowhere else.

Permit me to caution you, young men, since your period
of life and the whole drift of the times is likely to lead you
to sympathize with those who make liberality and broad
church their watchword, that you do not abuse liberty.   An
Apostle tells us there were those of old, and possibly there

may be some such now, who spoke "great swelling words
of vanity," and promised liberty to others, while they were
themselves "the servants of corruption." Always liberty
has been assailed in the name of liberty. There is nothing new in this claim of liberality and demand for it.
It has existed from the time that a holy God laid claim to
exclusive worship, and established a church that should
recognize that claim. In that claim was the root of a
conflict that has been waged, and will be, till one party or
the other shall triumph. Let men yield to that claim as
children, and we ask no more. We can be satisfied with
nothing less. In opposition to that claim there was always
a party among the Jews inclined to affinity in their religion
with the nations around them. Were not those religions
equally religion? Did they not bring into activity the
religious nature? Were not the people sincere? And
then the creed was less exclusive, and the worship more
attractive, and artistic, and compatible with freedom in
certain practices not allowed by the Jewish law. Why
should they be so narrow as to stand aloof from all others?
The whole history of the Jews under the Judges and the
Kings is little else than an account of the different phases
of this struggle, the liberal party being generally in the
ascendant ; and it was only through the Babylonish captivity that God vindicated his supremacy and eliminated
the tendency to idolatry.

Nor is Christianity, as claiming the absolute supremacy
of God over both the life and the heart, less exclusive than
was Judaism. It did, indeed, throw down all barriers
between the Jews and others ; but it abated nothing of the
moral claims of God. So Christ regarded it. He spoke
of the "strait gate and the narrow way ;" and there is
something ominous in the sound of "broad church" when
we hear Him saying, "broad is the road that leadeth to

destruction." So the Apostles regarded it; and when that same principle of exclusiveness that had been quiescent in Judaism became aggressive in Christianity, then a liberality that could tolerate and fellowship everything else revealed its quality in the bitter hate of ten bloody persecutions. And so it has been since. Of everything else but a church that represents the uncompromising and exclusive claims of God, liberality has spoken with a bland voice; but *that* she on the one hand, and bigotry and intolerance on the other, have equally persecuted. That it is that ecclesiasticism has frowned upon and imprisoned, and that literature and genius have caricatured and mocked at, and do still. Be it that in such a church there may be found hypocrisies, pretence, dishonesty, meanness, narrowness, and even inelegance. These are fair game, but can never account for the intense venom that has tipped the arrows that have been shot at the church; nor for the spiteful and persistent vigor with which they have been sped. These have come only as a part of that " irrepressible conflict " of all time, that has never failed to show itself where the claims of God have been set up.

In connection with this conflict, in which no man can be neutral, I wish for you, my friends, no needless antagonism. Whatever may stand in the way of a life under the inspiration of love to God and men, and in sympathy with the remedial power of Christianity, that meet and oppose ; but have no mere anti-isms, and make nothing a point unless required by loyalty to truth and to God. All wilfulness and false issues are mischievous, and suffering from them, or for them, is at best useless. But I do wish for you in this conflict such a belief, and such an attitude toward it, as not to imply that the martyrs were fools; and as to make it possible that you should yourselves become martyrs. No belief—no, I do not say belief, I say faith involving trust—no faith can give to life its highest inspiration that a man would not die for. Have such a faith. Live for it; if need be, die for it; for in losing your life thus you shall " keep it unto life eternal."

But shall we not, you say, belong to the party of progress? Yes, progress in light, in discrimination, in the detection of all shams and hypocrisies, and out of the church as well as in it; but especially progress in LOVE, love to God and love to man. In this only is the root of a liberality that is not pretentious and hollow, that will despise no one and persecute no one. Through this you shall grow into a liberality that will embrace all that can be embraced without defilement; and all narrowness, bigotry, sectarianism, will fall from you as naturally as its chrysalis covering falls from the insect that is finding its wings. Come out then from all incrustations of narrowness into full Christian light and liberty. Whomsoever God loves, love ye; whomsoever he receives, receive ye. Join that great party that is now seeking, as by a divine instinct, A HIGHER UNITY IN CHRIST. Ponder more the import and the implications of his prayer, " *That they all may be one.*" Progress? Yes, progress in all in which that is possible; but remember that our great business here, our whole business as practical, is progress in conformity to those fixed conditions of growth and well-being in which, as in the brightness of the sun, there is no progress, but which God has perfected forever. Learn what those conditions are. Accept your place under them as creatures and as children; comprehend, if you please, and if you can, how conformity to those conditions promotes growth, but know that except in conformity to them there can be progress only in barren knowledge, or in delusion and folly.

XVI.

ZEAL.

And why beholdest thou the mote that is in thy brother's eye, but considerest not the beam that is in thine own eye? or how wilt thou say to thy brother, let me pull out the mote out of thine eye, and behold a beam is in thine own eye? Thou hypocrite, first cast out the beam out of thine own eye, and then shalt thou see clearly to cast out the mote out of thy brother's eye. Woe unto you scribes and pharisees, hypocrites! for ye compass sea and land to make one proselyte, and when he is made ye make him twofold more the child of hell than yourselves.—Matthew, vii. 3, 4, 5; xxiii. 15.

THE most dangerous foe to Christianity to-day is not open infidelity, not a false liberality, but a zeal that puts on the form of Christianity, that works under its semblance, that seeks its own ends, not only reckless of the degradation and perversion of the religious nature, but through that very degradation and perversion.

What then? Shall we disparage zeal? No. We but need it the more. Without zeal for the enlightenment, the reformation and salvation of men, we have none of the spirit of Him of whom it was said, " The zeal of thine house hath eaten me up." Without zeal we can do no good. The danger is, that we shall not be zealous enough; and yet, if we consult either Scripture or history, we shall perhaps feel that there is equal danger of our being wrongly so. We do not need to disparage or diminish zeal, but we do need to understand the characteristics of that which is legitimate; and the causes and modes of possible deviation from it. It is to these that I now ask your attention :—THE CHARACTERISTICS OF A LEGITIMATE ZEAL ; AND THE CAUSES AND MODES OF POSSIBLE DEVIATION FROM IT.

Legitimate zeal has two great characteristics,—one, as it is related to the Intellect ; the other, to the Heart.

₊ JULY 26, 1868.

As related to the Intellect, zeal must be *enlightened*. This is the first great characteristic of a zeal that is legitimate.

And zeal must be enlightened, First, That its end may be good.

It is not that the end sought by a false zeal must be avowedly bad, or is even known in distinct consciousness to be so, for then the zeal would not be ignorant,—but that the real end, and that which a thorough honesty would discriminate as such, is not good. The origin of the ignorance is in the heart ; on moral subjects it generally is, but still it is ignorance. So was it with the Jews of whom the Apostle Paul speaks. " For I bear them record," says he, "that they have a zeal of God, but not according to knowledge. For they, being ignorant of God's righteousness, and going about to establish their own righteousness, have not submitted themselves to the righteousness of God." Avowedly they would submit to the mode of justification established by God, but really their end was to establish one of their own. So was it with the Scribes and Pharisees in compassing sea and land to make proselytes. Whatever their ultimate end was, it was not good, and they so far knew it as to be hypocrites. Still their zeal was not enlightened. They neither chose a good end because it was good, nor a bad end because it was bad, saying to evil, " Be thou my good ; " but, seeking to gratify their desires, they ignored the light of conscience and reason and revelation, and worked in a twilight which enabled them to call evil good and good evil, and at the same time maintain a good opinion of themselves. Such was the zeal of Paul which he enumerates among his Pharisaic accomplishments when he says, " Concerning zeal, persecuting the church." This was an ignorant zeal, for he says, " But I obtained mercy because I did it ignorantly in unbelief." The ignorance was from the heart, and therefore criminal, but still it was ignorance. Such was the zeal of the crusades that again and again precipitated Europe upon Asia. Such has persecuting zeal generally been. It is really some form of selfish desire becoming malignant, and blindly seeking to destroy whatever may oppose it.

Secondly, Zeal must be enlightened, that the means may be good.

We may not do evil that good may come. We may not enslave negroes out of pity to Indians. This, it is said, was the origin of the African slave trade. We may not deprive men of their rights in order to Christianize them. We may not do anything that will injure the bodies or degrade the souls of men that we may get money for the spread of the Gospel. We may not rob or defraud that we may be able to give in charity. The essential evil of this world, and of all worlds, is sin, and to think of destroying sin by committing it, is absurd.

Thirdly, Zeal must be enlightened, that its ends may be practicable.

Human power works within limits and under conditions that make it necessary to consider not merely what it is desirable we should do, but what we can do, and it is the part of wisdom to undertake only that. But men very early undertook the impracticable project of building a tower whose top should reach to heaven, and since then there has been no lack of visionary schemes, or of zeal in their prosecution. Mathematically and morally, individually and in communities, men have been at work to square the circle, and to make a weight lift itself. They have sought a universal solvent, and the philosopher's stone, and an elixir of health. They have sought universal empire, and uniformity of belief, and an equal division of property, and an absolute equality. Defeated as a race in raising a tower that should reach to heaven, individuals still make the attempt. With the original builders they say, " Let us make us a name." Let those do it who can. Effort that is not folly I would not discourage. Let zeal touch the limit of the possible, but let it be so enlightened as to waste no energy on what lies beyond.

Fourthly, Zeal must be enlightened, that it may not be sectarian or narrow.

Sectarianism is blind to good except under its own forms. When Eldad and Medad prophesied in the camp, Joshua said, " My lord Moses, forbid them." But Moses said, " Enviest thou for my sake ? Would God that all the Lord's people were prophets." Here, in the man who stood nearest to the founder of the Old dispensation, we have the spirit of sectarianism in all its elements, and the rebuke of it by that founder shows that it did not belong to the system. So too was it, and it is worthy of notice that it was so in each dispensation, with the man who stood nearest to Christ. " Master," said the beloved disciple, " we saw one casting out devils in thy name, and he followeth not us ; and we forbade him because he followeth not us." This man, whoever he was, cast out devils ; he did it in the name of Christ, but he did not " follow us." But Jesus said, " Forbid him not." " He that is not against us is on our part." That God's people should be prophets, and that devils should be cast out, were the things to be desired. It was for these that Joshua and John should have been zealous for their own sake and as good in themselves, whereas they were zealous for them only under a narrow aspect, and as related directly or indirectly to themselves, and under all other aspects they were opposed to them. That this spirit does not belong to the New dispensation, this rebuke of our Saviour will forever testify. Utterly alien is it from the whole spirit of its Founder and of the dispensation itself. And yet this it is that has so rent the seamless garment of Christ, and so rends it now. In the time of the Apostles even, so prevalent was this spirit that Paul asked, "Is Christ divided?" And from that time till this, the question has been pertinent. There has been, and is now, zeal for Christ, but for Christ divided ; for Christ, but only as he is related to the man through his own church. Men will be zealous in promoting the cause of Christ if they can do it under their own form ; but form and substance they cannot separate, and under any other form they have for it no eye and no heart.

For the removal and prevention of this great evil, greater than any other in the church, we need to substi-tute an enlightened for a sectarian zeal.

But again, Zeal needs to be enlightened that it be not partial, taking up some one object to the neglect of all others.

Would you then, you ask, disparage men of one idea? Yes, if they really have but one idea. Just so far as they fail of comprehending the true relation of the different branches of reform, I would disparage them. Intelligent concentration I would not disparage. That is a condition of efficiency ; it is wisdom. The want of it is the great want. Let a man say, if he will, This is my field ; here I will concentrate my efforts ; for this object I will labor ; but I will hold it in its true place. I will labor for it as a part of the great work to be done, central or incidental.

If central, I will labor for it as central; if incidental, as incidental; but I will not so estimate it as to be thrown from my just bearings as an intelligent Christian man toward any other part of the work. Let a man say this, and do this, and the more zealous he may be in any one branch of reform the better.

Once more, Zeal must be enlightened that it be not frivolous.

"Ye pay tithe of mint and anise and cummin." The Scribes and Pharisees held to the "washing of cups and pots and brazen vessels and tables." To eat with unwashed hands defiled them. To heal the sick on the Sabbath they esteemed a crime. In things external, ceremonial, unessential as not involving the state of the heart, they were precise and exacting. Want of conformity in these they visited with exclusion and persecution. They strained at a gnat, but passed over judgment and the love of God.

Marvellous it is how this folly and sin has repeated itself, and does still. The Apostles were men of large views working for spiritual ends. The New Testament, more than any other book, insists upon principles and ends, regardless of accessories and details. It is impossible that these latter should be less regarded, and be regarded at all. "What then?" said Paul, "notwithstanding, every way, whether in pretence or in truth, Christ is preached, and I therein do rejoice, yea, and will rejoice." And that was the spirit of all the Apostles. But passing from the New Testament to church history, we find ourselves in another atmosphere. We find men so contending and dividing on points incidental and trivial, that the "Big-endians" and "Little-endians" of Swift, whose controversy was at which end the eggs eaten at Easter should be broken, were hardly a caricature. And so, in large measure, it is still. Now, the zeal is for some shibboleth of doctrine ; now, for some form of church-government ; now, for the mode of an ordinance ; now, for vestments and the shape of a garment ; now, for church-architecture and altar forms ; now for the parapher-nalia and artistic arrangement of a liturgical service ; and now, for the sacredness of consecrated grounds and parish limits. Sometimes this zeal manifests itself in the earnest-ness of a genuine superstition, impetuous and uncompro-mising in proportion to its narrowness ; and sometimes it is modified by a predominating sentimentalism and dilet-tanteism and foppery.

These things may be thought trifles, and in themselves they are. " An idol," as the Apostle says, " is nothing in the world." It is nothing till it becomes an idol. And these things are nothing, unless, as they always have done and will do, they obscure the truth, and lead men to " omit the weightier matters of the law : judgment, mercy, and faith."

We have now considered Zeal as related to the Intel-lect. We proceed to consider it as related to the Heart.

As related to the Heart, the great characteristic of legitimate zeal is, that *it must spring from love.*

Love is the actuating principle in the divine mind. " God is love." Love moved him to create the world ; a greater love moved him to redeem it. The whole mission, and work, and sufferings of Christ, were from love ; the zeal that consumed him was from that, and from that the zeal of his followers ought to be. It is only a zeal spring-ing from love, and manifesting itself in self-sacrifice, that can make the professed followers of Christ really like him. Such a zeal—zeal from love—would be in opposition,

First, To an interested zeal.

"Ye seek me," said our Saviour, "not because ye saw the miracles, but because ye did eat of the loaves and were filled." They sought him ; they had taken shipping and crossed the lake to find him ; they had zeal, but it was inspired by the loaves and fishes. "Ye know," said Demetrius to the silversmiths of Ephesus, and to the workmen of like occupation, "that by this craft we have our wealth." This was the undertow that bore the mob of Ephesus on to that pitch of zeal which led them to cry out with one voice about the space of two hours, "Great is Diana of the Ephesians." How far this subtle element has mingled, and does now, with zeal apparently religious, man cannot know. In primitive times, when the confessing of Christ involved the loss of all things, it could hardly come in ; but let any system be once established and the pecuniary interests of large numbers will become involved in it, and will be affected by its prosperity or decline. From that moment there comes in a conservative element—mainly conservative, but sometimes aggressive and destructive—that is aside from the interests of truth and righteousness, and may usurp their place. From that moment it becomes possible that everything connected with religion should be conducted on mercenary principles, until the very temple of God shall pass into the hands of the money-changers, and it shall be supposed "that the gift of God can be purchased with money." Is there an established church ? Men are trained for its ministry with reference to its emoluments as they would be for the law. Is the system voluntary? The zeal of rival churches and the eagerness to secure converts to themselves, is often not without reference, conscious or unconscious, and sometimes painfully evident, to pecuniary interests. Religion is not discarded. It is professed. Everything is done in its name. There is zeal for it, more or less, but individual men and whole churches fall into the equivocal state of some of old, of whom it is said, "So these nations feared the Lord, and served their graven images, both their children and their children's children ; as did their fathers so do they unto this day." It is a state of things that perpetuates itself, only with a tendency downward. To overcome this tendency, to resist wholly this pervasive influence, requires a singleness of purpose and strength of zeal that can spring only from a deep love.

Secondly. Zeal from love will be in opposition to an ambitious zeal.

"They desire," says Paul, "to have you circumcised, that they may glory in your flesh." "Diotrephes, who loveth to have the preëminence," will be zealous for everything that will give him that. This is less general than an interested zeal, but often more intense. It belongs to heads of sects, or those who aspire to be, and to leaders, and men in place. It originates sects and divisions, and perpetuates them. Instead of giving due honor to that only name by which we can be saved, it perpetuates those distinctive names by which men so early began to call themselves, saying, " I am of Paul, and I of Apollos, and I of Cephas." Occasion for this is found in connection with all organization, but the more extensive and permanent the organization, and the greater the power to be gained under it, the stronger will be the temptation to this kind of zeal. Especially will this be the case if temporal be conjoined with spiritual power, thus adding to the fascinations of that, those of wealth and pomp. In this way the most tempting prizes of earthly ambition have been offered in the name of the Him who was meek and

lowly in heart and had not where to lay his head. But
with or without the temporal power, it is possible for an
ambitious zeal to hold the same place in the leading
minds of the church that an interested zeal may in the
minds of the many, and for the church thus to become
the arena to which shall be transferred, under another
name, the passions, and factions, and compromises, and
management of politics.

In opposition to this, how beautiful is the spirit of
Christian preëminence as presented in the Bible ! "Taking the oversight, not for filthy lucre, neither as being
lords over God's heritage, but as ensamples to the flock."
" And Jesus called a little child unto him, and set him in
the midst of them."

Thirdly. Zeal from love will be in opposition to an
ostentatious zeal.

"Come," said Jehu, " and see my zeal for the Lord."
Ostentatious, is to ambitious zeal, what vanity is to ambition. Vanity is the more common, but to gratify it by manifesting religious zeal, requires that we should meet with
some Jehonadab, as Jehu did, or be surrounded by those
who approve such zeal. This may seldom happen. Hence,
though vanity be more frequent, zeal from it is less so.
Being also a weakness as well as a sin, it tends less to
mischief, and may pass without further notice.

Fourthly. Zeal from love will be in opposition to that
from envy and personal ill-will.

" Some, indeed," says Paul, " preach Christ even of
envy and strife ; supposing to add affliction to my bonds."
That zeal is often heightened and embittered by personal
feeling is well understood. But what an exhibition of our
nature is this ! Truth is impersonal and immutable, the

capacity of knowing it is for the sake of goodness, and yet a rational being professedly pursuing both truth and goodness will sacrifice both from personal feeling. Controversialists turn from argument to vituperation. Luther and Henry the Eighth call each other hard names. The question between the champions of rival doctrines and sects, and between the sects themselves, comes to be, not, What is truth? and What does goodness require? but, Which party shall triumph? This is not peculiar to the church, but is there more intense and unseemly—more intense, . because religion is deeper and more central in man than anything else ; and more unseemly, because it is so utterly opposed to the whole spirit and end of the religion of Christ. So early and intensely did this form of zeal manifest itself in the church in the controversy about circumcision, that the Apostle Paul was constrained to say, " But if ye *bite* "—yes, *bite*—as if they had laid aside their rational nature and become dogs—" if ye bite and devour one another, take heed that ye be not consumed one of another." This is a point that needs to be specially guarded.

Fifthly. Zeal from love is in opposition to a malignant and persecuting zeal.

" Ye know not," said our Saviour, when the disciples would call down fire from heaven, " what manner of spirit ye are of." Of this zeal Paul, before his conversion, was a conspicuous example. He was in earnest ; so much so, that he was exceedingly mad against the disciples, and when they were put to death gave his voice against them. He was as sincere as a man can be who has the means of knowledge and yet is in the wrong. He verily " thought that he ought to do many things contrary to the name of Jesus of Nazareth." He was an example of what our Saviour had said, " He that killeth you will think that he

doeth God service." Here we have religious persecution.
What a phenomenon! A man arrogating the right to
come between other men and their God—the right to punish them for their offences, not against themselves or
against society, but against Him. A man who would produce conviction by stripes, and love by torture. A man
who thinks he is doing God service when he is putting his
servants to death. A civilized, educated, professedly religious man and religious teacher doing this. And in this
Paul was a representative man—representative of the
most envenomed and unrelenting class of persecutors from
that time onward—representative especially of priestly
persecutors clothed with civil authority. Strange that
there should be such a phenomenon—and yet not strange.
Strange, when we look at man as the child of God directly
responsible to him, and see that every man must stand or
fall to his own master. Strange, when we look at the
meekness and gentleness of Christ, and know that his religion—that all true religion is love. But not strange when
we see what power the heart, and custom, and a glozing of
fair names have to suborn and subsidize the conscience,
making it call evil good and good evil. Not strange, when
we see how intense and unscrupulous, and even self-complacent, selfishness and malignity may become when they
can thus seem to carry the conscience with them. And
when, in addition, we see how other forms of perverted
zeal, an ignorant, a sectarian, an interested, an ambitious
zeal may become tributary to this, swelling its rushing
tide, we no longer wonder that the most awful scenes this
earth has witnessed, the tortures of the Inquisition, the
massacre of St. Bartholomew's day, have been perpetrated
in the name of religion. Nor is it strange, while ecclesias-
tics, as Luther, have often been the first to catch the light,
that they, and especially those claiming to be priests,

8

together with all whose living may depend on their ministrations, should cling the most strongly to that which is
established, and, if not thoroughly Christian, should be the
most ready to persecute those who refuse conformity, or
would make innovations. So has it always been ; so is it
now. Do our missionaries meet with opposition, or their
converts with persecution, whether in heathen or nominally Christian lands? it is from the priests. Are sects
and divisions perpetuated in Protestant Christendom?
Who does it? Certainly the ministers of religion, of all
men, have need to pray to be delivered from a selfish and
persecuting zeal.

Sixthly. I will only add, that zeal from love will be
opposed to a temporary and periodical zeal.
"It is good," says the Apostle, "to be zealously
affected *always* in a good thing, and not only when I am
present with you." So early did this unsteady and falter-
ing zeal show itself. And there has been no lack of it
since. It is now one of the standing reproaches of Christendom. Its causes are many. It is, perhaps, better
than no zeal at all, but love is a principle, and as that
gains ascendency, zeal becomes pure and burns with a
steady flame. This is the perfection of Christian life—an
intelligent, affectionate, constant zeal for the glory of God,
and the good of men.

This, my friends, is the zeal and the life that I commend to you. Your value to the world will be from the
changes that you work in it—changes in the world of matter
around you, in yourselves, and in your fellow-men. You
are born into a state of perpetual and uniform on-going.
Nothing is still. The very stability of the earth, all stability but that of God, is from movement. Into this state we

are born, not simply to be borne alone with it, but as
agents, voluntarily and intentionally to produce changes
that but for us would not have been.   This we can do.
We can make two spears of grass grow where, but for us,
there would have been but one.   We can turn our own
thoughts, which otherwise would have wandered with the
fool's eyes to the ends of the earth, to the comprehension
of the works of God and of his attributes and character;
and our deepest love, which tends so strongly to earth, we
can fix upon God.   We can feed the hungry, and clothe
the naked, and instruct the ignorant, and lead lost men to
Christ.   The changes we can work are wide enough and
far-reaching enough to awaken our highest zeal.

But zeal distinctively, and that here contemplated, has
relation to the changes to be wrought in our fellow-men.
To work these rightly is the highest test of human power.
Not the direct control of will, which men so much seek,
but the transformation and moulding of character is the
highest test of human power.   And now, that you may do
this as you should, having pointed out the lines of possible
misdirection, I call your attention to a great principle laid
down by our Saviour, which will guard your from them all,
and secure to you the condition of successful work according to your power.   That principle is, that *if you would
hope to reform others, you must begin with yourselves.*
" *First cast out the beam out of thine own eye.*"   Failure in
this has been the great failure hitherto.   Till this is
adopted, there must be failure ; and for two reasons.

The first of these reasons is that he who would reform
others and does not begin with himself is a hypocrite.
" Thou hypocrite," says our Saviour.   The reason is, that
a genuine opposition to evil must strike at it wherever it
finds it, and there most directly and vigorously where it
can be most readily and effectually reached.   But this is

by every man within himself. For this every man is
especially intrusted to himself. His business is to keep
his own vineyard first. For the detection of evil within
himself, nothing is needed but a thorough honesty ; and
to its removal the only obstacle is in the will. Just so
far, therefore, as a man really hates evil, he will begin the
attack upon it within himself, and will carry it on as vigorously there as elsewhere. Not doing this, he is a hypocrite, and from hypocrisy no reformation of others can
come. How can it ? " Who can bring a clean thing out
of an unclean ? Not one." Reformation is not the thing
intended, and like produces like. There may be zeal,
persistent and self-denying. Proselytes may be made ;
but water does not rise higher than its source. They will
be proselytes to the principles and tempers of those who
make them ; only, with that vivacity of a new-born zeal
which belongs to all proselytes, they will be more active
and worse than they. "And when he is made, ye make
him two-fold more the child of hell than yourselves."

Do you say that this application of the principle will
extend fearfully the domain of hypocrisy? So be it. The
principle must be so applied. Truth requires it. If it be
not, reform has no starting point, and the condition of this
world is hopeless. Let me say then unequivocally, that
just so far as you shall profess a zeal to reform others
beyond the point at which you are honestly laboring to
reform yourselves, you will be hypocrites. Let me say
also that there must be a weak point in all attempts
at reform, and in all organizations for that end, where
the principle of reform is not, as in the church of God,
universal.

The second reason why you must begin with yourselves
if you would reform others is, that clearness of moral
vision can be attained in no other way. " First cast out

the beam out of thine own eye, *and then shalt thou see clearly.*" This involves the great principle that clearness of moral perception depends, not so much upon power of intellect, as upon the state of the heart. This is a great principle, and I ask your recognition of it in all your attempts to reform yourselves or others. I ask your aid in correcting the prevailing undue estimate of intellect alone. From that is knowledge only. From that, in a right combination with the heart, is wisdom. This it is, this only, that lifts us into the region of clear vision. Not from imbecility of intellect is the Babel of opinions on moral subjects. The power and the laws of intellect were not different on different sides of Mason and Dixon's line in the days of slavery. It is not from lack of intellect that the rumseller pleads for his nefarious traffic as right An intellect with a bias in it is an eye with a beam in it and however strong, cannot be trusted. First then purge your own vision, and then you shall see clearly how to remove even motes from the eyes of others. Your vision being clear, comprehensively so, your method will be right. Instead of a biassed intellect, applied to remove what intellect did not cause, the blind leading the blind, there will be " the meekness of wisdom." Instead of the weapons of controversy, there will be the pleadings of love instead of saying of your brother that you have gained him to your party or sect, you shall say of him, " Behold, he prayeth." Instead of the low and solitary joy of a selfish success, you shall have a pure joy, shared by angels, over sinners that repent.

Beginning thus with yourselves, being always as severe toward yourselves as toward others, permitting no severity to become harshness, but cultivating " the meekness of wisdom," your zeal for the reformation of others cannot be too great. Let such a zeal be fostered. Make your lives more and more fountains of good influences. As I have said, your value to the world will depend on the nature and extent of the changes you will work, and that, but for you, would not have been. But of all changes those wrought in character are highest in their nature, widest in their influence, and most enduring. Change matter if you will ; chisel the marble into a statue ; build palaces and pyramids. You do but change the relative position of particles and masses, and the moment the product is completed it is touched by the finger of decay. Not solidity, or that intrusted to it, is most enduring ; but the reverse. The blind old poet of Scio utters his words. The thin air receives them. Brass and marble have perished, but they live. It was mind changing mind in the realm of thought. Change mind there. You may and must ; but go deeper ; aim higher ; seek to change character. See all faults. Yes, see motes. See them, but not in a spirit of pride, or satire, or censoriousness. In these may be ability, but they do no good. See sins and faults and follies only in a spirit of love and helpfulness, desiring to remove them. So shall you enter the moral domain, and work changes there. And changes there shall not only be permanent but progressive, passing on farther, and spreading wider forever.

In this moral domain it is, that we find the stress and pressure of the battle that is being waged in this world. This is central. Of the seeming conflicts of matter this is the origin. They are but the reflection of this, and in it find their significance. Without this no waves of ocean would be proud, no tempest would wail, no thunder mutter wrath. Of this battle the forces are organized, and the Leader is in the field. On his hands, and his feet, and in his side, are the scars of that great conflict, in which by dying he conquered death, and " is now alive forever·

more." His voice it is that calls you, saying, "Follow me."
Follow Him. Add, if you may, your names to the list of
those who have gone to bear salvation to heathen shores.
But if that may not be, wherever you are, and in whatever
you engage, follow Him; He is the hope of the race.
Finding first for yourselves the light and strength that
come from Him, lead to the same source of light and
strength every ignorant, tempted, struggling brother.
Keeping near to Him, you need not fear to be in the
thickest of the battle, for above its tumult you shall hear
a voice saying, "Lo, I am with you." How long this
battle is to rage we know not, but He knows, and victory
is sure. When that shall come, this earth and these
heavens shall be reorganized in sympathy with moral
order. In their order and beauty they shall correspond
with the higher moral order and beauty of those who
shall dwell in them, and that order and beauty shall be
perfect.

But what place will there then be for your zeal?
Must it not fail with prophecies, and cease with tongues,
and with knowledge vanish away? In its present form
there will be no place for it. Beholding the countless
throng that shall walk in the smile of God, each perfect
in beauty, with no mote even in any eye, "without spot,
or wrinkle, or any such thing," zeal shall expire. But
expiring thus, it shall not perish. It shall be only to
revive and live again forever, transfigured, glorified, to be
known no more as zeal, but as the joy of a perfect complacency.

XVII.

SPIRIT, SOUL, AND BODY.

And I pray God your whole spirit, and soul, and body, be preserved blameless, unto the coming of our Lord Jesus Christ.—1 Thessalonians, v. 23.

IF man would know what he may hope, or attempt, under God's natural government, he must know what he is in his nature, and in the powers which God has given him. If, again, he would know what he may hope for under God's moral government, he must know what his character is. He must know his tendencies, and the direction of his voluntary activity.

Hence self-knowledge is in two directions. The question may be, What am I? What nature have I? What powers? Am I in the image of God as created by Him? Am I in the image of the brute as developed from him; or rather from that? Have these powers immortality as separate and conscious? Or are they mere upheavals of an infinite, underlying, unconscious force into which they will again sink, and all separate consciousness be lost? Or again, the question may be, What is my real character? Disguises aside, and the glozings of self-love. What are my deepest tendencies? What is that supreme end to which all else is subordinated?

If a man would know himself fully, both these questions must be fully answered. He must know his powers, and he must know the direction of their activity.

To which of these forms of knowledge the injunction

⁎ JUNE 20, 1869.

of the ancient oracle, " Know thyself," referred, or whether to both, it may be difficult to say. Probably to the
first chiefly, because a knowledge of character could have
no such place or importance under any heathen system
as under Christianity. Such knowledge would not have
been philosophy, and could have gratified no pride ; it
would not have been religion, and could have secured
no reward. There was among the heathen generally no
such knowledge of sin as to reveal to them either the
importance or the difficulty of this kind of knowledge.
Accordingly the current of speculation, so far as it had
man for its object, was in the direction of the powers.
So was it with Plato, and so has it been with the philosophers since. They have sought, and are still seeking, to
give us the constituents, and to unfold the nature of man.
Here, as in other sciences, the obstacle is chiefly ignorance, or a limitation of our powers.

    With Christianity, however, this is reversed. That
assumed that man is in the image of God, and is to live
hereafter. And then, assuming also sin, and making destiny turn upon character, it gives to the knowledge of
that an importance impossible under any other system.
Hence the apostolic precept, " Examine yourselves," and
the great standing duty of self-examination inculcated by
the church, refer, not at all to the nature and powers, but
wholly to the character and moral state of the man.
Here, however, the obstacle is not simply ignorance from
limitation of the powers, but from a liability to self-
deception. The most difficult honesty in this world for a
man to practise is to be honest with himself when he has
done wrong, or desires to do so.

    From this importance of character, and the difficulty
thus originating, there has arisen a great department of
Christian literature, that of self-examination for religious

                 8*

ends, to which there is nothing similar in heathen literature. There is, perhaps, something analogous to it, as the
blindness, and inconsistencies, and folly of vice and of
self-love have been made the objects of analysis and
of satire. Into this region of character, of desire and
passion and purpose, the satirist and the philosopher
look, and, according to their temperament, find food for
self-complacency, or scorn, or misanthropy. Not so the
Saviour. Into this region He looks, and beholding with
an infinite pity its agitations and turbid tossings as of a
troubled sea that cannot rest, he says, "Peace, be still."

But while the Scriptures thus magnify the knowledge
of character, and assume, rather than teach, the truths of
philosophy, they do not, in thus assuming, ignore those
truths. They rather receive them in the most radical
and effectual way, making them pervasive, as the atmosphere, so that while they will never be obtrusive, their
presence will be always felt, and their true nature will be
constantly though incidentally, gleaming out. So it is
with the Apostle Paul. Incidentally, he teaches us the
true theory of our nature. In opposition to the current
philosophy of our day certainty, if not of his, which
teaches that man is composed of soul and body, the Apostle
teaches that he is composed of spirit, and soul, and body.
"And I pray God that your whole spirit, and soul, and
body, be preserved blameless unto the coming of our
Lord Jesus Christ."

Let us then inquire for a little into the grounds of this
distinction—a distinction not new, but generally accepted,
in the primitive church. That we accept it is not necessary to our salvation ; still, if Christianity is to stand in
its full beauty, and reach its full power, its implied and
underlying truths must be rightly held. If they are not,
there will be constant outcroppings of errors and incon-

sistencies on which skeptics and scoffers will take their
stand, and jeer and mock the passing pilgrim.

The difficulties in the way of comprehending those
underlying powers or parts of our nature of which the
Apostle speaks, and which have thrown and still throw
obscurity around them, are found in three words, as they
are applicable to man and related to each other. These
are *unity*, *complexity*, and *progressiveness*.   Man is a unity ;
he is also complex, and progressive.

First, then, man is a unity.   This we know by our consciousness.   We affirm it by necessity, and cannot doubt
it.   He is a unity, but not a unit.   What a unit is, or
rather what is a unit, and whether there be one in this universe, I know not.   A grain of sand is no more a unit
than the universe is.   A unit has no parts.   A unity is
made up of parts that find their unity in their relation to
each other and to their common end.   The eye is a unity.
It is one thing, one eye, but it is made up of six principal parts, and if any one, or certainly two of these be
removed, it will cease to be an eye.   And so man is a unity,
commonly supposed to be constituted of soul and body.
The body is not the man, the soul is not the man, but the
two united.

Such is the unity.   But even as thus regarded, what
complexity have we.   For first, the body is a unity ; and
in it is a system for digestion, and that is a unity ; and
one for circulation, and that is a unity ; and there are systems for secretion, and respiration, and locomotion, and
sensation, and thought, and each of these is a unity.
Then also the soul is a unity.   But that is made up of intellect, and sensibility, and will ; and each of these is a unity,
while all are to be combined into the higher unity that is
to make the one man.

What now is that one thing which binds together these

several systems and makes them one? Whatever it be, the
complexity is so great that the mystery of the unity will
not be increased if we make it greater. It is to be said,
too, that beings are higher in the scale in proportion to
their complexity. This is on the principle that that which
is higher becomes so by having all that is below it with
something added. If, therefore, to body and soul we add
spirit, we raise man in dignity, and increase no difficulty
or mystery.

But besides this difficulty in comprehending man from
the complexity of his unity, we find another from his progressiveness. This requires the unity to be preserved not
only in the midst of complexity, but through such changes
in the mode of life and forms of the being that it is difficult
to recognize its identity. At birth, all the instrumentalities of a former life are dropped. At that point there is
not merely progression, but a new mode of being. There
are objects, and instrumentalities, and forms of being
inconceivable before. And then, from that point, what
progression! What a change from the infant uttering its
first faint cry, to a Newton trembling with joy as he grasps
the problem of the heavens! What a change again from
that same infant, still preserving its unity, to the coffined
dust, and to the possibilities for the spirit of the untried
and unending scenes that lie beyond death!

The full problem of man then is, first—first practically,
though not logically—that of his end and of his law as
derived from that. This is the problem of Moral Philosophy, and is for all. It is therefore explicitly revealed.
Here we have the moral law, the great law of love. We
have secondly the problem of what man has been, and is,
and may become, in the unity of a complex and progressive being that has undergone one entire change in the
mode of its life, and is destined either to undergo another,

or to go out in annihilation. This involves the problems
of metaphysical philosophy, around which a sea of controversy has always surged. To be truly man, the being
must retain throughout, the constituents which make him
man. Are these, then, body and soul? Or are they body,
soul, and spirit? Is there a spirit distinguishable from the
soul, though perhaps not separable from it, as the soul is
distinguishable from the body? When the ruins of the
fall shall be retrieved, and the ravages of a penal death
shall be repaired, is it these three, spirit, soul, and body,
instinct with an immortal vigor, and in a union attempered
to the harmonies of heaven, that shall go to make up the
one redeemed and perfect man? This is our inquiry, for
so the Apostle seems to say.

First, then, reversing, for convenience, the order of the
text, what is the body? and what is its relation to the soul?

The body is commonly supposed to be mere matter.
It is not. It is organized living matter built up by unconscious force, and includes both the matter and the force.
A tree is nothing but body. A tree is not the mere matter which we see. It is far rather that unseen force that
has worked from the first moment of germination, and de-
posited every particle, and protruded every branch, and
scalloped every leaf, and has made the tree to be a maple-
tree instead of an elm. In every living organism it is this
mimic soul working out the pattern of its home after its
kind, that is the wonder of nature and the ground of our
sympathy with her. This unconscious force it is, with the
organism it thus holds in its grasp and charge, that is the
body. This is the same in us as in the tree, except that in
us it is made movable, and is taken up into relation to a
higher life. In us, indeed, the body is a double set of
organs, one of which builds up and repairs by an involun-
tary force another set for the use of the soul.

This force then that builds the house I live in, that digests my food and circulates my blood, and fashions organs for my use, this house and these organs—are they a part of myself? For the time being, yes, and so a part of myself that without them I am not a man. They are not my personality, but without them that unity which makes me a man is gone. Except as a part of myself that house and these organs become a corpse and return to their original elements; and as separated from these the soul passes we know not where, and exists we know not how.

What the link may be between this life of nutrition and the higher life of the soul, I know not. Let those who are troubled by the mystery of a Trinity in unity, resolve the mystery of a unity of two hundred and four bones, each separately formed; and of the muscles, more numerous still, that cover them; and of the stomach and blood-vessels that build them up; and of the nerves that run through them; and of the brain that crowns them; and of all these, moved and built up by an unconscious force with the higher life of the conscious and intelligent soul, so as to become its servant. That was its purpose. It was that all these, in their unity, should become the servant of the soul. So it ought, but the reality and power of the higher unity is seen in the fact that the soul may, instead, become the servant of it. It is possible for the life of the whole man to be centred, and by deliberate choice, in the nutritive life and the passions that connect themselves immediately with that. So is it with whole tribes of savages, I say not nations, for at this point of elevation the idea of a nation does not dawn. So is it with gluttons, gourmands, epicures. The stomach is the centre of life, and the intelligence is used to serve that. The soul keeps house in its kitchen. This is the point to be noticed here, that that which gives unity to the whole, and

is truly man, can, and does take up its abode and find its
life in this lower part of our complex being to the neglect
of all that is above, and so becomes "of the earth, earthy."
In the language of Scripture, the man becomes " carnal."

With the intelligence thus employed, the higher æsthe-
tic, and moral, and religious powers can find no proper
objects or scope, and all their manifestations in the direction of art and of religion will be either fantastic or hideous. Voluntarily placing himself on a level with the brute,
passion will run riot, and through superstitions, and unnatural cruelties and lusts, the higher powers will avenge
themselves by degrading the man below the brute.

Such is the body, consisting of the power that builds
it, and the structure built. In its present materials and
functions—some of them at least—it cannot be permanent;
but with some material, and with some functions through
which the soul shall be in relation to a material universe
it must be forever a constituent of a complete humanity.

We next inquire respecting the soul. In inquiring
after the body, we simply needed to transfer to man the
nutritive life of plants, adding however the organs built up
by that life for the use of the soul. In inquiring after the
soul, we transfer to him again the sensitive, instinctive,
and directive life of the animal, adding all that is built up
by these and that may be conjoined with them for the use
of the spirit. Animals have instincts, and directive powers, and natural affections, and something of what Kant
and Coleridge call understanding. They have powers correlated to this fixed order of nature by which they provide
for themselves in it, and for the most part secure to themselves all the good of which they are capable. This is the
special characteristic of the soul, that under the guidance
of instinct and of intelligence in the form of prudence, it
deals consciously with a fixed order of things—a nature.

In respect to this, the animal and man run into each other by imperceptible shades. In its lower forms instinct is perfect. There is a tendency on the one hand, and a provision on the other, and well-being is secured. But among the higher animals there is diversity. Different animals of the same species will pursue different courses under the same circumstances. They have diversities of feature and of characteristics. They have some power of generalization and of inference. They assume what are called first truths. If an animal does not state to itself the proposition that causation and the laws of nature are uniform, it yet proceeds upon it. If a bee does not put it into a geometrical treatise that a straight line is the shortest distance between two points, it yet takes a *bee line* when it has freighted itself with honey, and would go to its home. Here man has all that the animal has and something more, though of the same kind. Rooted in the same soil, he is as the towering tree with its branches and leaves and tasselled blossoms tossing and fragrant, beside the lichen hard by on the rock, or the moss at its root. Through his understanding, and the instruments with which he is endowed, especially the hand, man is perfectly fitted to deal *intelligently* with a fixed order of things, to profit by experience, and to subdue such an order wholly to himself; and whatever powers may be necessary to put him into relation with this order, and to give him dominion over it, belong to the soul. To this belongs the recognition and articulate statement of what have been called the first truths of pure reason, those necessary affirmations, always the same, which are implied in reasoning, and through which alone reasoning can fully understand itself. On these, however, the brutes act as well as ourselves, and they have been unduly exalted into the highest ground of difference between man and the brutes. To this belongs the reasoning power, and so the power of controlling the mightiest forces through a knowledge of their laws, and of combining materials anew at the behest of use and of beauty. Through this, man can construct machinery, and use fire, and the metals, and steam, and lightning, and the printing-press; can act on the distant and the future, and can rise to the conception of law. Through language, experience and all knowledge can be diffused and transmitted, so that not only, as with the brutes, the individual may be improved, but the race may make progress.

Finding his centre and life in the soul and in nature, man looks no longer downward, but outward. At first he cowers before the forces of nature and deifies them; but at length he comes to know them as uniform and controls them; and how far this control may go it is impossible to say. Through machinery man is already laying off on to nature his heaviest burdens. Already he spans continents with the iron track. He makes the bed of the ocean the track of his thought. He evokes from a drop of water the power to send that thought with a speed that makes the swift-rolling earth but a laggard, and confounds our notions of time. He takes apart the mechanism of nature, analyzing it into its elements. He traces force through its subtle transformations. He seizes the light from the farthest star and wrenches from it the secrets of its home. He may yet, who knows? navigate the air, and parties be seen careering and bicycling through it. Through chemistry he may combine the elements into food without the labor of tilling the soil.

With such a world for his home, and such powers at his command, civilization will have ample materials and scope. Now there will be nations, and cities, and wealth, and art; now the Parthenon and the Coliseum. Now refinement will take the place of barbarism, manners will be polished, and nothing that can minister to comfort, or taste, or luxury will be wanting. Now the full capacity of man for achievement and enjoyment within the limits of nature will be reached. Here we have the sphere of what, in the Scriptures, is called " the natural man."

But in all this man can know nothing but this rounded, limited, necessitated frame-work of uniformities. Except in the mere notion of it, sapless and powerless, he can know nothing of anything that will put him in relation with what is above or beyond the horizon of time. What can such a system know, what can it utter, of anything beyond itself ? Hence the time has come for the reign of sense, and of experiment, and of positive science. Now, what man can see, and touch, he knows, and only that. What belongs to the on-goings of this visible system is real to him, and only that. Now art is not fantastic ; it may reach high perfection : but what of religion ? Religion ! what need have we of that ? God ! what need of him ? Have we not force, uniform force, and do not al' things continue as they were from the beginning of the creation, if it ever had a beginning ? Have we not the *To Pan*, the universal All, the soul of the universe working itself up from unconsciousness through molecules, and maggots, and mice, and marmots, and monkeys, to its highest culmination in man ? Certainly no God is needed, a miracle is impossible, or if possible it cannot be proved even by the senses, and the idea of a revelation is absurd. If the religious nature must find some resting-place, let it make the unconscious universe with its sleeping capabilities its god ; or let it frame to itself the conception of a god whose work is finished, and who is enjoying himself in everlasting repose. This is, indeed, just what those who practically ignore the spirit have always done and are doing now. Yearning and groping after something higher, yet recognizing only necessary relations as in mathematics, and the uniform and unconscious forces of nature, they transfer what they thus find, and only that, over to the infinite. Of this the result may reveal itself in different forms, and under different names. In India it may be Brahminism or Budhism. In Germany it may be transcendentalism, or positivism, or pantheism. In this country it may be an humble imitation and jumble of them all ; but the thing itself and its paralyzing effect on the religious character will be essentially the same, whether at Benares, at Berlin, or at Boston.

Such is the soul. Some would make it include only instinct and sensation. I would make it include the intellect of man, perceptive, and combinative, with those endowments which fit him to be a denizen of this world, to serve himself of its substances, and to have dominion over it by the adjustment of its forces for the accomplishment of his own ends. It knows of nature, and of science and art within that, but of nothing beyond.

We next turn to the spirit. We here pass into an entirely different region, and hence infer a difference of soul and spirit. If there be a distinct function, there must be a distinct organ ; and certainly sense is not more different from intellect than intellect is from the power of spiritual apprehension. We here pass entirely away from and above anything that belongs to the animal, or to which his acts can have relation, and come to the immediate knowledge of moral law, of a personal God, of our filial relation to him as made in his image, and of our responsibility to him. We come to all that is involved in prayer, in communion with God, in loving him, and in making him our portion. We come also to that brotherly kindness of which the Apostle speaks, and by which we love our fellow-men as the spiritual children of a common Father. This is the

region of the spirit, and of all this the brute knows aoso-
lutely nothing. He has nothing in common with us in it.
We here reach the region of personalities, and sanctities,
of that which calls for respect, and awe, and veneration,
and worship. Of all this the experience is impossible,
not only to the brutes, but to mere intellect, or to taste
knowing only beauty. The logical faculty with its concepts
and notions cannot compass it. The intuitions of the pure
reason do not give it, for "that which is spiritual is spiritually discerned." There is a discernment by the spirit,
not merely of ideas and relations, as by the intellect, but
of qualities as meeting a taste and a want. "O taste and
see that the Lord is good." The brute cannot say that;
the intellect cannot say it; nothing can say it but that
which has immediate apprehension in the region of spirit
as sense has in that of matter. Either this is, or there is
for us no personality, no God. It is through sensation,
which is feeling, and perception, which is knowledge, that
we are conversant with matter, and in our knowledge of
the material world these are blended. So they are in the
meaning of the words that express that knowledge. The
word house, includes both a sensation and a perception.
And so it is with the spirit in its knowledge of spiritual
things. There is intuition, apprehension, knowledge, but
so blended with feeling that they become one and receive
a common name. Only thus could we have such words
as obligation, righteousness, adoration, love, that is, rational
love, holiness, and godliness. These imply spirit in immediate communication with spirit, as sense-perception
and words from that, imply intelligence in immediate
communication with matter. And as we have from our
intercourse with matter, sense-perception, including both
feeling and knowledge, so do we have from our intercourse
with spirit, senti-*ment*, that is. from its etymology, imme-

diate apprehension of mind or spirit, and including both
intuition and emotion. This is the characteristic of spirit,
that it does not deal with gross matter, touching, tasting,
handling; that it does not analyze, and abstract, and combine, and induce, and deduce logically; but that it blends
and fuses the intuition of that which is highest, with
emotion; and so approves, and condemns, and loves, and
rejoices with a "joy unspeakable and full of glory," and
wonders, and adores. So does it become "the rapt seraph
that adores and burns."

This immediate apprehension just spoken of in the
region of the invisible and the spiritual, is said by some to
be by faith, and it is on this that they base their definition
of faith. But since evil as well as good spirits must have
this apprehension, such faith, if it be faith at all, cannot be
that required by the Gospel.

But would not man be a moral being without the knowledge of God? Yes. His moral nature would affirm obligation to choose as between higher and lower ends, but
it would, as I think, be so without light and sanctions,
that its impulses would either simply take their turn with
others, or be wholly disregarded as an impertinence. Such
a nature without God would be an organ and a function
without its proper element and sphere. Man is a spirit in
the image of God. It is as a spirit preëminently that he
is in that image. God is his supreme end and good; and
if this be not known there may be moral phenomena as
blind gropings, but no working in distinct light, and no
moral law recognized as supreme.

Such is the spirit. It gives us a sphere above that of
nature, in which there is intuition of personality, and of
what pertains to that; and in which emotion is always
blended with intuition. In it there may be a consciousness
of the immediate presence of God with us. In it we have

a basis for the operation in us of the Holy Spirit in his quickening and sanctifying and comforting influences ; and here it is that we find the sphere of those who, in the Scriptures, are called spiritual. And as we have seen it to be possible for man to concentrate his life in the lower region of the body, or again within the on-goings and fixed laws of nature, so also is it possible for him to concentrate his life in the region of the spirit. He may " live in the spirit, and walk in the spirit." He may not only look downward, and outward, but also upward. The failure to do this is the great failure and apostasy of man.

The view just stated seems implied throughout the Bible ; and whoever will notice it will find it implied in a large portion of the evangelical sermons he hears. If we accept it, besides throwing light on important doctrines which cannot now be specified, it will give us first, a clear distinction between man and the brutes. We can then give the brutes all that is claimed for them, and still not rank with them. Let them generalize, and contrive, and even reason if you will, it will yet not be claimed that they have the capacity of knowing, or loving, or worshipping God, or of working under moral law. It will not be claimed that the alternative necessary for moral freedom is possible for them. This distinction is of special importance just now. This view will also give us a clear distinction between nature and the supernatural. Nature is necessitated, spirit is free, and all operation of free spirit within nature is supernatural. This is the only consistent line that can be drawn. The operation is supernatural, but not miraculous. If it be directly by the will of God, and the course of nature be reversed or suspended by it, it is a miracle, and, if we admit a personal God, any supposition that this is impossible is absurd.

To the view now presented objections may be made—

some perhaps which would not lie against the common view. It may be asked whether the spirit can exist separate from the soul, as the soul from the body. It may be said that our Saviour spoke of the soul rather than of the spirit, asking what a man should give in exchange for his soul, and warning us to fear Him who can destroy both soul and body in hell. But it is to be said, also, that the words spirit, and soul, and their cognates, cannot, for the most part, be used interchangeably even in English, and that the contrast between the Greek words signifying these is much stronger, the word for spirit and its derivatives being generally used in a higher sense ; and that after the Holy Spirit was given, the use of the word spirit greatly predominates. It was his spirit, not his soul, that our Saviour commended into the hands of God ; and the first Christian martyr said, " Lord Jesus, receive my spirit." No angel, or devil, is said to have a soul. They are spirits ; and it is the " spirits of just men " that are " made perfect."

But whatever may be thought of this division of our nature by the Apostle, and I suspect the Apostle was right, it is certain that the three spheres of life based on this division are recognized, not only in the Scriptures, as they are most fully, but also by mankind generally. These spheres are, First, The Sensual, having its seat and centre in the body ; Secondly, The Worldly, in which life is centred within the compass of nature and of time, and in which, as I suppose, the soul may be greatly cultivated while the spirit is neglected and dwarfed ; and Thirdly, The Spiritual, in which man " lives in the spirit, and walks in the spirit." In the first of these spheres the appetites bear sway ; in the second, the desires ; in the third, the moral and spiritual affections. Into these three classes, in Scripture language the carnal, the natural, and the spiritual, mankind may be divided. These three spheres of life there are, and what-

ever may be their basis in our complex nature, it is to
these, my beloved friends, that I wish to call your attention
as you are about to enter upon the new and wider responsibilities of life.

But is it possible that any one of you shall go down
and abide on the low plane of animal life, and sink into its
indulgences and the vices that riot there? I trust it may not
be, and yet it is possible. Strange as it may appear, experience and observation hardly seem to diminish the number
of travellers in this road to destruction, and many educated
and strong men go in at the gate that stands wide open
at its entrance. Accordingly, we still see gluttons that
come to poverty. We still see those who "tarry long at
the wine," or what they suppose to be wine, and who have
"woe," and "sorrow," and "contentions," and "babbling,"
and "wounds without cause," and "redness of eyes;" who
say "they have beaten me and I felt it not, when shall I
awake, I will seek it yet again." Yes, and those lips of
the strange woman that of old dropped "as an honey-
comb," and the mouth that was "smoother than oil," are
speaking still; and the feet that went down to death, and
the steps that took hold on hell are still travelling the same
dreadful way; and there are victims who "mourn at the
last when their flesh and their body are consumed, and say,
How have we hated instruction, and have not obeyed the
voice of our teachers." But whoever may enter this gate
of sensuality, be not you of the number. Dally not with
the allurements at its entrance. "Avoid it, pass not by it,
turn from it and pass away."

But if I may be hopeful of your escape from low sensuality, what shall I say of worldliness—of that world which the
Scriptures put in opposition to God and to Christ? "Love
not the world, neither the things that are in the world.
If any man love the world the love of the Father is

not in him." What world is this? As an object of love, it is that world of nature and of time of which I have spoken, seen out of its relation to God, and idolized. As consisting of persons, it is those who thus idolize this world of nature and of time, whether speculatively recognizing God or not. They may be formalists, or superstitious, or skeptics, or even atheists, and yet the radical character be the same. Most men love and idolize the world in pursuing the ordinary objects of gain and of ambition, but do not justify it to themselves. This you will be tempted to do, and this is your great danger. But as educated, you may be tempted to do it, and to justify it, in the name, and under the authority of science ; and the temper of the times requires that you be specially guarded against this.

You live in a day when science is making great progress, and you are called upon to advance and honor science. Science is simply a knowledge of the works of God as they are revealed under uniform laws of succession and construction. This knowledge the Bible favors. It tells us that "the works of God are great, sought out of all them that have pleasure therein." Let them be thus sought out. They ought to be. But when men suppose that science is all ; when they begin to talk about the majesty of impersonal law in the place of a personal God ; when, instead of making this magnificent and amazing scene of uniformities but the outer court of God's temple, they make it a finality, cutting it off from the sanctities of religion and the higher glories of the upper temple ; they dwarf both it and themselves, and not only make that which is so beautiful in its place to be an insolvable enigma, but, as offering itself to meet the highest human wants, they make it to be a failure and a deformity. Science is good, but with no revealed system to meet the higher wants of

man, it is a pillar crowned by no capital, an avenue termi-
nated by no mansion ; and ignoring that which is highest,
it falls back into rejections and pettinesses. There is no
narrower man, often none more bigoted, than he who
thinks that science is all. With his spiritual faculties
undeveloped, self-complacent from defect, plodding and
sneering in his little round of uniformities, he is but half
a man. You may see him where scientific conventions
gather, with his plant-box across his shoulder and his
geologic hammer in his hand, on his way to spend God's
day as a naturalist, instead of honoring him by spiritual
worship with his people ; and as he goes he shall meet a
woman aged and blind, who can see no plants, who cannot
see even him, but whose lips move in prayer ; and he
shall think of her only as a poor specimen of Natural
History ; and he may be the greatest among naturalists,
and she may be the least in the kingdom of heaven ; but
she is greater than he. She is greater because she
belongs, and he does not, to a kingdom of purity and joy
and free service, having God for its light and centre, and
love for its gravitating force, and in which science but furnishes the ground under their feet from which its subjects
may rise into their true life. Science is good. It gives
control over nature. It is the basis of art. It ministers
to comfort and to taste. But it eradicates no evil passion.
It does not reach the deep springs of human action, so as
to control character ; and hence it cannot renovate society. It can assuage no grief. It stands at the door of
the tomb and is dumb. It knows nothing of sin, or of
redemption, or of prayer and communion with God, or of
a judgment day. It has not one property of a corner-stone
on which you can build for eternity. Give science then
its place and full scope. Study the works of God ; but

study them as his works, and so as to bring you nearer to
Him.

Nearer to God—that is what we need. God is a spirit.
We are in his image. A spiritual life pervaded by the
worship of Him in spirit and in truth is therefore our true
life. Away from the life of the flesh, and the love of the
world, I now call you to this. I call you to walk, like one
of old, with God. Failing of this you will fail of that
which is highest, and, severed from the source of life, your
failure will be final and utter. "To be carnally minded is
death ; but to be spiritually minded is life and peace." If
the race could but be lifted up to this, the great adjustments needed would take place of themselves. Knowing
himself, and knowing the Bible as God's provision for his
spiritual life as nature is for his animal life, the higher
and lower natures of man, man and nature, and nature
and the Bible would come into accord. Knowledge,
and the inventions and power that come through that,
would be greatly increased. Soliciting her by the hand
of a more skilful and loving science, man would be
nourished at the breasts of a nature more plastic and
richer than now. No longer infidel, like the Hebrew
mother of old, nature would take man as at once her own
and her foster child, and bring him up for God. The
region of spiritual life would no longer be, or seem to any,
one of mysticism, or uncertainty, or gloom. So it was
not to the Apostle. So it will not be to you, my friends,
if, holding body and soul, nature and science in their own
place, you shall centre your life in the spirit, and seek in
yourselves and in others the welfare of that. So doing,
all other ends must fall into subordination to moral and
spiritual ends, and your first and most urgent need will be
seen to be, not wealth or honor ; not even what you shall
eat, or what you shall drink, or wherewithal you shall be

clothed ; but that blamelessness of the " whole spirit and
soul and body " for which the Apostle prays. Guilt,
guilt, and not ignorance or poverty, you will see to be the
great obstacle to be taken out of the way.

And as moral and spiritual ends will subordinate all
things to themselves in your own life, so will they, as they
shape the future revealed in the Bible, shape all your
expectations of the future. You will not look forward, as
many do, to the continuance forever of a nature, embosom-
ing physical science indeed, and beautiful in many of its
aspects, but yet evidently out of harmony with man and sympathizing with his unrest. You will heed the prophecies in
nature herself from former upheavals and overturnings, of
another yet to come ; and you will look for this, not from
any upward movement of blind forces, but from the coming of our Lord Jesus Christ, who will raise the dead, and
judge the world, and bring in everlasting righteousness.

NOTE.

The doctrine of the foregoing discourse is not newly adopted by
me. On the 158th page of my Lectures on Moral Science it is
said :—" Here it is that we find the ground and necessity of a three-
fold division of man into body, soul, and spirit, which the Scriptures
seem to recognize, and which philosophy will be compelled to adopt."
The doctrine is now awakening increased interest, and I desire to
call attention to an able English work upon it which I have recently
seen—The " Tripartite Nature of Man," by the Rev. J. B. Heard.

XVIII.

LIFE.

For whosoever will save his life, shall lose it ; and whosoever will lose his life for my sake shall find it.—Matthew, xvi. 25.

NO less than six times is this passage, or its equivalent, given us by the Evangelists : " For whosoever will save his life, shall lose it : and whosoever will lose his life for my sake, shall find it." This indicates its deep significance and central position in the Christian system. This significance and position it has, whether we consider the subject spoken of, or the principle involved. The subject spoken of is Life. The principle involved is self-renunciation, even to the loss of life, for Christ's sake, and the gain through that of life eternal.

To this subject, and this principle, I now invite your attention.

And first, of Life. What is that life which we are to lose that we may gain one that is better? What is that better life which we are thus to gain?

Life ! What is life? Life is a force. What is force? With this, and the idea of it, we are early familiar. The infant knows it when it first stretches forth its little hand, or feels the pressure of its mother's arms ; and a large portion of the experience of subsequent life consists either in the putting forth of force, or in feeling and observing its effects. No change that we observe, no movement is produced without it. At first many things around us, as the

₊ June 26, 1870.

rock and the earth, seem devoid of force and at rest. But smite the rock and you will find a force of cohesion that will prevent its particles from flying asunder; and as for the earth, we know that it is rolled on its axis, and whirled in its orbit, by a force for which we have no measure. Investigating further, we find that without force, matter has no consistency, and that, in its wider relations, it has no stability except through uniform motion, produced by uniform force.

Thus does this familiar acquaintance of our infancy not only reveal itself where it was least expected, in the innermost constitution of matter, but it spreads itself through immensity, urging the planets on their way, and holding the stellar heavens in its grasp.

Here we have two things, matter and force, and it will be seen that force reveals itself only through motion or the resistance of motion, and equally through each. The motion, therefore, is not the force. The force is the cause both of the motion and of the resistance, and till we reach a power to originate motion we have no original force. To say, as some do, that motion is force, is to make motion the cause of motion, and any beginning of motion impossible.

As revealed through motion, force is manifested under three aspects—as aimless; as orderly, but necessitated; and as under the guidance of choice and will.

Of force as operating, or seeming to operate aimlessly, we have examples in chaos, in the winds, and in the ocean when it tosses and whirls matter, and causes it to heave and surge without order, and with no apparent reference to an end. So far as we can see, this might be, and go on forever. Here we have matter and force simply, and and all that belongs to them of their own right.

Before these, as thus exhibited, the human mind stands

hopelessly. It knows the spectacle as a fact, but can have no communion with it. There is in it no thought, and no basis for science.

We also see force necessitated, but acting, by what is equivalent to an instinct, in subordination to the idea of order. Order reveals itself in regularity of form, or of movement. Primarily it is regularity of movement. This may either petrify its material in fixed forms, as in the crystal, or become established, as in the heavens, and abide from age to age, a spectacle of force acting permanently in subordination to the idea of order.

With matter and force thus manifested, the human mind comes into sympathy. Form and movement now express ideas, and science becomes possible.

Groping among a shapeless mass, an explorer lights upon a crystal. It delights the eye by its brilliancy, but it delights the mind more by the regularity of its form. At once the man seizes the crystal. It satisfies no animal want, but he admires it, exhibits it, and lays it up among his treasures.

Searching now into the manifestation of force as seen in the crystal, we find a force in different kinds of matter tending to crystallize it in different forms. These forms we find to be geometric, as the cube, the rhomboid, the hexahedron. Toward one of these we find that the carbon of the diamond is striving, toward another the quartz of the rock cyrstal, and toward another the lime of the calc-spar. Thus do we find through this form of force, not merely ideas, but *ideals*, and we find each kind of matter striving after its own ideal. That ideal is seldom reached perfectly, but it is never lost sight of, and it is one of the delights of science to trace the doublings and disguises under which it is sought.

But while we thus find in the crystal a basis for science,

we also find that which baffles science. Analyze it. You have the same particles, the same weight, but they are only the corpse of the crystal. That you have not, and human power can no more restore it than it can raise a dead body to life. True, there is a power of reproduction which may be said to answer to the seed in the plant. Place these same particles so that they can move freely among themselves ; plant them, and they will again assume the same form. There will be a resurrection. There will be that, and that is all we know about it. No microscope, no test will enable us to discover any fitness or tendency in the particles to assume this form, or to detect the force which controls them. We may say, if we please, that it is a *property* of such matter to combine thus, but that is only another mode of stating the fact. We simply know from observation that there is an unconscious, necessitated movement subordinated to the idea of order. That movement and its result we record, and call it science.

And this is *nature* and the whole of it. Wherever we have a force that gives no evidence of self-comprehension, or of comprehending its end as compared with other ends, we have nature ; and physical science is nothing more than a record of the movements and results of matter controlled by such a force. With favoring conditions such a force will go on to its end with a precision that mocks human skill. Baffle it, and it will go on still, and work out monstrosities. Such a force is not aimless, but it is unswerving. It hears no cry, and recks of no consequences.

Of force acting thus there are as many varieties as there are forms of matter, perhaps more. Recently some forces of this kind have been supposed to be *correlated;* which means that they are fundamentally one thing manifesting ·tself under different forms of motion. It is supposed, and some think proved, that it is the same agent or force that, as heat, cooks the dinner of the mariner; and as magnet-ism, gives direction to the needle of his compass; and as electricity, runs of errands miles down under his ship; and as light, gives him promise of fair weather in the bow that is set in the sky. This may, or may not be. For our purpose it matters not, so long as they come within that unconscious necessitated sphere which we call nature.

It is among these forces, possibly correlated with them, that I have long ranked that of life. Thirty years ago I said in a public discourse that " the principle of life is one of the great principles of nature," and " when we see it acting with the same uniformity and at times with the same apparent blindness as the other powers of nature, we can neither doubt that it is to be ranked as one of those powers, nor that is among the greatest and most striking of them." It is the highest of those powers, and subordinates all others to itself. It breaks up strong cohesions; it picks the lock of chemical affinity; it mocks at gravitation as it lifts the top of its pine three hundred feet into the air. It is an artist, a Præ-Raphaelite. It gives the shell in the deep sea its voluted form, and its polish. It snatches colors from the faint light and ingrains them in lines and patterns of beauty. It scallops the edge of the leaf and paints the corol of the tulip; it brings from the shapeless mass of the egg the bird that is perfect in beauty; it builds up the huge form of the elephant, and chisels the lineaments of him who is made in the image of God. Still it has all the characteristics of a purely natural force. If not as wholly blind as the lower forms of force, it is never more than instinctive, or somnambulic in its ways, and will work at a wen as readily as at an eye. Except as we supply it with material it is wholly independ-

ent of our will, and builds up and takes down its structures
in its own way.

Like other natural forces, this of life is manifested
only in connection with a particular kind of matter. This
has always been known, but a sensation has been created
of late, by discovering what kind of matter this is, and
calling it *protoplasm*. This amounts to just as much as it
does to analyze the matter of a crystal and call it carbo-
nate of lime, and no more. Here, as in the crystal, analysis gives us only the corpse. Of the formative force we
know nothing in either case; but that it must be different
here is clear from the difference of the result. Before we
had a crystal; now we have organization. This is a new
thing, embodying the new idea of a whole made up of parts
that are mutually means and ends ; and also of the per-
petuation of the species while the individual perishes.
Here is a radical difference, and the attempt to slur it is
vain. So, also, is there a radical difference between the
two divisions of that force which we call life. Under one,
nutriment is taken directly from inorganic matter, and we
have the vegetable ; under the other, it is taken from food
prepared by vegetables, and we have the animal. In each
of these cases we have not only a new mode of working,
but a new idea and product, and these must be from something new in the cause. In that cause, whatever it is, is
our life. Working in the blind way of a natural force, it
builds up and takes down our bodies. In connection with
it we come to the knowledge of ourselves. In connection
with it we live this earthly life. It thus becomes *our* life
—the life of our bodies—and this is the life that we are to
lose, if need be, for Christ's sake.

What, then, we inquire secondly, is that better life for
the sake of which we are to lose the life of the body?

We here reach the phenomena to which the scalpel, the

microscope, and the chemical test have no relation.   We
reach the life of self-consciousness, of the personality, of
that in every man which he calls *I*, and which is, in truth,
the man himself.   Of this life the phenomena are known
immediately, as they are in themselves, and with a certainty
greater than facts of observation.   Here we find a unit.
There is no unit in matter.   It divides itself endlessly
into molecules and atoms.   But we are one.   We know
ourselves to be one being.   Here, too, we find permanence.   This we do not find in the matter of the body—
we call it the same, as we do a river, but its particles flow
like those of a river.   I hold myself to be the same being
I was thirty-four years ago, when I became president of
this College.   If I know anything, I know this.   But the
protoplasm is not the same.   That has changed many
times.   How, then, can the protoplasm of to-day remember what happened to that of thirty-four years ago?   It
would almost seem as if God had anchored this consciousness of permanence in a flowing stream of matter, to show
that it could not be the product of that matter.

In connection with this one, permanent, self-conscious
being, we find thought, feeling, love, hate, will.   We find
the idea of God, of eternity, of moral law, of retribution.
We find a power of comprehending ends, of freedom
in choosing between them, and of acting, not blindly,
or instinctively, but with a wisdom and adaptation in
emergencies of which no natural power knows anything.
In connection with this prerogative of freedom, we know
ourselves as having the power of originating motion, of a
true causation, of which we not only see no trace in
nature, but the very conception of which is opposed to the
definition of nature.   We are, moreover, able to overlook
and comprehend, as they are related to ourselves, all natural forces, and to make them our servants.

Through these powers it is, and their corresponding objects, that we find ourselves capable of living a permanent life of thought and of increasing knowledge ; a life of emotion, as of admiration, wonder, joy ; a life of the social affections, and of rational love in the appreciation of all that has value or worthiness, and a life of voluntary activity in the pursuit of chosen ends. This life, endowed by the beneficence, and irradiated by the smile of God, we feel that we are capable of living forever ; and this is the life for the sake of which we are to lose the life of the body.

But is not this life the same as that of the body? This is held. "The difference," says Mr. Huxley, "between the powers of the lowest plant or animal and those of the highest, is one of degree, not of kind." Except that plants take their nutriment from inorganic, and animals from organic matter, he says, "it may be truly said that the acts of all living things are fundamentally one." Indeed ! The act of a tree is to grow, of a worm to crawl, of a man to reason, to love and hate, and sin and repent ; and so growing, and crawling, and reasoning, and loving, and hating, and sinning, and repenting, are all fundamentally one ! The doctrine is that thought results from certain combinations of matter as hardness does, and is its property in those combinations in the same way. As well might we say that thought is the property of a telegraphic machine when in motion. Such a machine, not in motion, is as dead protoplasm. Here is a dead body. It is protoplasm ; it is organized. As mere matter, its combinations are the same as in life. But it is dead. It is a telegraphic machine before the electricity comes. That is the life of the machine. Let that come— not a property of the machine, remember—and it will go. Ah, you say, but is not electricity matter too ? Yes, but to say nothing of the origination of the machinery, you have no thought yet. It only clicks. At best it is but a vegetable. To have thought, you as much need an agent other than electricity, higher and totally different, as you needed electricity to start the dead machine. If the clicking were to go on a hundred thousand years it would not develop itself into thought. The machine would not come to self-consciousness and stand above itself, and interpret the product of its own working. No. What we say is that the moment you have a formative force that works under the idea of order, you have what mere matter cannot account for.

We say there is a difference in kind between a crystal and a vegetable, a vegetable and an animal, an animal and a man. A vegetable has life, a crystal has not, an animal has sensation, a vegetable has not, a man has a conscience, an animal has not. We say that there is a difference in kind between motion and thought, and that it is not "fundamentally one" to demolish the argument of an opponent, and to knock him down with your fist. We say, not only that there is a difference in kind between the mineral and the vegetable, the vegetable and the animal, the animal and man, but that the mineral, the vegetable, the animal, and the rational kingdoms are so ordered relatively to each other as to show unity of purpose, superintending wisdom, and an origin from an intelligent will. Admit this, and everything is accounted for. Deny it, and nothing is accounted for. You may observe, and record, and classify, but you account for nothing. And not only so, but you have the higher from the lower, unity from multiplicity, life from death, thought from motion, something from nothing; and you make God impossible. Whoever says, "no phosphorus, no thought," says there is no God. God cannot be matter or force and be God

He must be a person, rational, free, moral, causative, and so "the living God, and an everlasting King"—living in that life of which I have just spoken, and by partaking of which we are in his image.

Unless then we say that the higher in kind is from the lower, that is, something from nothing, that thought is motion, and that matter is God, we must allow that the self-conscious life is different in kind from that of the body.

But allowing that the self-conscious life is different in kind from that of the body, we have not yet reached the full meaning of the word *life*, as used by our Saviour, for this self-conscious life may itself differ in quality. It may be a curse. It may be death in its highest meaning, for death is not merely a cessation of existence, but moral putrefaction and misery. This is the second death, as the life spoken of by our Saviour is truly life—the life everlasting. That is not merely self-consciousness continued, but continued in holiness, in happiness from holiness, that is, in blessedness. It is a life of love, of fulness of joy in the presence of God, and of participation in those pleasures which are at his right hand forevermore.

Having thus seen what life is, we turn to that principle of self-renunciation by which we are to lose the earthly life, if need be, for Christ's sake, and gain one that is better. Whatever this principle may be, the text makes it certain that it is not one which requires the renunciation by us of our highest good. The self we are to renounce is the lower self, as the life we are to lose is the lower life. It is the selfish self. The self we are to deny is the self that is opposed to God. Our highest good, Christ everywhere calls upon us to labor for, and to secure at all hazards, even of the loss of life itself. We are to "lay up treasure in heaven," and Christ requires no renunciation of anything except in relation to that. This is universal with him, and peculiar to him. Does he forewarn his disciples of persecution for his sake, he tells them their reward shall be great in heaven. Does he call upon them to forsake all and follow Him? He promises manifold more in this life, and in the world to come life everlasting. Are they to seek first the kingdom of God? Other things shall be added. Does he command them to love their enemies, and do good, and lend hoping for nothing again? He immediately adds, "and your reward shall be great, and ye shall be the children of the Highest." Even the giving of a cup of cold water for his sake is not to be without its reward. Everywhere a recognition of enjoyment and of suffering as depending on conduct, is involved in his teaching and gives it weight. The first verse of his first discourse as recorded by Matthew is the promise of a reward, even the first word implies it ; and in the last verse of his last discourse as given by the same Evangelist, he speaks of everlasting punishment and of life eternal.

But is this prominence of reward thus held forth as a motive, compatible with an appeal to that which is noblest in man? Does it not make goodness mercenary?

This might be if the condition of the reward were other than it is. The essential good is holy happiness, or happiness from holiness. This can be increased only as the holiness is increased, and external rewards will be added in proportion. Christ had no fear of lowering the dignity of man, or the tone of morals, by a regard to that good the conception of which so underlies morals that without it no moral idea can be formed. If there be no sensibility, no possible enjoyment or suffering, there can be nothing right or wrong, nothing that ought, or ought not to be done.

It may be asked again, how this prominence of reward is compatible with the requirement to do what we do for

Christ's sake. If we are to do it for the reward, then not for Christ's sake; if for Christ's sake, then not for the reward. Is there not contradiction here? No, not contradiction, but one of those Christian paradoxes which abound in the New Testament, by which the many-sided wisdom of Christ brings our whole complex nature into harmony; and by which his teachings are so distinguished from those of abstractionists and logical system makers. Two things the Saviour does. He requires disinterested service, and he promises reward. But if happiness in any form was to be the reward, it was necessary that we should be required to seek it disinterestedly, that is, to seek, not that, but something else. This is a law of our being. Happiness is the spontaneous product of every faculty acting directly upon its appropriate object for the sake of that object. If we are to have happiness from knowledge, we must seek knowledge and not happiness. This would be seeking it, not uninterestedly, but disinterestedly, unselfishly. So of love, only that love is disinterested in its own nature. Knowledge may be sought selfishly, but love, to be love, must be disinterested. It must therefore produce happiness to ourselves as well as to others. It will always do this, and is the only thing we can always do that will. We can always love God and our neighbor. We can always work, or suffer for Christ's sake. If therefore we were to be happy at all through our own activity, or rewarded for it, the requisition of our Saviour could not have been otherwise. It is based on the deepest knowledge of our frame; and when we know the two facts, that happiness cannot be had by seeking it directly, and that love must be disinterested, the paradox is solved.

What has now been said is true of all moral love—of the love of enemies. But in loving Christ, and so suffering for his sake, there is something more. In him we

find every ground of love, whether from complacency or
personal relationship. In him all moral excellence is
marvellously combined, and marvellously expressed—all
the more so from that lowliness of form which has dimmed
its radiance in the eyes of men. In loving him, too, we
love a friend who has loved us, a benefactor through suffering unto death—a redeemer, a leader and captain of
our salvation, who is identified with a great cause ; and in
loving him we identify ourselves with that cause, as a
patriot soldier identifies himself with the cause of his
leader. Casting in our lot with him, choosing him, loving
him, we seek the promotion of that blessedness which is
the object of his kingdom. In the prosperity of that
kingdom is the hope of the world. Whatever we do for
that we do for Christ's sake, and the principle of self-renunciation is that we are to renounce and suffer whatever
the prosperity of that kingdom may require us to renounce
and suffer, and nothing else. Here are no negations, or
abstractions, or mere intellections ; no self-sacrifice as
meritorious, or for its own sake, but a universe of living
beings, personal beings, with glorious capacities and unspeakable interests, and Christ taught no self-renunciation
which should not find its inspiration in the well-being of
such a universe.

But what ! I think I hear you say to me, What ! seek
a higher end by renouncing the lower! Have you not
taught us that the lower is the condition of the higher,
and is best secured through that? Have you not taught
us that this is the law which gives unity both to nature
and to life ? Yes. But while I have taught you that
there is a natural law of self-denial based on condition-
ing and conditioned forces and faculties, and on the law
of limitation from that, I have also taught you that there

is a Christian law of self-denial that may become paramount to this. Christianity is a remedy. It deals with
sin, and it is the exceptional and atrocious nature of that
that brings in an exception to the great natural law of harmony. If there were no sin there would be no call for the
cutting off of a right hand, and the plucking out of a right
eye ; there could be no persecution for righteousness'
sake, no losing of life for Christ's sake. Sin is the primal
disorder. But for this, reflecting itself in the misadjust-
ment of nature to our physical being, this earthly life,
instead of being maintained by struggle and going down
at length into the darkness of death, would have passed
into the life of heaven as the morning twilight brightens
into day. What may be before you in this life I know
not, but I do know that if you are to gain that better life,
you must, in spirit, renounce this. You may not be persecuted for Christ's sake. You may be. In either case,
since the spirit of this world is opposed to that of Christ,
you must, in your inmost souls, renounce this world as a
portion, and not count your life dear if Christ calls for it.
This martyr spirit, ready to reveal itself in little things
as well as in great, as occasion may call for it, up to the
great height of the sacrifice of the earthly life, is what the
world needs in you ; is what you need for your own highest good. This spirit is itself that life eternal which all
external splendor waits to crown.

It is because this spirit, so the inspiration of all that
is noble in this life, and of all good hope for the future,
cannot co-exist, logically at least, with materialistic tendencies, that I have desired to draw your attention to
those tendencies as they now exist. In themselves they
are nothing new. More than two thousand years ago
they and their results were as well stated, by a writer of
that day, as they can be now. " For we are born," says

he, " at all adventure : and we shall be hereafter as though
we had never been: for the breath in our nostrils is as
smoke, and a little spark in the moving of our heart ;
which, being extinguished, our body shall be turned into
ashes, and our spirit shall vanish as the soft air ; and our
life shall pass away as the trace of a cloud, and shall be
dispersed as a mist that is driven away with the beams
of the sun, and overcome with the heat thereof." Now
the results : "Come on, therefore, let us enjoy the good
things that are present ; let us fill ourselves with costly
wine and ointment ; let us crown ourselves with rose-buds
before they be withered ; let none of us go without his
part of our voluptuousness." This, that is sensuality, is
the first result. The second is malignity and abuse of
power. "Let us oppress the poor righteous man, let
us not spare the widow, nor reverence "—why should
they reverence anything? How can they reverence a
mere piece of dissolving protoplasm ?—"nor reverence
the ancient gray hairs of the aged. *Let our strength be the
law of justice*, for that which is feeble is found to be
nothing worth." This is the inevitable logic and result
of materialism in whatever form. Let the spirit of this
people but become materialistic, and you insure, on a
scale proportioned to the bounties of God, if not a gross,
yet an utter sensuality, and either anarchy or despotism.

In itself, as I have said, this spirit is the same now as
in ancient times. It only differs in using the vocabulary,
and wearing the livery, and claiming the authority of
physical science. It claims, indeed, to *be* physical science,
but it is not. Force and life, and thought and feeling,
are not matter, and any assertion that they can be the
product or result of mere matter, must be hypothesis, and
not science.

Very different from this philosophy of dust and of death

is that which teaches that the beginning was from above, not from beneath ; that if there be everywhere the reign of law, there is, also, everywhere the reign of One who has originated, and who sustains all law, and who reigns by no law of necessity, but by that moral law which presupposes freedom. I trust you are convinced that there is a region of life and of knowledge above the uniformities of natural science, a region of self-consciousness, of personality, of freedom, of holiness, of perfect love, and of the fulness of joy in a social state unmarred by sin. In such a state the conscious life may be connected—it will be in the future—not as now with a body that lives only by dying, but with one that is unwasting, so as that it can " hunger no more, neither thirst any more." Such a body may have senses responding as ours do now, to the more glorious objects around it, it may be flexible to every touch of the spirit, and may be endowed with the untiring energy that we see in the great forces of nature.

It is, my friends, to a life in this region, and thus endowed, that the Saviour calls you from above ; and that call finds an echo and enforcement in every work of God beneath you. I have said to you that the carbon of the diamond, and the quartz of the rock-crystal, and the lime of the calc-spar are seeking their ideal. After this too it is that the oak and the elm are struggling and battling with the elements. It is the tendency to this in the movements of all things in nature that gives them their beauty, and they all call to you to come into harmony with them, and to struggle toward that higher ideal of your higher nature, which is the glory and crown of these lower works of God. It is to a life of struggle toward this ideal that the Saviour calls you, and he calls you to suffering only as it may be incidental to that. That ideal he himself

was, and is. You are to "grow up into him in all things."
Will you do this? Will you love him, and be like him?
Will you love his cause, and have his spirit, and devote
your lives, cheerfully, joyfully, to the good of men, and to
the glory of God?

XIX.

THE BODY THE TEMPLE OF GOD.

What! know ye not that your body is the temple of the Holy Ghost which is in you, which ye have of God, and ye are not your own?—1 Corinthians, vi. 19.

THERE are three great ideas, each resting back on the fact of sin, that have controlled the religious history of the world. As revealed in the Scriptures each of these has assumed three forms. It has first been presented as a type, then in its antitype, and then, in a modified form, in its consummation and results in Christian life. These ideas we need to see in their relation to each other, if we would apprehend fully the place and use which Christianity assigns to the body.

Of these the first and central idea is that of *sacrifice*. An innocent being comes directly to God, and needs no sacrifice. But a guilty being, not yet given over to despair, naturally asks, "*Wherewith* shall I come before the Lord?" The practical answer to this question given by those unenlightened by revelation, is the saddest and most awful chapter in the history of man. It reveals to us not only the sacrifice of animals with no conception of its true relation to the divine government, but also the sacrifice of human victims in vast numbers, and often the association of cannibalism with religious rites. It shows us a ferocious superstition combining itself with sensuality and a lust for power, with an utter disregard of human rights, and an utter subjection to it of every natural affection. It shows us how great the darkness in man may be when "the light that is in him has become darkness."

But to the question, "Wherewith shall I come before the Lord?" God himself gave an answer under the old dispensation by appointing a system of bloody sacrifices. These, it would seem, must have originated with God, for the thought of pleasing him by taking the life of an innocent being, which life God himself gave, and by destroying with fire everything left of that being that could be useful to man, is too alien from reason to have been suggested by it. As typical and inculcatory, nothing could have been more admirable than these sacrifices. Nothing could have so pointed forward to the Antitype.

The Antitype! The Lamb of God! Jesus Christ! In him we have the idea in its true form, the consummation and fulfilment of all that was signified by the sacrifices of the Old Testament. Whatever significance or efficacy there may have been in the idea of sacrifice, as expressed in preceding ages, it all centred in the one " offering of the body of Jesus Christ once for all." In him, and him alone, all sacrifices of the old dispensation find their Antitype.

But while the idea of sacrifice in its high sense, as making atonement, must be confined to the work of Christ, yet that work was not for its own sake, but for the sake of its spiritual results, carried over into Christian life. And those results are substantially the same to us as they were to those under the old dispensation. Did they, under the form of their sacrifices, recognize the holiness of God, and his perfect requirements, and their own sinfulness, and a forfeited life, and the idea of substitution, and of a perfect consecration? So do we. Did they, in the recognition of these ideas, bring to God sacrifices and offerings which were acceptable to him? So do we, even " spiritual sacrifices," the very things which are " acceptable to God," for their own sake. In these sacrifices

there is nothing outward, material, visible, but there is
that which has value in itself, and without which nothing that is outward, or material, or visible, has any value.
The dispensations of God do not go backwards. To the
eye of sense they may seem to, as outward forms disappear, but to the eye of reason and of faith, it is the real,
the permanent, the eternal taking the place of the sha-
dowy and the transient.

Thus have we the idea of sacrifice in its three forms—
as typical ; as seen in its antitype ; and as expressed in
spiritual worship and full consecration.

The second great idea which has controlled the history
of the world, is that of a *priesthood.*

This removes man still further from God. At first
men brought their own sacrifices and offerings, as Cain
and Abel, but when a priesthood was established, not
only could they not come directly to God without an
offering, but another, and one specially consecrated, was
required to bring the offering. And so consonant was
this idea, also, with the wants of man as conscious of guilt,
that a priesthood, however originated, became permanent
and universal. Everywhere there was a class of men
who intervened between the people and God, and the
exactions and oppressions from them, to which the people
have submitted, are an indirect testimony to their consciousness of alienation from God, to their felt need of
access to him, and to their sense of unfitness to approach
him directly.

This want God met under the old dispensation by
establishing the Levitical priesthood with its magnificent vestments and imposing ceremonial. That this was
wholly typical was obvious, because the priests were
obliged " to offer up sacrifices first for their own sins,"

whereas a real priest must be one who can stand before God in his own name, and that can offer a sacrifice that shall avail on the ground of its own merits. Therefore, magnificent though it was, and appointed of God, and national, and long continued, it yet availed nothing except as pointing to an antitype.

And here again this antitype is Jesus Christ. He was both the sacrifice and the priest. *"He offered up himself."* He was *the* priest, he offered *the* sacrifice. Whatever difficulty we may have in comprehending the mode of it, if the sacrifice of Christ did not avail as between God and us for our salvation, the Old Testament is an absurdity, and salvation by faith is impossible. Christ was the only real priest that ever stood on this earth, and without him no other sacrifices or ministrations could avail anything. " By one offering he perfected forever them that are sanctified."

But here, again, as in the case of sacrifice, the office of priest passes over to the people of God in a modified form. Every Christian is a priest as he is permitted to approach directly to God with no earthly mediator ; as he is permitted to offer up spiritual sacrifices, even himself, and as he stands between God and nature, the only intelligent being on the earth capable of gathering into articulate utterance the praises that go up to him from his works, and of offering them as incense to Him. In this high sense all Christians are priests, all are equally so, and the attempt to perpetuate a priesthood and a continued sacrifice, in distinction from a ministry for teaching and for edification, has not only been a dishonor to the one priesthood and sacrifice of Christ, but has been among the greatest sources of disaster and corruption to the church.

We thus have the idea of a priesthood in its three forms. We have the typical priests, the true Priest, and then Christ has made his followers " priests unto God."

The third great idea which has controlled the religious history of the world, is that of the *temple.* This removes man still farther from God. Not only must there now be a sacrifice and an intervening priest, but the sacrifice must be made in a consecrated place.

If this idea has been less universal and influential than the others, it has yet had such an affinity for the human mind, as to prompt some of the most astonishing labors that have been performed by man. With the exception of the pyramids, the grandest, the costliest, and the most permanent structures built by man, have been temples. So has it been in India and China, so in Asia Minor and Egypt, so in Greece and Italy, so in Central and South America. Nothing that art or labor could do has been spared in erecting and decorating the temples of the gods. To them pilgrimages have been made, and they have been among the wonders of the world.

This idea is also presented by God in the Scriptures under its three forms. As typical he presents it with peculiar magnificence, even more than that of the priesthood, thus showing not only his recognition of the idea, but the importance he attaches to it. There is no scene in history more striking than that in which God took possession of the temple built by Solomon. The building was more magnificent than the world had then seen, perhaps than it has ever seen. The religious feelings and patriotism of a nation, whose work it was, were centred in it. It was a marvel of architectural skill, having been so planned, and the materials so prepared in the mountains, that " neither hammer, nor axe, nor any tool of iron was heard in the house while it was building." When the building that went up thus quietly and as by magic was completed, the whole nation was assembled by special proclamation. Religious services were instituted, innumerable sacrifices

were offered.   The ark of the covenant was brought by
the priests in solemn procession and placed in the temple,
"in the most holy place, even under the wings of the cheru-
bims."   Then King Solomon stood on a brazen scaffold
which he had set in the midst of the court of the temple,
"and kneeled down upon his knees before all the congre-
gation of Israel and spread forth his hands toward heaven"
and prayed.   What a scene !   A whole nation assembled,
standing with bowed heads and in solemn silence !   Its
monarch, surrounded by a magnificence such as earth has
not seen, kneeling in prayer !   That prayer we have.   It
met the grandeur of the occasion, and closed by calling
upon God to take possession of his house.   " Now therefore, arise O Lord into thy resting place, thou and the ark
of thy strength."   This invocation God heard, for "when
Solomon had made an end of praying," while the hush yet
continued and every mind was expectant, " the fire came
down from heaven and consumed the burnt-offering and
the sacrifices, and the glory of the Lord filled the Lord's
house."

But if such was the type, what was the antitype ?   Ex-
ternally it was in wonderful contrast.   Looking forward a
thousand years we see, standing upon the banks of the
Jordan, surrounded by a rugged nature, a human form, a
man simply clad.   He prays, and the heavens are opened,
and the Holy Spirit descends "in a bodily shape like
a dove upon him."   He was the Antitype.   " In him dwelt
the fulness of the Godhead bodily."   In his body God
dwelt, and through that manifested his glory as in no other
way.   The glory of the first temple was simply a brightness showing the presence of God ; the glory of the true
temple was such a manifestation of the divine attributes,
especially his moral attributes, as the world had never

witnessed.   It was the "light of the knowledge of the glory of God in the face of Jesus Christ."

What now is the spiritual idea here to be carried over into Christian life? The Scriptures express it thus: " What! know ye not that your body is the temple of the Holy Ghost which is in you, which ye have of God?" There is now, there has been since the coming of Christ, no temple of God on the earth except the body of man. Christianity had no temple nor anything that resembled one. Christ stood before the old temple and declared that not one stone of it should be left upon another. That was fulfilled, and there was nothing to take its place. For hundreds of years Christians worshipped in obscure places, in concealment, in the catacombs, wherever they could find security.

But was not that a going back of the dispensations? So it would almost seem when we look at the vagueness of nature, and at the difficulty man has in apprehending a spiritual and an infinite God.   It was a great thing for God to manifest himself visibly and permanently as he did to the Israelites, and to choose a place where he might be found ; and it is not, perhaps, surprising that attempts have been made since, and are still made, to connect with Christianity temples, and a temple worship; to establish sacred places, and to localize the presence of God.   This has been done on the ground, or under the pretence, that spiritual worship was cold, and that something warmer was needed.   Warmer—yes, in the sense in which the ancient idolatries were warmer than the worship of a spiritual and holy God as instituted by him.

But all this proceeded on a misapprehension of the genius of Christianity and ended in its perversion.   As the types centred in Christ and had their significance in him, so we are not to go back of him in finding that significance. In him the letter that killeth was dropped, and all became spiritual. But instead of stopping at the anti-type and drawing Christianity wholly from Christ, the pomp, the show, the formality, the outwardness of the type have been carried over into Christian life, and each of the three great ideas mentioned has been the basis of a prevalent and disastrous superstition. A regard for places and forms, once legitimate, became, under Christianity, a superstition, and through it Christianity lost its spiritual power and took on the formality of Judaism blended with the license of paganism. The new wine of a spiritual religion was spoiled, and always will be, in the old bottles of places and forms. What we need, and all that we need, is the realization within us, in its full import, of the great, the precious, the indispensable doctrine of the indwelling of the Spirit of God with man.

That this is a doctrine of the Bible, there can be no doubt. The Apostle Paul is explicit on this point: "Know ye not," he says, "that ye are the temple of God, and that the Spirit of God dwelleth in you? If any man defile the temple of God him shall God destroy, for the temple of God is holy, *which temple ye are.*" This doctrine is also directly asserted by our Saviour, and everywhere implied. "If ye love me, keep my commandments, and I will pray the Father and he shall give you another Comforter, even the Spirit of truth whom the world cannot receive because it seeth him not neither knoweth him, but ye know him for he dwelleth with you and shall be in you." "If a man love me he will keep my words, and my Father will love him, and we will come unto him and make our abode with him."

Thus do these three great ideas result and culminate in making the body of man the temple of God. This is

the end, the consummation ; beyond this nothing can go.
With this the kingdom of God will be, as it must be if it
be at all, within every man, and formality and superstition will be impossible. God dwelling with man, working in him and with him !   Man yielding himself as a child
to God !   For this were the sacrifices, for this the priesthood.   Not by his own unaided strength, but through this,
and this only, will man reach whatever of perfection and
happiness is possible for him.   Christ opened the way for
the presence and indwelling of the Holy Ghost in every
man who will receive him.   Let him be received, and let
the " fruit of the Spirit, which is love, joy, peace, long-suffering, gentleness, goodness, faith, meekness, temperance,"
be manifested in their fulness, and there will be a glory
shining through this temple of the body transcending that
of the Shekinah.   Where these thus produced are, there
the temple of God is, and where these are not, there the
temple of God is not.

I have thus presented to you, my friends, the place
which the body holds under the Christian system.   According to Christianity, it is the office of the body to
stand over against the ancient temple, magnificent as that
was, and to be the dwelling place of God under this dispensation as that was under the old, the only temple of
God now on earth.

And lightly as we may esteem it in our familiarity and
want of spiritual insight, this body is worthy to stand
there.   It is the only temple worthy of God.   Be it, that
it is that which is lowest in man ; it is yet highest in the
handiworks of God.   The heavens do, indeed, " declare
the glory of God and the firmament showeth his handi-
work."   For the impression they make upon us of grandeur and of a broad order, there is nothing that can be
compared with them.   But these heavens are made up

of unorganized bodies floating in space with adjustments relatively simple. They can never manifest the skill required for the construction of the eye which beholds them, and which, in beholding them, epitomizes infinity within a space less than the half of a square inch. But the eye is only a single organ of that body, so complex in its unity, which is set over against the universe to be acted upon by it, and to react upon it. Moreover, the parts of the universe, so far as they are related to the body, are for it, it is not for them ; and we might expect that greater skill and wisdom would be found in that for which the things are made than in the things themselves.

And as the body of man thus transcends all arrangements of inorganic matter, so does it all other forms of organization. Naturalists are agreed that from the first appearance of organization on this planet there was a movement onward and upward till man was reached. They are agreed that of the four great classes in Zoology, that to which man belongs is the highest, and that man stands at the head of that class. In the first fin of the first fish they find a foreshadowing of the hand of man ; but while that fin was perfectly adapted to its use, they find in the hand, as more complicated and capable of wider uses, an instrument vastly more perfect. And so of the body of man as a whole. When it is perfect and of the highest type, there is nothing like it. Whatever superiority any animal may claim in some specialty, there is no one whose body can be compared with that of man in the combined delicacy and strength and beauty of its organization, in its wide range of possible activities, in its erect posture, in its power of articulate speech, and in that general power of expression by which it may become as the æolian harp to the wind, and give forth the whole range of emotion that nature can awaken, or that can stir the depths

11

of a being that is above nature. It was in the form of man that the ancients represented the gods, and it was in the form of man that He appeared who "thought it not robbery to be equal with God." And if he could say of the simple lilies of the field that " Solomon in all his glory was not arrayed like one of these," much more may we say of the body of man, which was the body of Christ, that the temple of Solomon, in all its magnificence, was not to be compared with it.

Has Christianity, then, assigned the body, thus fitted to be the temple of God, its true place? We say, Yes. We say that it has revealed its highest end, and that, in doing this, it has given us the clue to its whole regimen and use. According to the law of limitation this must be so. The higher can be attained only through the lower. Society can make no permanent progress in connection with habits and practices that deteriorate the body. This should be understood. The body is so a part of ourselves that it reacts upon us, and we become enfeebled, degraded, para- lyzed by its abuse. The effects of such abuse, perhaps unsuspected, may pervade society as a choke-damp, lower- ing its susceptibility to truth, and stifling its higher life. This will be so with society ; it will be so with you. Hence I call your attention to it. If you are to be men, and to do the work of men, the relations of the body to the spirit must be known, and the laws of physical well-being must be conformed to.

Looking at the systems of which the body is composed, we see that there are two to which all others are subordi- nate. These are the muscular and the nervous systems— muscle and brain. As an instrument, and controlled by us, each of these has its great function. That of the mus- cles is motion, giving power and expression ; that of the brain is thought: and whoever can so control the body as to produce all desired movements in the easiest and most graceful way, and so as to think by it with all possible facility and power, has attained perfection in the control of the body.   He will only need the choice of right ends, to the attainment of which his thoughts and movements shall be directed.

These two systems, that of thought and of movement, are capable of being developed in harmony.   They are also capable of separate, and in a measure, antagonistic development.   A man may make it his main object, so to cultivate his muscles that he may walk, or run, or wrestle, or row, or fight better than others.   He may train himself to be a prize-fighter, and so draw off the energy of the system in this direction, that there shall be none left for thought and the higher feelings.   To this there is a tendency, and of it a danger in modern physical culture, in gymnasiums, and boating, and ball-playing, and muscular Christianity, which is no Christianity at all.

On the other hand, the nervous system may be developed to the neglect and attenuation of the muscles.   It is not my belief that this is often done by sheer study, with no self-indulgence or wrong physical habits otherwise, but it is done ; and when it is, the end is lost by the means taken to attain it.   With brains over-wrought, and nerves over-sensitive, and digestion impaired, the man is too feeble to carry out into expression and act, the thought and the will that are in him.

But in whichever line the body is to be developed, there must be a submission to fixed conditions.   This they understand who train it solely with reference to its muscular power.   They require men to rise at such an hour, to eat only such food, to exercise so much, to abstain from intoxicating drinks, from tobacco, perhaps from other things.   And this men submit to.   These trainers have understood, as the athletes of old did, what the Apostle means when he says, "Every man that striveth for the mastery, is temperate in *all* things." He does nothing, and indulges in nothing which will unfit the body as an instrument for that for which he is to use it.

Now this is what we ask, and all that we ask, with reference to the use of the body for higher ends. In the interest of learning and of thought, as you are scholars and beneficiaries of the public through an institution endowed by them, we ask you not to fall back into a mere animal life. Except from the exigencies of want, we ask that no muscular development shall be sought beyond the point where the best conditions of thought are reached; and also that such training and regimen, such diet and abstinence shall be submitted to as shall make you athletes in the field of intellect. Here also we ask you to be "temperate in all things," and to keep your body under, not in the way of austerity, but as rational, self-controlled beings acting for higher ends. The end will determine the limit of your liberty. Whatever use you can make of your body and not deteriorate it as an instrument of thought, that, as under the law of thought, you are at liberty to make.

And this is, perhaps, the highest law that could be known to philosophy. Philosophy could see that the intellectual was higher than the animal life, and that it must be a degradation to use the body simply as an instrument of sensation when it might be an instrument of intelligence, comprehension, reason. Philosophy might lay down rules, as the old philosophers did, as may well be done now, for the regulation of the body for the ends of philosophy, but it could know of nothing higher than itself. If man might consecrate his body as a temple for God to dwell in, and God would accept it, that could be known only from God. But while philosophy could not know the fact, because, as the act of a personal God, it is outside of its sphere, that fact is yet fully in accordance with philosophy. It just meets a want, and carries out the doctrine of divine aid in such a way as to restore in substance the communion with God that was lost in Eden, and as to complete Christianity as a redemptive system. Anything else would make God external to us, and Christianity a form. But now God is the living God, present with us, working with all who will work with him; and Christianity is so the dispensation of the Spirit that every Christian may properly be said to be the temple of God, and that every man who will, may so consecrate his body as a temple to God that God will dwell with him.

I am aware of the little favor with which what I have said, and am to say, will be received by many. I know how much there is in the deformities and diseases, and perversions by men of their bodies to cast discredit, perhaps ridicule, on this doctrine. I know it will be said that it is mystical, and not adapted to a practical age, and that it trenches too much on the enjoyment of life. But I know, too, that the apprehensions of men respecting what God has designed for them here are still greatly inadequate; that their standards, and tone of feeling, and whole plane of action are low: and I believe they will hereafter be looked back upon as we look back upon barbarism. I know that civilized, and cultivated, and nominally Christian men use their bodies, if with more sagacity, yet on the same principle as pagans and savages, for mere animalism. They eat and drink and to-morrow they die. I know, too, that except as you bring your bodies, as well as your spirits, under the law of that which is highest for them, you will walk all your lives in disastrous eclipse, you will go halting through your pilgrimage.

It is this *principle*, that of bringing your bodies under the law of their highest end, that is in question here. Will you accept it ? No hard service is required of you, no austerity, no penance, no maceration of the body for its own sake, but simply the application of the principle on which the athlete trains himself. So the Apostle puts it ; he kept his body under and brought it into subjection, but only that he might "so run, not as uncertainly," and " so fight, not as one that beateth the air." Precisely as the old athletes placed the regimen of the body under the law of its end so did he its Christian regimen. " Now," says he, " they do it to obtain a corruptible crown, but we an incorruptible." Whatever use you can make of the body and not impair its fitness and efficiency in enabling you to obtain that incorruptible crown, you are at liberty to make. That crown will come, if it come at all, in con- nection with an incorruptible body ; and you are to in- quire what would be the fitting antecedents of such a body and such a crown.

Shall then, your bodies be brought under the law of that which is highest, and so become the temples of God ? If so, you must submit to the regimen required by that; just that, and nothing more. And here we should expect that while the positive training would be different, yet that whatever would be excluded by the lower as obstructive of perfec- tion, would also be excluded by the higher. I believe that whatever would be excluded in the best training for the physical perfection of the body, would also be excluded from that for intellectual power ; and much more for spir- itual insight and communion with God. But this is ques- tioned theoretically, so far as intellect is concerned, and dis- regarded practically throughout. It is said that a German professor can soak his system in lager beer, and saturate it with tobacco, and be as profound a student, and live as long as he would otherwise. Be it so. The question here is not that. It is on a higher plane. It is whether he can do these things and consecrate his body as he might otherwise to be a temple of the Holy Ghost. A temple may stand as long as it would otherwise, and be as strong, and yet be *defiled*. It is of defilement rather than of impaired strength that a temple is in danger, and he who would hold his body as a temple must study and heed in its broadest import the injunction "keep thyself pure."

At this point it is not for me to judge others. I would make every allowance for prejudices of education and differences of temperament. If there are exceptions I would admit them. But I may express my conviction, that habitual alcoholic or narcotic stimulation of the brain is not compatible with the fullest consecration of the body as a temple of God. Good men may do this in ignorance, as other things prevalent at times have been done, and not offend their consciences, but I believe that greater earnestness, more searching self-scrutiny, fuller light, would reveal its incompatibility with full consecration, and sweep it entirely away. The present position on this point of the Christian Church as a whole, and largely of the Christian ministry, I regard as obstructive of the highest manhood, and of the spread of spiritual religion. I know that strong men have, in this connection, been bound as in fetters of brass, and cast down from high places, and have found premature prostration and premature graves, and that this process is going on now. Let me say, therefore, to those who expect to be ministers, that I believe that sermons, even those called great sermons, which are the product of alcoholic or narcotic stimulation, are a service of God by "strange fire ; " and that for men to be scrupulous about their attire as clerical, and yet to enter upon religious services with narcotized bodies, and a breath that "smells to heaven" of anything but incense, is an incongruity and an offence, a cropping out of the old Phariseeism that made clean " the outside of the cup and the platter." Not that abstinence has merit, or secures consecration. It is only its best condition.

But whatever may be said of particular practices or habits, or conditions, what I ask your attention to is the thing itself, the principle, the consecration of your bodies, under the law of that which is highest, and according to your best light, to be the temples of God. If they are to be temples they must be consecrated. Will you do that? When this is done on the part of any one it involves that which is of higher significance and more acceptable to God than the consecration of any cathedral that ever has been or will be built on the earth. How grand a thing it is for any one in the freshness of youth and the fulness of strength to say, " This body, which God has given me, I hold as a temple for his indwelling. These senses, these hands, these feet, this whole organization shall be held as sacred, and shall be devoted to no purpose that I do not conscientiously believe will be pleasing to God." Can you do better? Does God, indeed, come to you and offer to dwell with you, and will you not welcome him? Welcome Him, and his presence shall be to you an infinite joy. When the high and lofty One that inhabiteth eternity, whose name is Holy, who dwelleth in the high and holy place, says that He will also dwell with him that is of a contrite and humble spirit, it is not for dismay, or sadness, or repression, but in sympathy, and with an unutterable tenderness, to " revive the spirit of the humble, and to revive the heart of the contrite ones."

I have only to add that whatever course you may take, whether you do, or not recognize the claims of God, " you are not your own." You may seek, as most do, to appropriate yourselves to your own selfish ends, and thus rob God, but "ye are not your own." These are the words that I would leave sounding in your ears, "Ye are not your own." You do not belong to yourselves. You belong to God. You belong to humanity. You belong to a world that is waiting for your help. You belong thus to God and to humanity as the creatures and children of God, and members in common of his great rational and moral family and kingdom. You also belong to God and to humanity by a more tender tie. Not only are you not your own as the creatures of God, but "Ye are not your own, *for ye are bought with a price*—therefore glorify God in your *body* and in your spirit, which are God's."

11*

XX.

THE CIRCULAR AND THE ONWARD MOVEMENT.

That which hath been is now, and that which is to be hath already been ; and God requireth that which is past.—Ecclesiastes, iii. 15.

WE are told by astronomers, that our planetary system has two movements ; one circular, by which the motions return upon themselves ; and the other, onward in infinite space. By the first of these the system is maintained as a system. The circling bodies composing it now approach each other, and now recede till they return to their first position, thus perpetuating from age to age, the mystic dance of the heavens.

Of these movements, those that are circular can be calculated, and in regard to them the astronomer, relying upon the stability of the order of nature, may say, " That which hath been is now, and that which is to be hath already been." But the onward movement cannot be calculated. By that the whole system, the sun and all his train of planets and secondaries and comets, is moving on in space, perhaps in a right line, perhaps around some centre at an inconceivable distance ; and of this movement, its object and its limit, we know nothing. We have no data for calculation, and the mighty secret must rest with God till He shall please to reveal it.

Not unlike these are the two great movements of human life. There is a succession of events, making up much of what we call life, constantly beginning, never ending, which is repeated over and over every generation. There is also a progressive movement, both of the individual and of the race, which does not return upon itself, the objects and limits of which are known to man only as it has pleased God to reveal them. It is with this latter movement that man is connected as responsible under the moral and permanent government of God. That which is once past here, is fixed forever, and God requireth it.

It is only as we keep in view these two movements, that we have a key to the apparently discrepant assertions of the wise man. Now we hear him say that "all things come alike to all ;" that "there is one event to the righteous and to the wicked." And so, for the most part, there is in the circular movement. But again we hear him say, " I know that it shall be well with them that fear God, which fear before Him ; but it shall not be well with the wicked." And so it always is with the onward movement.

Looking at the circular movement, permanent indeed in its successions, yet so transient for the individual, Solomon speaks of· all things as "vanity and vexation of spirit," and "full of labor." And, regarding life in this aspect, how striking are the emblems chosen by him to represent it. He compares it to the sun that "ariseth, and goeth down, and hasteth again to the place where he arose ;" to the wind "that goeth toward the south, and turneth about unto the north, that whirleth about continually, and returneth again according to its circuits ;" to the rivers that "are taken from the sea, and return again to the place whence they arose." But not so does he speak when he surveys the whole of life. Looking also at the onward movement and its issues, he condenses all wisdom into one brief utterance, and says, " Let us hear the conclusion of the whole matter. Fear God, and keep his commandments, for this is the whole duty of man. For

God will bring every work into judgment, with every secret thing, whether it be good or whether it be evil." "God requireth that which is past."

It is as they are brought within the sweep of this circular, or, if you please, iterated movement, that the generations come and go, each another, and yet the same. In its great features the succession of events is recurrent, and "that which hath been is now." To those who went before us there were the same senses and the same gifts of intellect as to us. Their eyes beheld the same sun; they watched the same seasons as they came and went; the trees, the mountains, the streams, the flying clouds, the stars of night, were the same to them as to us. There was to them the same period of helpless, ignorant infancy; of curious, wondering, wayward childhood; of inexperienced and perilous youth, and then the time came, which among some ancient nations was celebrated as a festival, when the manly robe was put on, and they were committed to their own guidance. And, "That which hath been is now." As young men you now stand where others have stood before you, and the same doubts, and hopes and fears that agitated them now agitate you. The same veil of futurity that once rested over their prospects, now rests over yours. Can that veil be raised? In some measure it may, for we are told not only that "that which hath been is now," but that "that which is to be hath already been."

In illustrating this part of the subject I observe, First, that it is to be with you as it has already been with those who have gone before you, in the diminution of your numbers by death, and in the physical changes that are to pass upon you.

It has been in time past that one and another from the ranks of those who have been associated as friends has been

14

arrested in his career at no distant period, and has found
an early grave. And so it will be with some of you. By
consumption, by fever, by accident, slowly, or suddenly,
the grasp of the destroyer will be fixed upon you. And can
it be that to any of you the bright morning shall be over-
cast, and your sun go down before it is noon? Ah, if we
could but know whose eye must first be dim, whose heart
first cease to beat, whose account must first be rendered
up! We cannot know, but there is One who does, and
the days may be few that shall reveal the fearful secret to
the startled consciousness of him who least expects it.
Thus one will go, and the time of another, and of another
will come. Meanwhile the finger of Time will begin to trace
its furrows upon the brow of those of you who remain, and
his hand to scatter its frosts upon your heads. You will
see another generation coming up to take your places, and
will think it wonderful how fast they come. You will begin to be called old men, and be surprised at it ; you will
begin to be old men, till one and another shall pass away
and the last man shall be left alone bending with years,
and tottering upon the brink of the grave.

In view, then, of the certainty of death, and the uncertainty of the time, lay no plan of life into which provision for it as possible at any time, does not enter. " Watch,
for you know not at what hour the house may be broken
through."

And as there are physical changes which are common
and inevitable to the race, so also there are mental
changes.

It has been said that when the mind takes its own
course, the ruling passion in youth is pleasure, in middle
life fame, and in old age avarice. And probably, if the
character be not formed on fixed principles under the
moral government of God, some such change of object does

usually take place.   Certainly as age comes on the ardor
of the passions will cool, the imagination will be chastened,
and the judgment will predominate more.   Then the power
of habit will reveal itself more strongly.   Your thoughts,
your feelings, your associations, your pursuits will run on
in settled courses that will not be easily broken up.   The
metal now so ready to fluctuate and so impressible, will
harden, and will be taking its final· impress for eternity.
As the body decays so will the mind, or seem to, just as
the sun seems to be going out when the cloud thickens
before him.   First, the perceiving faculties will fail, then
the memory, then the judgment, and then second childhood
will have come.

Whether it is desirable for any one to reach this point
God only knows, but they are to be pitied who do reach
it, having earned no title to the respect and love of those
who come after.

I observe, again, that it is to be with you as it has
already been with those who have gone before you, in your
failure to carry out your plans of life.

Young men generally form to themselves some plan of
life, and this is right, but it should be only in a general
way.   The two forces by which the direction of human life
is determined, and which act and react upon each other,
are the human will, and the course of events.   But the
course of events is under the control of God, and it is by
means of this that " He turneth the hearts of men as the
rivers of water are turned."   So influential, indeed, is this,
that the Prophet could say, " I know, O Lord, that it is
not in man that walketh to direct his steps."   By the
course of events God can hedge up your way in any particular direction ; He can take off the chariot-wheels of
your ambition, and can open to you new and unexpected

vistas of hope and of effort. Few are there, much advanced in life, who cannot look back to unexpected events that have so become turning-points in their lives that they have been led in a way they knew not.

And so, doubtless, it will be with you. While, therefore, you heed duly the fixed course of God's providence, and use vigorously your faculties in studying its indications, falling into no indolence or imbecility as those do who wait for things to turn up, you are yet not to map the future with unchanging lines. Mistake not for a long line of coast, the headland that may round you into another sea. Go up no hill before you come to it. Live in the spirit of the petition which asks for daily bread Thus doing, the failure to carry out your plans may be the source, not only of no regret, but of thankfulness and joy.

These things have been in times past; they will be in time to come. They do not depend upon chance, or the will of man, but upon the settled laws of Divine Providence. There are, however, other things which "have been" so universally that we expect them with almost the same certainty as the rising of the sun, and yet we see no necessity for them. Of these it may be said, as our Saviour said of offences, " it must needs be that they come, but woe to the man by whom they come." We may certainly expect them, but they may be avoided by each individual.

Judging, then, from the past, it will be that some of you will so far find in the circular movement the chief objects of study as to become one-sided and narrow.

It is the circular movement that is the ground and sphere of science ; and as we found in the two movements a key to the seeming discrepancies in the Book of Ecclesiastes, so do we find in them a key to the alleged want of harmony between science and religion. Science, that is, natural science, which alone is in question here, has its basis in those works of God which are the expression of his natural attributes, as his intelligence and power, and which reveal themselves in the circular movement. Religion, on the other hand, has for its basis the moral attributes of God, which find their scope and distinctive sphere in the onward movement. The harmony, therefore, between science and religion must be, and must ultimately be found to be, just as perfect as it is between the natural and the moral attributes of God.

In science, as based on the circular movement, the instruments are observation, experiment, and experience. Making use of these, and assuming the uniformity of nature, science claims the right to proceed outwards in space, and from that which is here, and can be observed, to affirm uniformity of agency and of structure where observation cannot go. It also claims, and on the same ground, to proceed onwards in time, and from that which is observed now, to affirm uniformity of succession in events yet to come. And this is all that natural science can do. It knows of force, stability, order, uniformity; it bases itself on these, but of a Being back of all, of a cause, of uniformity with a purpose and as the result of will, it knows nothing. Of a miracle, of anything free and supernatural, it knows and can know nothing. These are, indeed, the very things that modern science seeks to ignore and exclude.

Religion, on the other hand, has revelation in the place of observation and experience ; and, as has been said, has the moral attributes of God finding their distinctive sphere in the onward movement, for its basis. It is within this sphere that we find occasion for the supernatural. Indeed, the movement itself is supernatural. To this the circular movement, nature, uniform, improgressive,

necessitated, is wholly subordinate.   It is but as the
staging to the building, the theatre to the drama, the field
to the battle.   Therefore any, the least miracle for a moral
purpose, is of higher significance than the whole of nature
as indicating the presence and supremacy of a personal
being who is other than nature, and is its Lord.   The harmony, therefore, of the natural with the supernatural, and
so of science with religion, will be found in the subordination of the lower to the higher ; and when this subordination shall be seen to be complete, the harmony of science
with religion will be perfect, and not till then.

But if this be so, how obvious is it that those who recognize only the lower movement must be one-sided and
narrow.   Nor is this always the worst.   Not a few votaries
of mere science, especially positivists, become not only
narrow, but bitter, and make it their special function to
stand at the entrance of the paths to the higher knowledge
and scoff at those who would enter in.   While, therefore,
you give science its proper place, and that a high place,
you will not, I trust, fail to find enlargement and completeness in that which is higher.

But if there is danger that you will find within the circular movement the sole objects of the intellect, much
more is there that you will find in connection with that the
sole objects of affection and of choice.   Not apprehending
rightly the relation between the circular and the onward
movement, it is greatly to be feared that some of you will
either pursue some phantom that cannot be grasped, or
will grasp that which will turn to ashes in your hand.
Then will come disappointment, and a temper irritated
against Providence, and soured towards the world.   Then
the chill and the gloom for which nature knows of no
morning, will begin to set in.

So has this been with many in the past.   Shall it be

so with you ?   Shall not the experience of the past benefit
you ?   Do you not live in the ninteenth century, after two
hundred generations of men with their hopes and fears and
follies have come and gone, and shall you be no wiser for
witnessing the things that have been ?   Most obvious is it
that mankind as a race, have not been thus made wiser.
Is not vanity as much enamored of itself as it was at the
beginning ?   Are the votaries of fashion, and the slaves of
conventional forms, diminished in number ?   Is the race
of mere pleasure-seekers coming to an end ?   Do not
young men start in the race of ambition, and strive to be
great men as much as if there had not been a great man
in every town and neighborhood since the time of the
flood ?   Is not unhappiness still imputed to the condition
in life rather than to the moral state ?   And hence, do not
men still say, " When we have removed such an inconve-
nience, have attained such an object, we shall be happy " ?
Are there more than of old who come to a pause in all this,
and deliberately say to themselves, as most men might,
" So far as worldly good is concerned, I am as happy now
as I can expect to be.   Having food and raiment, I will
therewith be content."   Is there less than formerly of
insane disregard of death, and judgment, and eternity ?
In all these respects the experience of others seems to do
the mass of men little more good than it does the fishes
and the birds ; for, " as the fishes that are taken in an
evil net, and the birds that are caught in the snare, so,"
even yet, " are the sons of men snared in an evil time,
when it falleth suddenly upon them."   Notwithstanding
the experience of the past, when the necessary result of
their own conduct reaches them, when the net comes over
them, it comes suddenly ; they are amazed ; they supposed
that *they* should escape.   But shall this be so with you ?
You may succeed in the lower sense of that word.   You

may become rich ; may come to be the first man in a vil-
lage, or a member of Congress, or the Governor of a State,
or the President of the United States, and may suppose
yourselves to be engaged, as ten thousands have before
you, in the most important and momentous concerns that
have ever transpired. But, however high you may rise,
you will be borne up by a wave that has risen quite as
high before, and when it subsides it will strand you where
it has stranded others, and leave you to neglect, while the
popular gaze is waiting for him who is to succeed you.
Thus have all schemes of life based on the circular movement, failed hitherto. They must in the time to come.
" The thing that hath been, it is that which shall be."
    Do I, then, disparage the world ? Far from it. It is
God's world. He made it: not in mockery of his creatures, or for their disappointment, but for their use. It is
just such a world as is adapted to man in his present condition, and, so viewed, every creature in it is good. It is
marvellous in its adjustments and in its provisions. It is
pleasant to live in it. It is pleasant to behold the sun, to
investigate truth, to feel the glow and warmth of the domestic and social affections, to be in sympathy with the interests and struggles of our humanity in this transient state,
and to work for its advancement. The world is good for
what it was intended to be ; but an inn is not a home.
It is no disparagement of it to say so ; and when he who
would make it one is disappointed, it is his own fault. If
the world shall disappoint you, it will be your own fault.
It will be because you attempt to make of it what He did
not intend it should be; and what you may know, if you
will, that He did not intend it should be. The great mistake of men is, that they do not rightly adjust their plans
to the relation between the circular and the onward movement. The relation here, as in the intellect and in science,

is one of subordination.   Here the law of limitation comes
in and gives you your key.   Make as much as you will of
the objects and interests of the circular movement if you
do but so subordinate them to those of the onward movement that they shall contribute in the highest degree to
the interests involved in that.   This it is that Christianity
would teach you to do ; and in thus harmonizing the two
movements to reach the highest results possible in connection with each.   The circular movement is subordinate.   It was intended to be.   If that movement were all ;
if life were but the same round over and over ; we might
well go about, as Solomon did when he looked at it in this
aspect, to cause our hearts to despair of all the labor that
we take under the sun.   But that is not all—

> " 'Tis not the whole of life to live,
> Nor all of death to die."

There is an onward movement in which that which
hath been, is not now ; and that which is now, shall never
be again.   It is that which gives to life its dignity.   Connected with that are the higher hopes, the nobler purposes,
and the supreme end of man.

And here there opens to us the grandest subject of
thought in the universe of God.   It might seem, when we
dwell upon infinite space that has no centre and no circumference, and upon those worlds of light within it which the
night reveals, and upon those myriads more which the tele-
scope calls up, that the feeling of grandeur must arise to
its highest point.   But no ; that all belongs to the circular
movement.   It is but matter and its forces—the domain of
mere science, with no power to reveal anything outside of
itself, or above itself.   View it as you will, investigate it as
you will, and what can any progress man may make in the

14*

knowledge of processes and results within this movement amount to? Progress ! Is not death a part of this same movement? and is not all progress here accompanied by a progress towards that?

Yes, Death ! That is a word at the sound of which science is dumb. Here is a man standing under the array which ·night reveals. By his side is a new-made grave. He has come there to mourn ; and pointing to that grave, and looking up, he asks of the blue depths, and of the starry hosts, "What does that mean?" The heavens do not hear him ; the depths and the stars are silent ; no tele-scope can pierce so far as to read an answer. Turning then, from these vast spaces and forces to that opposite sphere of science, where she delves and peers, and seems to be seeking for that nothing out of which all things were made, and pointing to the same grave, he asks the microscope, and the crucible, and the retort, " What does that mean?" and they make no reply. Then, looking around, and below, and above him, he cries out, " O thou mysterious circling, pitiless, all-engulphing Nature, speak. What does that mean?" And the moon glides on in her course, and the stars shine, and "there is no voice nor any that regardeth." But who is this that has heard the question, not of this man only, but of humanity, and stands by his side? He wears the form of a man, but his words imply the resources of omnipotence, and He says, " Thy brother shall rise again." " I am the resur-rection and the life : he that liveth and believeth in me, shall never die." Now Nature and its laws, matter and its forces, death and its terrors, are under our feet. We have now found Him "who has abolished death, and brought life and immortality to light." Now, being lifted above the circular movement, and released from the bonds of necessity, we come up into the region of freedom and

of personality.   Now we find a personal God ; now a universe, not merely strewn with suns and planets, fixed, or
in orderly movement, but peopled with intelligences in the
likeness of God—an innumerable company of angels and
the spirits of just men made perfect.   Now we reach the
true sublimities ; now the onward movement.

As has been said, the onward movement connects
itself with the moral government of God, and with man as
responsible.   It is within this that we find the supernatural.
Within this, and as a part of this, we find miracles.   Here,
also, we find prophecy, properly so called.   Science can
prophesy, but only within her own domain.   She can tell us
that the sun will rise to-morrow, and can predict an eclipse.
She can even foretell the weather, because "the wind returneth again according to his circuits," but she could not
foretell the coming of Christ, nor his crucifixion, nor his
resurrection and ascension ; nor does she know anything
of the time of his second coming, or of his coming at all.   It
was as a part of this movement, and wholly in its interest,
that Christ came ; and He is its central figure.   This precludes comparison between him and any philosopher.   Except as a condition of something higher and as holding it
in subjection, he had nothing to do with the circular movement.   As that movement is known by science and controlled by its methods, he had nothing to do with it.   His
method of knowledge within it was not induction, but
insight ; his method of control was not through law, but
through will manifesting itself in miracle.   He simply said
to one and another of the elements and forces of nature,
as the centurion said to his servant, " Go," and it went ;
" Come," and it came.   For Him to have discovered, or to
have propounded scientific methods, or to have controlled
nature after the manner of science, would have been a
degradation.   With Him everything was on another plane,

and only as his miracles were subservient to the interests
within the onward movement, to the establishment of truth
within that, and to moral progress, are they lifted practically above juggleries and mere wonders.

Moral progress—character, a character radically right,'
and then improvement in that—this gives us progress in
connection with a movement that turns not back upon
itself, that always records itself, and in which the past is
always required.   It is to this progress that I wish to call
your special attention, and concerning it, I have three
things to say.

The first is, that it is the only progress worth making ;
or, at least, that without this all other progress is relatively
worthless.

The second is, that this progress will draw after it all
other progress, and make it permanent ; and that nothing
else can.   And just here it is that we find the special wisdom and glory of Christ, in that while he seems to ignore
science and art, and in a sense to disregard the interests
of the circular movement, he yet initiated and put himself
at the head of a movement that has but to become universal to draw within its sweep the most rapid and only permanent progress in all things else.   The planets follow
the sun.   The greater includes the less, the higher the
lower.   In that saying of his, " Seek ye first the kingdom
of God and his righteousness, and all these things shall be
added unto you," there is not only the sum of religion,
but more of philosophy than in all heathendom.   It shows
a knowledge of the structure of God's universe from foundation to turret ; and of its administration from the beginning throughout all ages.   Moral progress must take the
lead.   This is Christ's method.   With this, progress in all
else will follow ; will be permanent and perpetual.   With
out this, the generations will but perform the labor of

Sisyphus. When a given point is reached there will be retrogression. Itself the one thing needful, it involves the wisdom and method of all reform that can avail much ; and when reformers learn this, and begin at home, the wheels of progress will begin to revolve rapidly, and their grating and jarring, now so dissonant, will cease.

The third thing which I wish to say is, that as this progress must be through Christ's method, so also must it be through his power and leadership. He must be recognized as the head of the race. He is its head. For all who shall fulfil, and, under Him, more than fulfil the destiny of our original humanity, He is the second Adam; and the one thing needed by those who would make progress in the onward movement, is a personal relation to Him, through which they may receive His guidance and aid. For the race in its anticipations of a happier future on earth, no less than for the individual in the great future, He must be " the Captain of our salvation." Without Him we can do nothing.

In connection with what social or physical convulsions this progress is to go forward, or whether in quietness, we can know only from revelation. Unaided by that, we find ourselves, in our attempt to take the bearings of this onward movement, without a chart in the open sea. It is all sky above with no polar star, and all ocean below. Respecting this movement science knows nothing. But from revelation we do know, whatever may intervene, that there is to come at some point an arrest to the present order of things, a solution of the perplexing problems connected with it, and a new adjustment on the basis of a final separation of the righteous and the wicked. It is by revelation alone that we know the astronomy of the moral heavens, and that the movement of our whole system is towards a day of reckoning and a judgment seat. Upon that seat—the throne of His glory—we know that He will be seated who was once crowned with thorns, and that "before Him shall be gathered all nations." We shall be there ; and God will require of each one of us that which is past.

To me, the thought of this responsibility, in the onward movement, is especially solemn as I look back. Oh, how much that needs to be forgiven ! How much that might have been more wisely, and faithfully, and better done ! But for you, while the thought must indeed have solemnity as you look back, yet, entering as you are upon life, with the power to make of that which is to be your past what you please, it will, perhaps, have more solemnity as you look to the future. The past which you will thus make, you will look back upon without regret in proportion as you subordinate, in accordance with the doctrine of this discourse, the circular to the onward movement—as you seek first the kingdom of God.

Nor, if you understand the relation of these two movements as Christianity presents them, will the doing of this diminish your interest in anything that pertains to the lower and circular movement. Here, again, it is the glory of Christianity, and a demonstration of its truth, that it so brings these two movements into harmony, that, while it presents in the strongest possible light the vanity of passing objects and scenes considered as an end, it does not lessen our interest or activity in them. Not only, as has been said, does Christianity make the most of the two movements in their result—so that we gain our lives by losing them—it also makes the most of them as they call forth our energies, so that we become more active in the duties of time as we care less for its objects. It makes us more "diligent in business " as we become "fervent in spirit, serving the Lord." It is thus that all human employments may become equal in the sight of God, for He regards them as there is manifested through them a pur- pose and temper that conspire with the onward movement of his moral government.   Whatever stands related to that, and as it stands thus related, has grandeur in it.   What man is this who is so earnestly at work in the very humble employment of making a fine powder still more fine by constant attrition?   It is Michael Angelo, grinding the paints with which he is to paint for eternity.   The humble duties must be done ; the paints must be ground ; but they will be ground all the better if we feel that we are to paint for eternity with them.   There are duties towards God, in- dispensable, the highest of all, but they can never be ac- ceptably performed in the wilful disregard or neglect of any duty toward man.   You are never to forget that the best preparation for heaven is in that character which will fit you for the greatest usefulness on earth.

Since, then, the problems—the great problems in life —that come from the intersection and blending of the circular and onward movements are solved theoretically by Christianity ; and since, through that, you can make the most practically, of the interests involved in each move ment, the one thing needful for you is to be Christians. At this hour, when so many voices are calling you, the one voice which you are to hear is that of Him, who says, " FOLLOW ME."   Hear that voice, and then you wil take your places under His banner by the side of those who are waging with Him the great battle of all time.   It is around Him that the thick of this battle has always been.   Around Him it always will be.   Take, then, your places. You are needed.   The veterans are falling.   Who shall take their places?   The strong men are fainting. Who shall succor them?   Go ye, and the earth shall be better and happier for your having lived in it.   Go ; and when the time of your departure shall come, you will be able to say what he said who was a standard-bearer in this College for more than forty years, and for whom both its chapel and this desk are now draped in mourning.* When consciously dying, and but just able to speak, he said— "If we view it scripturally, death is but stepping out of one room in our Father's house into another; and, in this instance, without doubt, into a larger and pleasanter room."

---

* Professor Albert Hopkins.

XXI.

MEMORIAL DISCOURSE ON PRESIDENT GARFIELD,

Prepared at the Request of the Trustees of Williams College.

ONE year ago to-day ! Who does not remember the scenes of that Fourth of July, and of the two days preceding? Who does not remember the darkness and chill of that eclipse into which our Commencement passed so suddenly from the sunshine of brightest hope?

One year ago to-day—and to-day it is the heart that should speak. It is only the tribute of our hearts that is called for in response to a heart that then beat warmly for us, but now is still. Certainly no further biography or encomium of President Garfield can be needed for his own sake. Probably—I think I may say certainly—no equal number of spoken and published tributes was ever called forth by the life and death of any man within so short a time. The chosen orator of the nation has spoken—grandly spoken. The Archbishop of Canterbury, the head of the English Church, has spoken. The most eloquent pulpit orator of France, Father Hyacinthe, has spoken, and repeated his discourse. Embassadors, senators, the pulpit, the bar, friendship, admiration, patriotism, have spoken, and no words of mine, were that my aspiration, could reach the height of those already uttered.

Nor is anything more needed for the general public. The excitement, wonderful as it was, and long-continued,

---

⁎ Because of sickness in the family of the Author, read before the trustees and the alumni at Williamstown, Mass., by Rev. Dr. S. I. Prime, July 4, 1882.

is past. When President Garfield, as he lay on his bed of suffering, was told how intense and extensive the sympathy for him was, he said : "This cannot last. No one man can long hold the attention of the nation." But it did last. For *seventy-nine* days the tension was not relaxed. Every day the beating of his pulse was felt from Maine to Florida, and from the Atlantic to the Pacific. Everywhere there was the anxious look, there was secret weeping, prayers went up, and there was the constant alternation of hope and fear. And not only did it last in this country, but throughout the civilized world. In England and on the continent, as I can testify, the daily and eager inquiry among all classes was for the health of President Garfield. It did last as long as the life of the heroic sufferer lasted, and then it reached its culmination. The cities in this land and in other lands were darkened by tokens of mourning. In every town through which the body passed from Elberon to lie in state under the dome of the Capitol the people gathered in crowds and stood with uncovered heads. As he lay under that dome the long procession passed to view his face for the last time. There, too, at an appointed hour, while the city held its breath, the stricken wife was alone with her dead. On the day of the funeral business was suspended ; the people gathered in their places of worship; there was a hushed sympathy throughout the Union ; to this the Atlantic was no barrier, and it has been estimated that not less than 300,000,000 of people were reached by the shadow, and touched by the spell of that hour. Every State was present at Cleveland by its representatives. Twenty governors of States, each with his staff, were present. Side by side with those of the Union, the Queen of England laid her floral tribute on the bier. And so, with an attendance of 60,000 people, his body was borne to its final resting place.

But nothing violent or intense can last always. The tomb had received him, and the gloom became less. There were rifts in the clouds. The waters began to return to their accustomed channels. The government, as only such a government could have done, moved on without a ripple. The period of mourning appointed for the army and navy passed away, and the second great tragic scene in the drama of our historic life came to its close.

But though the general course of nature after storms and floods may be as before, yet how often is it found, not only that hopes are blighted by harvests destroyed, but that here a field, and there a garden, that before had been green and fruitful, or beautiful and fragrant, have been swept by a desolation from which they can never recover. And so it has been here. Ours is not the desolation of the home, but our most illustrious graduate, a member of the board of Trustees, whose interest in the subject of education was special, and who greatly loved and honored the college, has been taken from us at a moment when he had attained the highest honor in the gift of the nation. He has been taken from us at a moment when we hoped for inspiration from his zeal, and guidance from his counsels, and that his annual visits here, where he had arranged that his sons should tread the same walks trodden by himself, would make the college conspicuous throughout the country. Be it then that all has been said that can be said, all that is demanded by the fame of President Garfield, or by the general public, it has yet seemed to the Trustees to be most fit that at this their first meeting since his death, at this first gathering of the alumni since then, there should be some commemorative service in which we may place ourselves by the side of those more deeply bereaved, may look for a little at that in him which so fixed the attention of the world ; may recognize his love for the col-

lege ; and, possibly, may gather from his career some lessons for our own guidance.

I have spoken of the intense and extended sympathy
there was in connection with the sickness and death of
President Garfield. That sympathy made him the conspicuous figure in the opening of a new chapter—perhaps
I may say a new era—in the history of our race. There
was never anything like it. There never could have been.
Up to that time that quick and diffusive element in nature
which symbolizes human sympathy had not so lent itself to
man that such sympathy had been possible. For ages the
gambols of electricity in the clouds had awakened the thunder, its bolts had smitten the earth, it had streamed up in
long lines in the aurora, but it had waited for a Franklin, a
Henry, a Morse, a Field, so to tame it and bring it under
the yoke of service to man that its slightest whisper
should far outleap the thunder, and that the long wires
for its instantaneous transit should become bands of steel
to bind and hold fast in amity nations whom oceans had
separated. Up to that time such sympathy could not
have been. Then it could be ; and through it new possibilities of the union of the whole race through common
sympathies in one brotherhood, were revealed.

When a new era is to be opened there is needed pre
vious preparation. There must be, first, the essential
conditions. There is then needed the right man to stand
at its opening—one in whom its elements shall be in-
carnated, and who shall illustrate its spirit. And not
more signally was Luther fitted to stand at the opening of
the Reformation, or Washington at the opening of a new
era of civil liberty, than was Garfield to stand at the opening of this new era in that movement toward brotherhood
which had been originated nearly 1900 years ago.

How well fitted he was thus to stand will appear in

part if we look at the number of points in himself, or in his career, at which he touched our common humanity or some one of its phases. In this he was without a parallel.

There were first, his early struggles. In these—and perhaps it is the only point—he had an advantage not common to all. For some, for the many, early poverty is a misfortune ; but in this country, or at least in this part of it, a poverty with no taint of low vice or of vulgarity, an incident of pioneer life having often in it a heroic element, and inherited by one who has the strength to face and overcome the obstacles it brings, is an advantage, especially if he is to enter political life. When party capital was to be made, Lincoln was the railsplitter, and Garfield was the canal-boy. This could not have been among an ignorant people, or one where society was stratified by caste or class distinctions, and where honest labor was not honored. But among an intelligent people pervaded by the ideas of liberty and equality, the coming up from a log cabin of a barefooted boy—barefooted because of poverty—was a delight, and the more so as they saw it to be a legitimate result of free institutions by means open to all.

In these early struggles President Garfield resembled President Lincoln, but his struggles were more steady in their aim and more diversified in their means, and so were adapted to awaken a wider sympathy. President Lincoln was a rail-splitter, but he was not a carpenter, or a schoolmaster. He did not aim at high literary culture, and sweep the floor, and make the fires, and ring the bell, for his tuition. But these things President Garfield did. He did them cheerfully, faithfully, as means to an end, pushing them behind him as the swimmer pushes the water that bears him forward. In doing this he conferred a benefit upon the whole people by giving new emphasis to the truth that high aims ennoble all legitimate means for their attainment. This truth Christianity teaches in connection with the higher aims and deeper struggles that pertain to a future life ; but we need to have it taught, also, and illustrated in connection with political and social life. With this truth practically accepted we have a *people* self-respecting, stable, capable of self-government ; with it ignored, we have a *populace*, with no steady aim, the prey of despotism, or the seat of anarchy.

But as President Garfield had, from his early struggles, in common with President Lincoln, a ground for the sympathy of the masses, so had he, from his broad scholarship and varied attainments, in common with John Quincy Adams, a ground for sympathy with persons of the highest culture. It was a common remark, at the time of his inauguration, and has been since—I heard it from a Judge of the Supreme Court—that no President except John Quincy Adams had been equally equipped in scholarship and statesmanship. He was president of the Literary Society of Washington. If a rare book was absent from the congressional library, Mr. Spofford was wont to say that either Mr. Sumner or Mr. Garfield must have it. He not only kept up his classics, but studied the old Latin authors. Hence his high appreciation of the scholarly sympathy of Mr. Evarts, in sending him from England, when he was on his sick bed, a copy of a rare edition of Horace. He acquired modern languages, and while he was leader of the House, and during its stormiest times, he wrote for the magazines. It was but twenty-five years after his graduation, and yet in that brief time he had not only risen to be the chosen ruler of 50,000,000 of people, and thus the peer of the greatest monarch on earth, but by his speeches and his words, that have been

caught up and made imperishable, he has already taken
his place among

> " The great of old,
> The dead, but sceptred sov'reigns who still rule
> Our spirits from their urns."

Between these two extremes, the early struggles of
which John Quincy Adams knew nothing, and the broad
scholarship and literary culture of which President
Lincoln knew nothing, President Garfield was in positions and performed duties of which neither of them
knew anything, and which brought him into that special
sympathy with large classes which comes from being
one of them.   He was an under-teacher ; the head
of a college; after the manner of the disciples, a
preacher ; a member of the State Senate ; a colonel in the
army ; a brigadier-general ; a major-general ; a member-
elect of Congress ; and all this before he had been out
of college eight years.   A rise so rapid in both civil and
military life is without example in the country.   He was
thus brought into close sympathy with the great body of
teachers, and especially with the great body of soldiers
who were then, from the prevalent war spirit, and who
continue to be, a controlling element in the country.

His election to Congress in 1863 was while he was in
the army, and from no agency of his ; and it was only by
the earnest wish of President Lincoln and Secretary
Stanton that he was induced to abandon his military career
and prospects.   He was poor, the pay of a major-general
was double that of a member of Congress ; he had been
successful, the soldierly element was in him, and he felt
within himself the power to succeed ; but at the call of
duty he made the sacrifice.

Entering the House of Representatives at the age of
thirty-two, with a single exception its youngest member,

he soon became prominent, and on the election of Mr. Blaine to the Senate, became the leader of the House. In Congress he continued seventeen years, having been elected nine times in succession by a constituency as intelligent and exacting as any in the Union. During that time he was far more a statesman than a partisan, and both by his speeches and his labors on committees became known and felt throughout the country as one of the controlling forces of the government.

It was during this period that he became known as a lawyer; and here again his course was without a parallel. His first plea was before the Supreme Court of the United States. There, without fee or reward, in a case that endangered his popularity, but in the cause of civil liberty, with the Attorney-General and General Butler opposed to him, and associated with Judge Black and the Hon. David Dudley Field, he made his first plea. The cause was won, and this plea gave him at once a high standing and continued practice in the Supreme Court.

Of his election to the Senate of the United States, and his nomination for the presidency, both unsought by him, I will not speak, but pass to his campaign speeches, for in them we have our best illustration of the versatility of his powers, of their perfect training, and of that hidden force which brought his hearers into sympathy with him. Of his making these speeches Mr. Blaine speaks particularly. There were seventy of them—not ordinary campaign speeches that could be prepared and repeated, but speeches impromptu, made to delegations and assemblies of the utmost diversity. They were made in opposition to the advice of his party friends, in disregard of the discreet and successful silence of General Grant and of the failure of others ; made at a time when the opening of his mouth by a candidate was eagerly watched for by his opponents, and dreaded by his party. But Gen. Garfield knew his own powers and made no mistake. He met every occasion freely and frankly, till at length apprehension passed into confidence and confidence into surprise and admiration. Probably not another man in the Union could have done that.

From this uniform, and equal, and great success in such diversified lines, it will appear that there must have been in the powers of President Garfield not only strength but symmetry. That is what we need—strength and symmetry—a combination of these. Without this in him sympathy must have been impaired, and this he had in an eminent degree. Hence his greatness was not that of the Swiss Matterhorn—the elevation of a single shaft, inaccessible in its height, and that dwarfs everything about it. It was rather that of a broad table-land, where there is equal elevation, but by gradual ascent, and with verdure all the way up. Hence, too, though his rise was so rapid, there was no point of transition where he lost the sympathy of those about him. There were emergencies and crises. They came thick and fast. But when the hour struck that called for the man, the man was there, and *he* was so the man that it seemed perfectly natural he should be there and rule the spirit of the hour.

In thus touching our humanity at so many points and so evenly, there was nothing in President Garfield, as there has been in so many other great men, that awakened repulsion or was obstructive of sympathy. There was no affectation, or assumption, no coldness of manner. There was just the simplicity and earnestness and sincerity, the naturalness and true gentility of an unspoiled and large manhood.

We have thus a remarkable combination of qualities in connection with great achievements. Was anything more needed to account for the sympathy mentioned ; or to fit President Garfield to stand at the opening of the new era of brotherhood now made possible ? Yes, two things. There was needed, first, a wealth of affection—a development of the heart on the same plane with that of the intellect and the will. And this there was. Of this the first sphere was the home. Into that we may not enter, but we know how he honored both his mother and his wife, and the kiss which he gave them on inauguration day was not more a token of affection than a public and deserved recognition of their helpfulness in the struggles through which he had passed. His attachments were strong, his friendships faithful and lasting, and there was a general kindliness that impressed all with whom he was associated.

And here, perhaps, I may be permitted to mention, especially since I have seen a statement of it in print not entirely accurate, how I first came fully to the knowledge of this affectionate element as taking its equal place in the trinity of his nature. He had become one of the great men of the nation, had returned to visit the college at its commencement, and, the evening after, attended the reception at my house. In the midst of the throng he put his arm around me and said, "I don't believe you know how much we love you." Few men who have ever lived could have done that.

But the illustration especially in point here is from the regard he showed for his classmates and the alumni in connection with his inauguration. Quite a number of his classmates were in the city, and when we remember the cares that had been on him, and the scenes that were before him, it is not a little remarkable that, in accordance with his own wish and suggestion, he should have met with them the evening before the inauguration at a social supper where he was one among them precisely as of old. Still more remarkable was it that he should have arranged for a reception of the alumni of the college at the White House immediately after the inauguration. To appreciate this rightly one must have witnessed the scenes of the day. In the morning, escorted by the élite of the army, he passed through the huzzahing crowd from the White House to the Capitol. There, in the presence of each department of the government, and of a multitude, vast and surging like the sea, he took the oath of office and pronounced that grand inaugural. Returning as he went, he stood before the White House with uncovered head while the gleaming forest of bayonets that filled Pennsylvania Avenue from end to end passed in review before him. Then, before the sun went down, he turned and gave his first reception to the alumni of his college. No one who was present can ever forget it. Beautiful it was, and next to the kiss of his mother.

One thing more was needed. He who had never known defeat, whose physical powers were exuberant, who had such a family about him, who had just reached the highest position this great country had to give, and who had such prospects before him was to be struck down in a moment by the hand of an assassin, and be obliged to look death in the face for seventy-nine days, under the gaze of two continents. That was such a test as no man had before been brought to. He needed the power to stand that test, and that power he had. He had had a Christian mother, and from a child had known the Holy Scriptures. At eighteen he had intelligently accepted and professed Christianity, and had sought to commend it to others. On the top of Greylock, when the hour came to read a chapter in the Bible with his absent mother, he proposed to his companions to read it aloud, and called for prayer. He did

not know Christianity simply as a creed, but also as a service and a ground of support. He put his hand into the
hand of one who had said, "When thou passest through
the waters I will be with thee, and through the rivers they
shall not overflow thee; when thou walkest through the
fire thou shalt not be burned, neither shall the flame
kindle upon thee." And so it was. The waters did not
overflow him, neither was there the smell of fire on his
garments. Deprived, as I think, unwisely, of the presence
of his pastor, and of the near friend with whom he had
been wont to hold Christian communion, his hope in God
did not falter. The anchor had been cast within the vail,
and it held. There was no bravado, or stoicism, or indifference. He wished to live. When told there was but
one chance he said, "I will take that chance." But he
also said : "I am not afraid to die ; " and so, with no movement or word that could impair sympathy, but with the
sympathy and admiration of the waiting continents constantly augmenting, he passed into the shadow of that
valley which we call dark, but which was light to him.

Thus was his life rounded out up to that point. There
are those who think that if he had lived he would have
been less distinguished for executive, than for intellectual
power. For this I see no reason except the rarity of the
combination it would have required. I know, indeed, no
instance in history of a man great in debate, or as an
orator even, who has been equally distinguished for executive capacity. One reason for this may have been that the
opportunity for distinction in both is seldom offered to the
same man ; but the chief reason is that the habits of mind
required for debate and for prompt and decisive action in
emergencies are entirely different, and in most men incompatible. Still, they are no more incompatible than strong
imagination and sound judgment, or than coolness and in-

tense action, and from every indication of his military
life, and his bearing before dissenting conventions and
opposing majorities, especially from the speeches he made
and the stand he took on the vital question of finance, we
may well believe that in him intellect would have found
its true function in ministering to both wise and efficient
action, and that his administration would have been as
efficient as it would have been wise.

And while President Garfield touched our humanity at
so many points, it is noticeable how entirely he touched it
by that in him which is essential to our humanity.   It
does not seem possible that any one should reach the position he attained with less that is extraneous or factitious.
He did not attain wealth.   He was not in the ranks of
fashion.   He did not disregard its conventionalities, but he
was not their slave.   In everything pertaining to his religious life there was the utmost simplicity.   He was of a
denomination little known in the country at large ; the
Bible was his creed, and during the whole time he was in
Washington, and while he was President, surrounded as he
was by elegant and fashionable churches, he worshipped in
a house hardly equal to the ordinary school-houses in New
England.   There was in him simple manhood battling as
best it might.

I make no attempt to interpret the providence which
permitted the death of President Garfield at such a time
and in such a manner.   To me clouds and darkness are
round about it.   But that he was eminently fitted in himself, and in the circumstances of his death, to be the object
of a gaze which should illustrate the power of sympathy in
the new conditions under which the race is placed will not
be denied.   Through their common sympathy with him
men were brought into sympathy and permanent kindly
relations with each other.   The good accomplished by this

we have no means of measuring, but that it was great we know. The common sympathy with him united the North and the South as nothing else could. That was a great thing. It so loosened the fastenings of old grudges between this country and England, and allayed more recent irritations, as to make war at that time impossible, and to diminish the probability of it for a long time to come. The messages of the Queen will not soon be forgotten, and the fragrance of the flowers which the telegraph enabled her to lay upon the bier will last for a generation. In other countries of Europe, as Germany, and Austria, in Turkey even, there was a similar sympathy through which there was a fuller apprehension and a better appreciation of our free institutions than could otherwise have been.

Under former conditions, it has been impossible to unite men of distant countries and different nations. There has been no common centre of a sympathy through which divisive elements might be dissolved, and no quick and effective means of transmitting any sympathy there may have been. But now, if there were such a centre of sympathy, the possibility of a felt brotherhood and of a unity of the race through the heart would be indicated by the results of which I have just spoken. Such a centre of sympathy we believe there will be, and that the short-sighted views of interest, and the antipathy of races, and difference of religions and of creeds under the same religion, will melt away in a common sympathy with Him, and a common love for Him, who has been lifted up and will draw all men unto Him, and in drawing them unto Himself, will draw them to each other.

We have thus seen what President Garfield came to be and some of its results. *How* he came to be what he was is of little moment except as it may aid others who wish to make full men of themselves, and may aid the friends of education in providing the best means to enable them to do that. In neither respect does his career suggest anything absolutely new, but in both respects much that needs enforcement.

What he did will aid others chiefly as a fresh illustration of two principles that no successful student can ignore. One is, that nothing that lives can grow except by its own activity. This is because, in all growth, life works from itself outward. That is its law. The other principle is, that all mental discipline and symmetrical growth are from activity of the mind under the yoke of the will or personal power. Activity of the mind in which the attention is held steady to one point, going out it may be in many directions, but always holding the thread and returning, is mental labor. It is work, and may be of the hardest and most exhausting kind. Say what you will of genius, or of gifts and aptitudes in particular directions, no man can come to the front in any line of business or of thought and hold his position there without a thorough study of principles and of details under them. Especially can no man become a legislator, or debater on the broad field of statesmanship, without a wide knowledge, not only of principles, but of what has been, of what ought to be, and of what, under the circumstances, is the best that can be. As no two cases are precisely alike, strict experience cannot be a guide. The man must be governed, not by rules, but by principles, and the power to comprehend principles and to apply them under new and varying circumstances, is the last result of patient and comprehensive thought. It is through such processes as I have mentioned, silent and long continued, that great efforts are made that seem extemporaneous. In a sense they are, but the reservoir must have been filled before the waters could flow. It is, too, by such processes that what are called self-made men are made ; but no man reaches high power in this line who is not essentially self-made. The two principles I have mentioned were perfectly understood by President Garfield. Of strenuous and persistent work in accordance with them we have no more conspicuous example than was he, and that example will, no doubt, be a stimulus and a guide to very many.

Suggestions from his career that would aid us in training upon this ground such men as he was, there is little time to consider. By such men I do not mean men who shall fill similar positions. The positions men are to fill must be determined by the times in which they live. I mean men who shall make the most of themselves, and be equal to any position to which they may be called. Whether such men shall be formed here will depend partly on the material furnished from which to form them, and partly on the college. In President Garfield, when a student, we had the right material. Eighteen years ago, writing to Mr. Gilmore, who desired to write his life at that early day, I said : "Gen. Garfield gave himself to study with a zest and delight wholly unknown to those who find in it a routine. A religious man and a man of principle, he pursued of his own accord the ends proposed by the Institution. He was prompt, frank, manly, social in his tendencies, combining active exercise with habits of study, and thus did for himself what it is the object of a college to enable every young man to do—he made himself *a man*. *"He pursued of his own accord the ends proposed by the Institution."* Give us students who will do that and it is all we ask. To teach a class of such young men would be a joy. Full co-operation throughout between teachers and students is the one thing needed for the best results of a college. For this nothing can be a substitute. But this cannot be unless the students have been well trained at home. The family, not the school or the college, is the seed-plot of society. If the students sent us are indifferent, or averse to study, if they are of the calibre and taste to do hereditary tricks, and perpetuate hereditary annoyances, if they tend to mischief or dissipation and vice, or even to distinction in inter-collegiate games rather than in collegiate studies, they may be advised to leave college, or patience and hope may tide them over the four years, but the ends proposed by the founders and benefactors of our colleges, and sought by their trustees and teachers, will not be reached.

But while so much depends on the student, much also depends on the college. Be it that every man is self-made through his own mental activity, yet his processes will vary with his associates, his teachers, and his surroundings. The affection of President Garfield for this college was based on what it had done for him. Of this he often and freely spoke. The years he spent here were formative, and years of rapid and extensive acquisition. And what the college did for him we would have it do for others, only more and better. The problem of the college, by no means solved as yet, is to furnish the best possible means of growth during its period of education.

As furnishing such means of growth during that period, the college may be compared to the nutriment that surrounds the living germs in a seed during the first period of the growth of a plant. During that period of vegetable life the proper nutriment is provided. The germ does not select it for itself. It is *provided*, and the germ feeds upon it till it forms roots and leaves, and the plant is ready to enter, as its second stage, upon its own independent life. Then it selects its own food, it explores the soil for it, it absorbs it from the atmosphere, it battles with the winds, and the promise with which it enters upon this second stage of its life will depend on the vitality of the germ, and the fitness and abundance of the nutriment it has received.

The two things, then, to be attended to are the surrounding nutriment, and the living germ.

In the surrounding nutriment—in whatever goes to make up opportunity, in buildings, and apparatus and cabinets, and the library, there has been a great advance in this college within my remembrance. These we must have to some extent, and we need them to such an extent and in such a form as shall keep us in close relation with advancing literature and science, and as shall correspond with the tastes and wants of our day. To these, additions have just been made in the Clark building, presented by an alumnus and trustee of the college, and remarkable for its combined solidity and elegance; in the Wilder cabinet that worthily fills it; in the Field observatory, an addition to various gifts that have gone before ; and, through a donation unexampled in its amount in the history of the college, an addition that will be magnificent when it is finished, has been provided for by Governor Morgan. In these the friends of this college, and the friends of education everywhere, have reason to rejoice.

But the student is not an unconscious germ with no alternative possible. These provisions being made, and teachers being provided, how far shall we go in prescribing the use to be made of them ? Here wisdom is needed. No doubt the changed relation of the sciences, and the ample and more diversified fields for action, demand changes in the course of study. But, if the course of study is to be *liberal*, rather than professional and technical, it would seem that, from the wealth of new fields, and the pressure of new studies, there would be more need than ever before of a wise selection and proportion-

ing of the studies to be chosen, and that, aside from indolence and caprice, this could be better done by those who
had been over the ground than by those who had not.
Some room for option there should be, especially in
branches where original bent counts for much, and in the
later years. I could wish the range for it enlarged to
include at least music and drawing, but would not have
it interfere with a fixed course that should *secure breadth*.
Breadth was a special characteristic of President Garfield,
and I should hope that the tendency to that in college
education might not be impaired. I would not have
the college become a school for training specialists instead of men. I would neither have a blur cast upon
the meaning of its diploma, nor have that diploma degraded to the level of a certificate of progress in specific
studies.

We now turn to the living germ. It is for this that
provision is made ; on this anxiety centres. Can anything
be done directly to quicken and strengthen this ? If so,
it must be by the teacher. Only life acts directly upon
life. We here reach the vital point in a college, and also
a special difficulty. Up to this point what was required
money could buy, and there are some things required in
a teacher that money can buy. A teacher needs to *know*.
With money enough we can secure teachers who know the
subjects they are to teach. But that is not enough. It
may be, especially on some subjects, that the more a man
knows the poorer teacher he is. He needs not only to
know, but to know *how*—how to teach, and how to manage
a class. Can this be bought? Not always. The teacher
needs aptitude, and discrimination of character, and
patience, and self-control, and these money will not always
secure. In general, however, it may be said, that with
proper provision for salaries—and this is the point at which

our colleges need money—the culture of the intellect and of taste may be, in a good measure, secured.

But it is the moral nature, and not the intellect, that lies deepest in man. That is central. In that we find the living and immortal germ. Quickened by the beams of the Sun of righteousness it is from that that we have the blossom, the fragrance and the fruit of our humanity. The intellect may be stimulated by appetite, or desire, or passion, and the results in literature and the arts may be admirable, but without the inspiration and guidance of the moral nature there will be no broad wisdom. In ignoring that, an attempt is made to educate the man with the man left out; and theorists and educators, with their endless systems and methods, will continue to roll the stone of Sisyphus up the mountain to have it return upon themselves. It is that, then, in the student that needs to be quickened and strengthened. But if this is to be done by the teacher it cannot be by any action of the mere intellect. It must be through the action of his moral nature. There must be love exerting itself wisely with reference to the whole good of the student. This will be valuable in the individual, but where it exists in a body of teachers working together there will be an atmosphere that can be created in no other way, and that is invaluable in education. This money cannot buy. But without it our colleges are liable to become hotbeds of corruption ; and they never can become what they should be till both teachers and students hear the voice of the great Teacher, saying, ''*Learn of Me.*'' That voice President Garfield heard before he came to college. " That," as he said, "settled canal, and lake, and sea, and everything." Under the influence of that his whole nature came into harmony. Not the intellect only, but *the man*, the whole man together, with the powers in right relation, entered on a

course of education. Hence the temptations of college
life he scarcely knew as temptations, and with such aids as
every one may have, he went on from step to step till he
became the man he was. Encouraged by such a result, due
in part and so largely to the college, it remains for us, the
alumni and the friends of education, to make provision on
this ground such that the college shall continue to be honored as it has been, or even more, in its alumni, and shall do
its full proportion in the time to come, in raising up for the
country and the world such men as President Garfield was.

I have thus, in accordance with the wish of the Trustees, sought to pay, in some measure, the tribute of affection and honor due from the College, and I may add, especially from myself, to one who so honored the College,
a beloved fellow alumnus, one of its trustees, one who was
honored and mourned by the nation and the world. On
the day of his inauguration, addressing him in behalf of
the alumni then present, I said to him that I was the only
president of a college who had ever lived to see one who
had graduated under him President of the United States.
How little did I then think that I should survive him, and
be called to such a service as this! But so it is, and in
view of the mystery that enshrouds his assassination as
permitted under the Providence of God, I can only adopt,
in closing, the words used by him on a great occasion
in immediate connection with the assassination of President Lincoln : "Fellow-citizens ! Clouds and darkness
are round about Him ! His pavilion is dark waters and
thick clouds of the skies ! Justice and judgment are the
habitation of His throne ! Mercy and truth shall go before His face ! Fellow-citizens ! God reigns, and the
government at Washington still lives." Yes, God reigns ;
and, " Therefore will not we fear, though the earth be removed, and though the mountains be carried into the
midst of the sea."

www.ingramcontent.com/pod-product-compliance
Lightning Source LLC
Chambersburg PA
CBHW032003120726
47898CB00005BA/1476